THE CAMBRIDGE COMPANIC

One of the founders of literary realism and the serial novel, Honoré de Balzac (1799–1850) was a prolific writer who produced more than a hundred novels, plays and short stories during his career. With its dramatic plots and memorable characters, Balzac's fiction has enthralled generations of readers. *La Comédie humaine*, the vast collection of works in which he strove to document every aspect of nineteenth-century French society, has influenced writers from Flaubert, Zola and Proust to Dostoevsky and Oscar Wilde. This *Companion* provides a critical reappraisal of Balzac, combining studies of his major novels with guidance on the key narrative and thematic features of his writing. Twelve chapters by world-leading specialists encompass a wide spectrum of topics such as the representation of history, philosophy and religion, the plight of the struggling artist, gender and sexuality, and Balzac's depiction of the creative process itself.

OWEN HEATHCOTE is Honorary Senior Research Fellow in Modern French Studies at the University of Bradford. He researches on the relation between violence, gender, sexuality and representation in French literature from the nineteenth century to the present. His many publications include *Balzac and Violence. Representing History, Space, Sexuality and Death in 'La Comédie humaine'* (2009) and *From Bad Boys to New Men? Masculinity, Sexuality and Violence in the Work of Éric Jourdan* (2014).

ANDREW WATTS is Senior Lecturer in French Studies at the University of Birmingham. His research focuses on the representation of provincial life in *La Comédie humaine* and, more recently, on the adaptation of nineteenth-century French novels in different artistic media. He is the author of *Preserving the Provinces: Small Town and Countryside in the Work of Honoré de Balzac* (2007) and the co-author (with Kate Griffiths) of *Adapting Nineteenth-Century France: Literature in Film, Theatre, Television, Radio and Print* (2013). He has also co-edited (with Michelle Cheyne) a critical edition of Balzac's *Le Nègre* (2014).

A complete list of books in the series is at the back of this book.

THE CAMBRIDGE
COMPANION TO
BALZAC

EDITED BY

OWEN HEATHCOTE
University of Bradford

ANDREW WATTS
University of Birmingham

CAMBRIDGE
UNIVERSITY PRESS

CAMBRIDGE
UNIVERSITY PRESS

University Printing House, Cambridge CB2 8BS, United Kingdom

Cambridge University Press is part of the University of Cambridge.

It furthers the University's mission by disseminating knowledge in the pursuit of education, learning, and research at the highest international levels of excellence.

www.cambridge.org
Information on this title: www.cambridge.org/9781107066472
10.1017/9781107588929

© Cambridge University Press 2017

This publication is in copyright. Subject to statutory exception and to the provisions of relevant collective licensing agreements, no reproduction of any part may take place without the written permission of Cambridge University Press.

First published 2017

Printed in the United Kingdom by Clays, St Ives plc

A catalogue record for this publication is available from the British Library.

Library of Congress Cataloging-in-Publication Data
Heathcote, Owen, editor. | Watts, Andrew (Andrew J.), editor.
The Cambridge companion to Balzac / edited by Owen Heathcote, Andrew Watts.
Cambridge ; New York : Cambridge University Press, 2016. | Series: Cambridge companions to literature | Includes bibliographical references and index.
LCCN 2016031770 | ISBN 9781107066472
LCC PQ2181 .C36 2016 | DDC 843/.7–dc23
LC record available at https://lccn.loc.gov/2016031770

ISBN 978-1-107-06647-2 Hardback
ISBN 978-1-107-69128-5 Paperback

Cambridge University Press has no responsibility for the persistence or accuracy of URLs for external or third-party Internet Web sites referred to in this publication and does not guarantee that any content on such Web sites is, or will remain, accurate or appropriate.

CONTENTS

List of Illustrations	*page* vii
Notes on Contributors	viii
Acknowledgements	xii
Chronology	xiv
Balzac's Work: An Overview of 'La Comédie humaine'	xviii
Abbreviations	xxiii

    Introduction   1
    ANDREW WATTS

1 Balzac: A Portrait of the Novelist as Social Historian and Scientist   11
    ELISABETH GERWIN

2 Balzac's Early Works   27
    MICHAEL TILBY

3 Balzac's Correspondence   40
    EWA SZYPULA

4 Fantasy and Reality in *La Peau de chagrin*   52
    DAVID F. BELL

5 Balzac, Money and the Pursuit of Power   67
    ALLAN H. PASCO

6 *Le Père Goriot: Arrivisme* and the Parisian Morality Tale   81
    ARMINE KOTIN MORTIMER

7 *Illusions perdues*: Writers, Artists and the Reflexive Novel   97
    SOTIRIOS PARASCHAS

CONTENTS

8	Balzac, Gender and Sexuality: *La Cousine Bette* DOROTHY KELLY	111
9	Space, Religion and Politics in the *Scènes de la vie de campagne* OWEN HEATHCOTE	127
10	BALZAC'S SHORTER FICTION TIM FARRANT	140
11	Adapting Balzac ANDREW WATTS	157
12	Balzac's Legacy SCOTT LEE	175
	Epilogues	189
	Dual Balzac	189
	CHANTAL CHAWAF	
	Living Balzac	193
	ÉRIC JOURDAN	
	Guide to Further Reading	200
	Index of Characters	207
	General Index	210

ILLUSTRATIONS

1 The Château de Saché in Touraine, where Balzac wrote some of his most celebrated works. © Ed Buziak / Alamy Stock Photo. *page* 9
2 Rudolph Valentino (Charles) with Alice Terry (Eugénie) in *The Conquering Power* (1921, dir. R. Ingram). © Kobal Images. 160
3 The police arrest Vautrin (Pierre Renoir) in *Le Père Goriot* (1944, dir. R. Vernay). © René Chateau Vidéo / www.renechateauvideo.com. 162
4 Alice Sapritch (Bette) and Jacques Castelot (Hulot) during filming of *La Cousine Bette* (1964, dir. Y.-A. Hubert). © INA via Getty Images. 167

CONTRIBUTORS

DAVID F. BELL is Professor of French at Duke University. His recent research focuses on the relation between science and literature, and in particular on the notion of embodied cognition with an emphasis on the concept of touch in its broad cultural and neuroscientific contexts. He is the author of *Real Time: Accelerating Narrative from Balzac to Zola* (2004), *Circumstances: Chance in the Literary Text* (1993) and *Models of Power: Politics and Economics in Zola's* Rougon-Macquart (1988), as well as numerous articles on the nineteenth-century novel and on contemporary critical theory. He is co-editor of *SubStance*, a review of theory and literary criticism, and also co-directs the PhD Lab in Digital Knowledge at Duke University, where he has been active in exploring new modes of digital publishing and archiving.

CHANTAL CHAWAF is the author of some thirty novels, a volume of essays and critical articles. Since her first book, comprising *Retable* and *La Rêverie* (des femmes-Antoinette Fouque, 1974), she has been writing sometimes exploratory, sometimes transgressive, texts, giving voice to the pain – and the joys – of women. Her writing denounces the inhumanity of war and its aftermath on the lives of both men and women. While a number of her texts deplore the depredations of the natural environment (*Mélusine des détritus*, signed Marie de la Montluel, Éditions du Rocher, 2002), others evoke the tragedy of Syria (*Syria. Le Désert d'une passion*, Éditions de l'Icéa, 2012; *Ne quitte pas les vivants*, des femmes-Antoinette Fouque, 2015).

TIM FARRANT is Reader in Nineteenth-Century French Literature at the University of Oxford and Fellow and Tutor in French at Pembroke College. His research centres on nineteenth-century prose fiction, in particular in relation to press, publishing and cultural contexts. His publications include *Balzac's Shorter Fictions: Genesis and Genre* (Oxford University Press, 2002), *An Introduction to Nineteenth-Century French Literature* (London: Duckworth, 2007) and an introduction to three novels by Jules Verne (London: Everyman, 2013), as well as numerous articles on nineteenth-century French literature and culture. He is currently preparing two books on nineteenth-century French short fiction, funded by the University of Oxford and the Arts and Humanities Research Council.

NOTES ON CONTRIBUTORS

ELISABETH GERWIN is Associate Professor of French at the University of Lethbridge, Alberta, in western Canada. A comparatist by training, she researches on the representation of difference, and in particular of sexual difference, in nineteenth-century French literature and in critical discourses such as psychoanalysis. She has published articles on Derrida and Freud and has written several articles on Balzac, including on Napoleon and *Le Colonel Chabert* (2013), on *La Duchesse de Langeais* (2012) and on *La Fille aux yeux d'or* (2010). Her current research project concerns the representation of narcissism in early nineteenth-century French literature.

OWEN HEATHCOTE is Honorary Senior Research Fellow in Modern French Studies at the University of Bradford. He researches on the relation between violence, gender and representation in French literature from the nineteenth century to the present and has published on many writers such as Cardinal, Chawaf, Duras, Garréta, Guyotat, Hyvrard and Wittig. His books include *Balzac and Violence. Representing History, Space, Sexuality and Death in 'La Comédie humaine'* (2009) and *From Bad Boys to New Men? Masculinity, Sexuality and Violence in the Work of Éric Jourdan* (2014). He is on the advisory committees of the *Groupe international de recherches balzaciennes* and the *Groupe d'études balzaciennes* and a contributor to the forthcoming *Dictionnaire Balzac*.

ÉRIC JOURDAN has written over twenty novels, collections of short stories, poetry and plays. His first published novel *Les Mauvais anges* (Éditions de la Pensée moderne, 1955) was banned for nearly thirty years, before appearing finally in 1984. He is noted, particularly, for his 'trilogy', *Charité* (La Différence, 1985), *Révolte* (La Différence, 1986) and *Sang* (Seuil, 1992) and for more autobiographical texts such as *Trois cœurs* (Pauvert/Fayard, 2008) and *Le Jeune soldat* (Pauvert, 2009). His short stories include *Barbe Bleue, Croquemitaine et compagnie* (La Différence, 1985) and *Anthologie de la peur. Entre chien et loup* (Seuil, 1989). In addition to an early volume of poetry, *Éclairs*, published under the name of Rochefalmer (Éditions Saint-Germain-des-Prés, 1969), he has also written a wide range of articles, prefaces and screenplays.

DOROTHY KELLY is Professor of French at Boston University. Her research centres on gender and nineteenth-century French narrative viewed through various theoretical lenses such as psychoanalysis, sociology and gender theory. She has authored three books: *Fictional Genders: Role and Representation in Nineteenth-Century French Literature*, *Telling Glances: Voyeurism in the French Novel* and *Reconstructing Woman: From Fiction to Reality in the Nineteenth-Century Novel*. She has recently turned to Baudelaire's works and is now in the midst of writing a book on the metaphor of the living dead in Balzac, Zola and Baudelaire.

SCOTT LEE is Associate Professor of French at the University of Prince Edward Island (Canada). He has published on Balzac's shorter fiction, both in *La Comédie humaine* and *Les Contes drolatiques*. He is the author of *Traces de l'excès: essai sur la nouvelle philosophique de Balzac* (2002). He has also published articles examining the work of contemporary French writers such as Patrick Modiano and Marie-Hélène Lafon.

ARMINE KOTIN MORTIMER, Emerita Research Professor of French Literature at the University of Illinois at Urbana-Champaign, has published numerous articles on French narrative literature, mostly of the nineteenth and twentieth centuries, with particular expertise on Balzac, Sollers and Barthes. Among her seven books are *For Love or for Money: Balzac's Rhetorical Realism* (2011) and her co-edited *Proust en perspectives: Visions et révisions*, published by Classiques Garnier (2015). She has translated two of Sollers's books: *Mysterious Mozart*, published by the University of Illinois Press in 2010, and his *Casanova l'admirable*, which appeared in 2016 under the title *Casanova the Irresistible*. She is now translating contemporary French novels. In 2009, she was awarded the Palmes académiques by the French government.

SOTIRIOS PARASCHAS is Lecturer in French Studies at the University of Reading. His research focuses on nineteenth-century fiction, with particular emphasis on realism and the aesthetic, economic and legal aspects of authorship. He is the author of *The Realist Author and Sympathetic Imagination* (2013). He is currently preparing a monograph entitled *Reappearing Characters: Originality and 'Property in Ideas' in Nineteenth-Century France* for publication and working on a monograph project entitled *Genius and Celebrity in the Nineteenth Century*.

ALLAN H. PASCO is a Hall Distinguished Professor at the University of Kansas. Although he specialises in French culture, his critical and historical orientations are both rooted in literature. His next book focuses on Balzac's attempt to grasp the sociological implications of the new, post-revolutionary world. Professor Pasco's articles have appeared in such journals as *French Studies, Modern Language Review, PMLA, New Literary History* and the *Revue d'histoire littéraire*. While serving on seven editorial boards, he has published two books examining the structures of the novel, and others on Proust, Balzac, romanticism, allusion and concepts of affection in the eighteenth and nineteenth centuries. The second, expanded edition of his thoroughly edited anthology of nineteenth-century French short stories recently appeared.

EWA SZYPULA is a Teaching Affiliate and MHRA Research Scholar at the University of Nottingham. Her research focuses on nineteenth-century literature and correspondence, with a special interest in Balzac. She completed her doctoral thesis on Balzac's letters to Madame Hanska in 2013 at King's College London and has taken part in many conferences on Balzac, French literature, letter-writing and the nineteenth century. She has published a monograph entitled *Balzac's Love Letters: Correspondence and the Literary Imagination*, a project funded by the Modern Humanities Research Association.

MICHAEL TILBY has been Fellow in French at Selwyn College, Cambridge since 1977. He has published on a range of nineteenth- and twentieth-century French authors, especially Balzac, and on the relationship between nineteenth-century French literature and the visual arts. Among his recent publications is the chapter on Balzac in the *Cambridge Companion to European Novelists* (2012). He has recently completed a study of the early Parisian *flâneur*. His current projects include a short biography of Balzac (for Reaktion Books), a comprehensive study of Balzac's early novels and a book provisionally entitled *Playing with Words: Language, Fiction and Text in Balzac's 'Comédie humaine'*.

ANDREW WATTS is Senior Lecturer in French Studies at the University of Birmingham. His research focuses on the representation of provincial life in *La Comédie humaine* and, more recently, on the adaptation of nineteenth-century French novels in different artistic media. He is the author of *Preserving the Provinces: Small Town and Countryside in the Work of Honoré de Balzac* (2007) and the co-author (with Kate Griffiths) of *Adapting Nineteenth-Century France: Literature in Film, Theatre, Television, Radio and Print* (2013). He has also co-edited (with Michelle Cheyne) a critical edition of Balzac's *Le Nègre* (2014) and is currently working on a monograph entitled *(Re)Writing 'La Comédie humaine': Balzac and the Practice of Literary Adaptation*.

ACKNOWLEDGEMENTS

This book represents for me the fruit of almost twenty years of working on Balzac. Since writing my first essay on *La Comédie humaine* as a second-year undergraduate, I have been enthralled by its larger-than-life characters and the extraordinary genius that produced this great literary monument. Writer, lover, debtor and inveterate coffee addict, Balzac has, in all his contradictions and rich diversity, never lost his power to fascinate me. My enthusiasm for his work owes much to the many inspirational scholars who have shared their knowledge with me so generously over the years. At the University of Bristol, the late Dr David Meakin encouraged me to consider undertaking postgraduate work on Balzac, an option that I later pursued under the guidance of Dr Richard Bolster, who kindly agreed to supervise me in his last year before retirement, and Professor Tim Unwin, who oversaw the successful completion of my doctoral thesis in 2004. Since that time, I have benefited from the advice and expertise of numerous colleagues in nineteenth-century French studies, many of whom I am lucky to count among my closest friends. In particular, I would like to record my warmest thanks to Anne-Marie Baron, Michelle Cheyne, Lisa Downing, Kate Griffiths, Bradley Stephens and Tim Unwin, for their unfailing generosity and scholarly insights. I am especially grateful to my co-editor Owen Heathcote for his many years of kindness and support, not least in introducing me to the Balzac studies community in France. This volume would have taken considerably longer to complete without him. As always, my friends and family have been instrumental in helping this book towards completion. My wife Claire, who has heard more about Balzac than she might ever have envisaged when we first met as undergraduates, has provided encouragement and practical wisdom throughout, and in my parents, Janet and John Watts, I know that I can always count on my two most steadfast supporters. My contributions to this volume are for my mother, whose energy, willpower and unflinching courage Balzac himself would have surely admired.

Andrew Watts

ACKNOWLEDGEMENTS

We would like to express our warmest thanks to all of the contributors to this volume for their collegiality, responsiveness and hard work. We are particularly pleased that Chantal Chawaf and Éric Jourdan have been able to share their appreciation of Balzac in these pages. We would also like to record our thanks to Bradley Stephens for the time and scholarly care he invested in reading and commenting on the final draft of this book. We are especially grateful to Linda Bree at Cambridge University Press for giving this *Companion* her full support. Finally our thanks go to Anna Bond and Isobel Cowper-Coles and the editorial team at Cambridge University Press for their guidance in the production of this volume.

Owen Heathcote
Andrew Watts

CHRONOLOGY

20 May 1799	Honoré Balzac is born in Tours to Bernard-François and Anne-Charlotte-Laure Balzac. The infant Balzac is sent immediately to a wet nurse in the village of Saint-Cyr-sur-Loire.
29 September 1800	Birth of Balzac's first sister, Laure-Sophie.
18 April 1802	Birth of Balzac's youngest sister, Laurence.
21 December 1807	Birth of Balzac's brother Henry, whose father is presumed to have been Jean de Margonne, owner of the Château de Saché in Touraine.
1807–13	Balzac attends the Oratorian boarding school in Vendôme.
1814	Having been named director of military supplies in Paris, Bernard-François moves his family to the capital, setting up home in the Rue du Temple.
1816	Balzac completes his secondary education and registers at the Paris Law Faculty. He is also apprenticed to a lawyer, Jean-Baptiste Guillonnet de Merville.
1819	Balzac obtains his degree but rejects a legal career in favour of writing. He rents a garret room in the Rue Lesdiguières and starts work on a five-act tragedy in verse entitled *Cromwell*, followed by an epistolary novel, *Sténie ou les Erreurs philosophiques*, which he later abandons.
1820	*Cromwell* fails to impress Andrieux, a professor at the Collège de France, who advises Madame Balzac that her son should pursue any career other than literature.

1821	Balzac agrees to produce a series of novels in collaboration with Auguste Lepoitevin de l'Égreville.
1822	Balzac publishes his first five novels under the pseudonyms Lord R'Hoone (an anagram of Honoré) and Horace de Saint-Aubin. *Le Vicaire des Ardennes* is banned for offending morality and religion.

Embarks on an affair with a married woman, Laure de Berny, who would remain a cherished friend and confidante until her death in 1836. |
1823	Balzac completes another play, *Le Nègre*, which is rejected by the Théâtre de la Gaîté.
1825	Frustrated by his lack of success as a writer, Balzac bids farewell to literature in the preface to his novel *Wann-Chlore* and decides to set himself up as a printer and publisher. His youngest sister Laurence dies in August.
1826–28	In partnership with André Barbier, Balzac runs a printing workshop in the Rue des Marais-Saint-Germain. The venture proves a commercial disaster. Narrowly avoiding bankruptcy, Balzac is left with a debt of 60,000 francs.
September 1828	Having decided to return to writing, Balzac travels to Brittany to research a historical novel, *Le Gars*, which would later become *Le Dernier Chouan ou la Bretagne en 1800*.
1829	Publication of *Le Dernier Chouan ou la Bretagne en 1800*, the first novel that Balzac signs with his own name. The publication of a second version of *Physiologie du mariage* (1826) reinforces Balzac's growing popularity with readers.
1830	Publication of *Scènes de la vie privée*, six short fictions that Balzac would later incorporate into his *Études de mœurs au dix-neuvième siècle*.
1831	Publication of *La Peau de chagrin*.
1832	Balzac receives an admiring letter from a Polish countess, Eveline Hanska. The couple embark on a romantic relationship which continues, mainly by correspondence, for the next eighteen years.
1832–34	A period of intense creativity in Balzac's career as he completes several of his most celebrated works,

	including *Le Colonel Chabert* (1832), *Eugénie Grandet* (1833) and *Louis Lambert* (1833).
26 January 1834	Meets Madame Hanska for the first time in Geneva.
1835	Publication of *Le Père Goriot*, in which Balzac inaugurates his system of reappearing characters.
1836	Publication of *Le Lys dans la vallée* and *La Vieille fille*, the first novel ever serialised in a French daily newspaper.
1837	Balzac narrowly avoids the debtors' prison following the collapse of the *Chronique de Paris*, a newspaper of which he was the editor and majority shareholder.
1838	Travels to Sardinia, where he considers becoming involved in the silver mining industry.
1839	Becomes President of the Société des Gens de Lettres, and argues for stricter laws for the protection of intellectual property.
1840	Balzac's play *Vautrin* is banned after only one performance for appearing to mock King Louis-Philippe. Balzac searches for a suitable publisher for his collective works, to which he gives the title *La Comédie humaine*.
1 October 1840	Balzac rents an apartment in Passy, where he would live for the next seven years. The Maison de Balzac (47, Rue Raynouard) is Balzac's only surviving Parisian home, and is now a museum and research centre.
November 1841	Death of Madame Hanska's husband, Venceslas Hanski. Balzac becomes increasingly preoccupied with attempting to persuade the newly widowed Madame Hanska to marry him.
1842	The first three volumes of *La Comédie humaine* go on sale. Balzac writes a preface, the 'Avant-propos', in which he explains the underlying principles of his literary enterprise.
1843	Travels to Saint Petersburg, where he meets Madame Hanska for the first time in eight years. Publication of *Une ténébreuse affaire* and *La Muse du département*.
1846	*La Cousine Bette*, the last great literary success of Balzac's career, is serialised in the newspaper *Le Constitutionnel*.

23 February 1848	Another revolution breaks out in Paris as the July Monarchy is overthrown. Balzac is present to witness the sacking of the Tuileries palace.
1849	Spends the year at Wierzchownia, the home of Madame Hanska in the Ukraine. An adaptation of *La Cousine Bette* is staged in Paris.
14 March 1850	Balzac marries Madame Hanska. By now in poor health, he departs Wierzchownia for Paris with his new wife on 24 April.
18 August 1850	Balzac dies at his Paris home in the Rue Fortunée (now the Rue Balzac).
21 August 1850	Balzac's funeral is held at Père-Lachaise. Victor Hugo pays tribute to his friend's genius in a graveside eulogy.
1854	Posthumous publication of *Le Député d'Arcis*, completed by Balzac's former secretary Charles Rabou.
1855	Posthumous publication of the unfinished novel *Les Paysans*.

BALZAC'S WORK: AN OVERVIEW OF 'LA COMÉDIE HUMAINE'

La Comédie humaine (The Human Comedy)[1]

Avant-propos (Foreword) (1842)

Études de mœurs (Studies of Manners)

Scènes de la vie privée (Scenes of Private Life)

La Maison du chat-qui-pelote (At the Sign of the Cat and Racket) (1830)
Le Bal de Sceaux (The Ball at Sceaux) (1830)
Mémoires de deux jeunes mariées (Letters of Two Brides) (1842)
La Bourse (The Purse) (1832)
Modeste Mignon (1844–45)
Un début dans la vie (A Start in Life) (1842–44)
Albert Savarus (1842)
La Vendetta (The Vendetta) (1830)
Une double famille (A Second Home) (1830)
La Paix du ménage (Domestic Peace) (1830)
Madame Firmiani (1832)
Étude de femme (A Study of Woman) (1830–31)
La Fausse maîtresse (The Imaginary Mistress) (1841–42)
Une fille d'Ève (A Daughter of Eve) (1838–39)
Le Message (The Message) (1832–33)
La Grenadière (1832–33)
La Femme abandonnée (The Deserted Woman) (1832–33)
Honorine (1842–43)
Béatrix (1839–45)
Gobseck (1830)
La Femme de trente ans (The Woman at Thirty) (1832–34)
Le Père Goriot (Old Goriot) (1834–35)

Le Colonel Chabert (1832–35)
La Messe de l'athée (The Atheist's Mass) (1836)
L'Interdiction (The Commission in Lunacy) (1836)
Le Contrat de mariage (The Marriage Contract) (1835)
Autre étude de femme (Another Study of Woman) (1832–42)

Scènes de la vie de province (Scenes of Provincial Life)

Ursule Mirouët (1841–42)
Eugénie Grandet (1833)

                Les Célibataires (The Celibates)
Pierrette (1840)
Le Curé de Tours (The Vicar of Tours) (1832)
La Rabouilleuse (The Black Sheep) (1841–42)

                Les Parisiens en province
L'Illustre Gaudissart (The Illustrious Gaudissart) (1833)
La Muse du département (The Muse of the Department) (1843)

                Les Rivalités (The Jealousies of a Country Town)
La Vieille fille (The Old Maid) (1836–37)
Le Cabinet des antiques (The Collection of Antiquities) (1836–39)

                Illusions perdues (Lost Illusions)
Les Deux Poètes (The Two Poets) (1837)
Un grand homme de province à Paris (A Distinguished Provincial in Paris) (1839)
Les Souffrances de l'inventeur (The Trials of the Inventor) (1843)

Scènes de la vie parisienne (Scenes of Parisian Life)

                Histoire des Treize (The Thirteen)
Préface (1834)
Ferragus (1834)
La Duchesse de Langeais (The Duchess of Langeais) (1834)
La Fille aux yeux d'or (The Girl with the Golden Eyes) (1834–35)

Histoire de la grandeur et de la décadence de César Birotteau (The Rise and Fall of César Birotteau) (1837)
La Maison Nucingen (The Firm of Nucingen) (1838)

Splendeurs et misères des courtisanes (A Harlot High and Low) (1844–47)
    Comment aiment les filles (How Young Women Love)
    À combien l'amour revient aux vieillards (What Love Costs an Old Man)
    Où mènent les mauvais chemins (The End of Evil Ways)
    La Dernière incarnation de Vautrin (Vautrin's Last Avatar)

Les Secrets de la Princesse de Cadignan (The Secrets of the Princess of Cadignan) (1839)
Facino Cane (1836)
Sarrasine (1830)
Pierre Grassou (1839)

        Les Parents pauvres (The Poor Relations)
  La Cousine Bette (Cousin Bette) (1846–47)
  Le Cousin Pons (Cousin Pons) (1847–48)

Un homme d'affaires (A Man of Business) (1846)
Un prince de la bohème (A Prince of Bohemia) (1840–44)
Gaudissart II (1844)
Les Employés (The Government Clerks) (1837–38)
Les Comédiens sans le savoir (The Unwitting Comedians) (1846)
Les Petits Bourgeois (The Middle Classes) (1855)

  L'Envers de l'histoire contemporaine (The Seamy Side of History)
  Madame de La Chanterie (1842–44)
  L'Initié (The Initiate) (1848)

Scènes de la vie politique (Scenes of Political Life)

Un épisode sous la Terreur (An Episode under the Terror) (1829)
Une ténébreuse affaire (A Murky Business) (1843)
Le Député d'Arcis (The Deputy for Arcis) (1847)
Z. Marcas (1840)

Scènes de la vie militaire (Scenes of Military Life)

Les Chouans ou la Bretagne en 1799 (The Chouans or Brittany in 1799) (1829)
Une passion dans le désert (A Passion in the Desert) (1837)

Scènes de la vie de campagne (Scenes of Country Life)

Les Paysans (The Peasantry) (1844–55)
Le Médecin de campagne (The Country Doctor) (1833)
Le Curé de village (The Village Priest) (1841)
Le Lys dans la vallée (The Lily of the Valley) (1836)

Études philosophiques (Philosophical Studies)

La Peau de chagrin (The Wild Ass's Skin) (1830–31)
Jésus-Christ en Flandre (Jesus Christ in Flanders) (1831)
Melmoth réconcilié (Melmoth Reconciled) (1835)
Le Chef-d'œuvre inconnu (The Unknown Masterpiece) (1831)
Gambara (1837–39)
Massimilla Doni (1839)
La Recherche de l'absolu (The Quest of the Absolute) (1834)
L'Enfant maudit (The Hated Son) (1831)
Adieu (1830–32)
Les Marana (The Maranas) (1832–34)
Le Réquisitionnaire (The Conscript) (1831)
El Verdugo (1830–31)
Un drame au bord de la mer (A Tragedy by the Sea) (1834)
Maître Cornélius (1831–32)
L'Auberge rouge (The Red Inn) (1831–32)

Sur Catherine de Médicis (About Catherine de Medici)
Le Martyr calviniste (The Calvinist Martyr) (1841)
La Confidence des Ruggieri (The Ruggieri's Secret) (1836–37)
Les Deux rêves (The Two Dreams) (1830–44)

L'Élixir de longue vie (The Elixir of Life) (1830–31)
Les Proscrits (The Exiles) (1831)
Louis Lambert (1832)
Séraphîta (1834–35)

Études analytiques (Analytical Studies)

Physiologie du mariage (Physiology of marriage) (1829)
Petites misères de la vie conjugale (Little Miseries of Conjugal Life) (1830–46)

Pathologie de la vie sociale (Pathology of Social Life)
Traité de la vie élégante (Treatise on Elegant Life) (1830)
Théorie de la démarche (Theory of Walking) (1833)
Traité des excitants modernes (Treatise on Modern Stimulants) (1839)

NOTE

1. The dates of individual works by Balzac presented in this overview are based on those given by S. Vachon, *Les Travaux et les jours d'Honoré de Balzac: chronologie de la création balzacienne* (Paris: Presses du CNRS and Presses universitaires de Vincennes; Presses de l'Université de Montréal, 1992). Given the complexity of dating Balzac's works, which often have a highly checkered production and publication history, some contributors to this volume foreground a date which corresponds to their own chapter requirements.

ABBREVIATIONS

The following abbreviations are used throughout the volume. Unless otherwise stated, references to works by Honoré de Balzac are parenthesised in the main text, using the relevant abbreviation followed by the volume and page number.

AB	*L'Année balzacienne*
CH	Honoré de Balzac, *La Comédie humaine*, eds Pierre-Georges Castex et al., 12 vols (Paris: Gallimard, 'Bibliothèque de la Pléiade', 1976–81)
Corr.	Honoré de Balzac, *Correspondance*, eds Roger Pierrot and Hervé Yon, 2 vols (Paris: Gallimard, 'Bibliothèque de la Pléiade', 2006–)
LH	Honoré de Balzac, *Lettres à Madame Hanska*, ed. Roger Pierrot, 2 vols (Paris: Laffont, 'Bouquins', 1990)
OC	*Œuvres complètes de Honoré de Balzac*, eds Marcel Bouteron and Henri Longnon, 40 vols (Paris: Conard, 1912–40)
OD	Honoré de Balzac, *Œuvres diverses*, eds Pierre-Georges Castex, Roland Chollet and René Guise, 2 vols (Paris: Gallimard, 'Bibliothèque de la Pléiade', 1990–)
PR	Honoré de Balzac, *Premiers romans*, ed. André Lorant, 2 vols (Paris: Laffont, 'Bouquins', 1999)

Quotations are preceded by a translation into English where appropriate. Translations are those of individual contributors unless otherwise stated. In chapter 12 ('Balzac's Legacy') quotations are given only in English for the sake of clarity. All ellipses are editorial unless otherwise specified.

ANDREW WATTS

Introduction

Honoré de Balzac stands as a true giant of world literature. One of the founding fathers of realism, Balzac was a prolific writer who produced more than a hundred novels, plays and short stories during his career, together with numerous essays, pamphlets, reviews and thousands of letters. At the heart of this vast corpus is *La Comédie humaine*, a collection of ninety-four novels and shorter fictions set principally against the backdrop of nineteenth-century French society. A towering literary edifice in which Balzac sought to document every aspect of the period in which he lived, *La Comédie humaine* has enthralled successive generations of readers with its dramatic plots and memorable characters. Moreover, the scale and richness of this project have inspired – and sometimes intimidated – writers since the nineteenth century. Among Balzac's compatriots, Flaubert, Zola and Proust all cited him as a key influence on their own artistic endeavours. Outside of France, Edgar Allan Poe, Henry James, Fyodor Dostoevsky, Benito Pérez Galdós, Oscar Wilde and Italo Calvino have also featured among his most enthusiastic literary admirers. In addition to its enduring impact on writers, Balzac's work has been theorised extensively, garnering the attention of Marxists, structuralists, psychoanalysts and gender theorists, to name but a few. His writings have appeared in countless translations and re-editions, and continue to provoke scholarly debate, with new books and articles constantly being added to the already-extensive body of critical material devoted to his work. Finally, his stories have spawned numerous adaptations across film, television, radio and, less obviously, *bande dessinée*. From the earliest stage adaptations of the author's work during his own lifetime to the Bolshoi Ballet's recreation of *Illusions perdues* in 2014, Balzac has never ceased to fascinate the cultural imagination.

Balzac's achievements as a writer were certainly hard-won. He was born in Tours in 1799 to middle-class parents who were well respected in the city. His father, Bernard-François, had risen from the peasantry of southern France to become Secretary to the King's Council before the Revolution, while his mother, Laure, was the daughter of Parisian haberdashers. Balzac did not enjoy a particularly happy childhood, and after spending the first four years of his life in the care of a wet nurse, he was sent to boarding school in Vendôme. This monastic institution discouraged parental visits, and during his six years as a pupil there, the young Honoré saw his mother only twice. When Bernard-François relocated the family to Paris in 1814, Balzac moved with them, completing his secondary education in the capital before registering to study law and embarking on an apprenticeship with the lawyer Jean-Baptiste Guillonnet de Merville.

Balzac's real ambition, however, was to write for the theatre. After persuading his parents to allow him three years to succeed in his chosen path, he set to work on a five-act tragedy in verse, *Cromwell*. Upon reviewing the finished manuscript, Andrieux, a professor at the Collège de France, advised Madame Balzac that her son should pursue a career in any field other than literature. Undeterred, Balzac turned instead to writing novels under the pseudonyms Lord R'Hoone (an anagram of Honoré) and Horace de Saint-Aubin. When these, too, failed to bring the success he craved, he attempted to establish himself as a printer and publisher, a venture that ended in financial disaster in 1828, leaving him with debts that would plague him for the rest of his life. The collapse of his printing firm nevertheless prompted him to return to writing with renewed determination. Inspired by the works of the historical novelists James Fenimore Cooper and Walter Scott, in 1829 Balzac published *Le Dernier Chouan ou la Bretagne en 1800* (later retitled *Les Chouans*). The story of a peasant insurrection in Brittany, it was the first novel that he signed with his own name, and marked his definitive arrival on the literary stage.

In *Le Dernier Chouan*, Balzac inaugurated a new approach to novel-writing that would shape the rest of his career. Drawing on the example of Walter Scott, who had set some of his works as far back as the Middle Ages, Balzac decided to situate his own fiction against the backdrop of recent historical events through which many of his readers had lived: the Terror, the rise and fall of Napoleon, and the restoration of the Bourbon monarchy. As his career developed during the July Monarchy of the 1830s and 1840s, he combined this emphasis on contemporary history with his predilection for recounting stories of domestic life. Among readers in the early nineteenth century, Balzac quickly established his reputation as an author who specialised in tales of private tragedy that but for his intervention would have remained hidden from view.

Balzac's importance as a writer nevertheless extends well beyond his ability to relate what he described in the 1833 preface to *Eugénie Grandet* as 'silent dramas' ['drames dans le silence'] (CH III 1025). With the publication of *Le Dernier Chouan*, followed in 1830 by his first series of *Scènes de la vie privée*, Balzac began to lay the foundations of the mammoth portrait of French society that would eventually give rise to *La Comédie humaine*. Drawing inspiration from the natural historians Buffon and Geoffroy Saint-Hilaire, he explained the underlying principles of his literary enterprise in the 1842 'Avant-propos' to *La Comédie humaine*, stating his ambition to classify human types like species in the animal kingdom. Famed for his acute powers of observation, Balzac aspired to construct a total vision of the society in which he lived, one in which every person and place would be catalogued, and from which no detail would be omitted. His obsession with exhaustiveness, reflected in the many passages of dense description for which his work is so often remembered, have caused him to be identified as one of the great social historians of the nineteenth century. As Friedrich Engels proclaimed in 1888, in what has since become one of the most well-known appraisals of *La Comédie humaine*, 'I have learned more [from Balzac] than from all the professed historians, economists and statisticians of the period together.'[1]

If Balzac's ambition to document society identifies him as a key precursor of realism, he was also deeply influenced by the Romantic movement. His career was contemporaneous with the second wave of French Romanticism, whose most celebrated exponents included Victor Hugo, Théophile Gautier, Charles Nodier and Alexandre Dumas *père*. In 1830, Balzac was also present at the Comédie-Française to witness the first performance of Hugo's *Hernani*, a play which broke with the time-honoured conventions of classical drama and heralded the triumph of Romanticism in French theatre. Not surprisingly, then, Balzac's fiction engages with many of the defining themes of Romanticism, most notably the idealisation of love, and the *mal du siècle* or sense of disillusionment that the Romantics saw as having engulfed French society in the wake of the 1789 Revolution. Moreover, Balzac shared the Romantic fascination with earlier writers such as Shakespeare and Rabelais, and with literary genres as diverse as the historical novel, medieval romance and Gothic literature. Traces of these elements can be found throughout his work, and feature strongly in the pseudonymous novels that he produced during the 1820s, when the Romantic movement in France was gaining in strength and momentum.

To attempt to categorise Balzac as realist or romantic – as many early critics of his work did – is nevertheless to underestimate the ways in which he transcended such labels. Although he disliked the term 'novelist', which he associated with frivolous entertainment, Balzac possessed a vibrant creative imagination, and was well aware of the need to captivate readers with engaging stories. Accordingly, his fiction abounds in moments of intense drama featuring characters who in many instances have become cultural landmarks in their own right. From the ambitious student Rastignac to the master-criminal Vautrin, from the budding poet Lucien de Rubempré to the vengeful spinster Bette, Balzac created a cast of characters with which readers could identify, and whose individual stories have continued to resonate across time and space. Just as importantly, his fictional universe heralded the introduction of narrative techniques that would have a profound impact on prose fiction, and subsequently other media as well. Balzac was a pioneer of the use of flashback, a technique readily appropriated by film and television in the twentieth century. More famously, starting with *Le Père Goriot* in 1835, he linked his works by having characters reappear in different stories in *La Comédie humaine*, thus giving readers the impression of catching up with old friends as they might in the real world.

Alongside these artistic developments, the vision of nineteenth-century France that Balzac presents in *La Comédie humaine* reveals that he was not simply the dispassionate, scientific observer he so often purported to be. 'French society was to be the historian,' he declared in the 'Avant-propos', 'I had only to be the secretary' ['La Société française allait être l'historien, je ne devais être que le secrétaire.' (CH I 11)] Yet Balzac's representation of this society was also underpinned by his own ideological principles. Disillusioned by the failure of the 1830 Revolution to bring about meaningful reform, he abandoned the liberalism of his youth soon afterwards, embracing instead what he termed the 'two eternal Truths' ['deux Vérités éternelles'] (CH I 13) of Throne and Altar. In the sometimes pessimistic vision advanced by *La Comédie humaine*, France had never recovered fully from the upheavals of Revolution and Empire, and could be saved only by a return to the core values of monarchy, religion and the family. Despite his political conservatism, when Balzac died in 1850 he was lauded by Hugo as a revolutionary, a writer who had transformed the art of prose fiction, and who had not been afraid to oppose what he perceived as the decline and disintegration of French society.

However, Balzac did not instantly become the canonical author we recognise today. While his works were undoubtedly popular during his lifetime, critics were often quick to condemn his supposedly poor style, tendency towards melodrama and apparent obsession with the sordid underbelly of society. Balzac also scandalised many of his first readers in Britain. In 1844, the literary critic George Henry Lewes described him as a 'very dangerous writer',[2] while Charlotte Brontë told her friend Elizabeth Gaskell that Balzac's novels 'leave such a bad taste in my mouth'.[3] The prevailing attitude of condescension towards Balzac softened only in the final quarter of the nineteenth century, when a number of developments combined to bring about a reappraisal of his literary legacy. First, the publication of his general correspondence in 1876, followed in 1894 by his letters to the Polish countess Eveline Hanska, revealed a more human, and indeed romantic, Balzac than readers had encountered before. Second, some of the most prominent members of a new generation of writers began to champion *La Comédie humaine* as an artistic achievement to be admired and emulated. While eager to stress his own originality, Zola proclaimed Balzac a forerunner of Naturalism, and a key inspiration behind his own twenty-novel *Rougon-Macquart* cycle. As his reputation was gradually rehabilitated by these developments, Balzac also became an object of academic study. Between 1895 and 1900, the eminent British scholar George Saintsbury edited and introduced a forty-volume translation of *La Comédie humaine*, as finally Balzac's work began to be judged on its artistic qualities rather than by strictly conventional moral criteria.

Balzac's status as a canonical author also owes much to the numerous theorists who have engaged with his work from a panoply of different perspectives. One of the earliest political thinkers to find support for his own theories in Balzac was Karl Marx. Marx saw in Balzac a writer who had documented the decline of the old nobility and the struggles of the individual in an increasingly capitalist society. In *Das Kapital* (1867), Marx returned repeatedly to Balzac, and cited the latter's unfinished novel *Les Paysans* as a compelling illustration of the dangers of exploitative money-lending in a rural economy. Such was Marx's admiration for the French novelist that he planned to write a study of *La Comédie humaine* once *Das Kapital* was complete.

Marx and his disciples also recognised some of the fundamental contradictions in Balzac's own political thought, not least the fact that he was an ardent royalist who simultaneously exposed the failings of the aristocracy. As Engels remarked of Balzac to the radical British writer Margaret Harkness in 1888, 'his satire is never keener, his irony never bitterer, than when he sets in motion the very men and women with whom he sympathises most deeply – the nobles'.[4] The Marxist view of Balzac as a contradictory figure continued to resonate well into the twentieth century, reaching an apogee in the 1950s and 1960s in the works of Georg Lukács, Pierre Barbéris and André Wurmser. For this later generation of Marxist critics, *La Comédie humaine* presented a society riven by class inequalities and monetary greed, and thus championed the cause of a new proletariat whose rise Balzac had actually feared.

Alongside Marxist interpretations of Balzac, the late 1950s saw the emergence in France of the New Novelists, who contemplated *La Comédie humaine* with a mixture of fascination and disdain. For the *nouveaux romanciers*, foremost among them Alain Robbe-Grillet, Balzac represented an outmoded tradition of nineteenth-century storytelling based on perfectly linear plots and third-person narration. As Robbe-Grillet complained of the Balzacian mode of novel-writing in his 1963 essay *Pour un nouveau roman*, 'everything aimed to impose the image of a stable, coherent, seamless, unequivocal, totally decipherable universe' ['tout visait à imposer l'image d'un univers stable, cohérent, continu, univoque, entièrement déchiffrable'].[5] However, like Marx and Engels before them, the New Novelists also recognised that Balzac was by no means a one-dimensional writer. While deriding *La Comédie humaine* for the supposed artificiality of its narrative techniques, Robbe-Grillet conceded that Balzac's realism was still capable of enthralling twentieth-century readers, many of whom, he claimed, looked upon his work as 'a lost paradise of the novel' ['un paradis perdu du roman'].[6]

During the 1960s and 1970s, the question of how Balzac's texts created such a powerful illusion of reality was taken up by structuralist and post-structuralist critics, most notably Roland Barthes. In *S/Z* (1970), his reading of the short story *Sarrasine*, Barthes argued that Balzac's work conformed to a 'simple representative model' ['simple modèle représentatif'][7] in which linguistic codes and signifiers were used to convey meaning. However, the somewhat ironic effect of *S/Z*, as Scott Lee explains in this volume, was that it brought Barthes into contradiction with himself. By dividing *Sarrasine* into 561 distinct fragments or 'lexies', *S/Z* demonstrated that Balzac's story was not merely 'modestly plural' ['modestement pluriel'],[8] as Barthes had claimed initially, but that it was founded on a much richer interplay of allusions and discourses. Having identified *Sarrasine* at the outset of his study as a 'readerly' text in which meanings are fixed and pre-determined, Barthes unconsciously revealed it as a 'writerly' text which lends itself to multiple possible interpretations.

By exposing the fundamental plurality of Balzac's writing, Barthes helped to lay the foundations of key theoretical approaches that have shaped Balzac studies since the 1980s. Over the past forty-five years, *La Comédie humaine* has garnered the attention of countless theorists, including Bourdieu, Derrida, Genette, Foucault and many others whose contributions to the field are reflected in this volume. Among the critical movements that stands out as retaining a particularly vibrant interest in *La Comédie humaine*, however, is gender theory. Echoing Marxist and Barthesian readings of Balzac, gender theorists have helped to reveal some of the complexities and paradoxes that underpin the novelist's work and, more specifically, his portrayal of sexual difference. As Dorothy Kelly, Michael Lucey and Lawrence R. Schehr among others have argued, Balzac appears to perpetuate

Introduction

stereotypes of male dominance and female vulnerability while at the same time demonstrating that the boundaries between male and female, heterosexual and homosexual, are uncertain and constantly shifting. Similarly, narratological approaches to Balzac have shown that *La Comédie humaine* is far from a textual monolith, and that its representation of the world is rarely uniform or consistent. During the 1990s, Éric Bordas, Nicole Mozet and Franc Schuerewegen all showed – more deliberately than Barthes – that the Balzacian text incorporates multiple voices and discourses which often compete with each other, a concept reflected in the title of Schuerewegen's 1990 volume, *Balzac contre Balzac*.

The present volume bears the imprint of the many theories and critical developments that have advanced understanding of Balzac since the nineteenth century. However, far from offering a purely theoretical reappraisal of his work, our principal aim here is to provide an introduction to Balzac, focusing on the key narrative and thematic features of his writing, and on aspects of his literary output that are typically neglected or under-discussed. The volume comprises twelve chapters by acknowledged Balzac specialists, and ranges over an extensive corpus of his works from both inside and outside *La Comédie humaine*. In the first chapter, Elisabeth Gerwin re-evaluates the notion of Balzac as a historian of nineteenth-century society, emphasising in particular his ability to synthesise the discourses of history, science, philosophy and religion. In chapter two, Michael Tilby reflects on Balzac's early works and their key role in the subsequent evolution of his writing. Tilby's reading of the *œuvres de jeunesse* is followed by Ewa Szypula's discussion of Balzac's correspondence, in which she explains how the author used letters – particularly those to Madame Hanska – to experiment with themes and narrative situations that he developed subsequently in his fiction.

Following Szypula's discussion of Balzac's correspondence, the volume presents readings of five key novels from *La Comédie humaine*, with each approached from a different thematic perspective. From David F. Bell's chapter on the relationship between fantasy and reality in *La Peau de chagrin*, we proceed to Allan Pasco's study of money and power in *La Comédie humaine*, as reflected principally in *Eugénie Grandet*. In her chapter on *Le Père Goriot*, Armine Kotin Mortimer turns to the question of morality and the corrosive influence of Paris on the novel's young protagonist Eugène de Rastignac. To complete our reassessment of this selection of Balzac's major novels, Sotirios Paraschas contemplates the representation of writers, artists and the creative process itself in *Illusions perdues*, while Dorothy Kelly examines the themes of gender and sexuality in *La Cousine Bette*.

The closing chapters of the volume focus on the broader dimensions of *La Comédie humaine*, and the evolution of Balzac's literary reputation since his death in 1850. In his chapter on the *Scènes de la vie de campagne*, Owen Heathcote explores the interaction between space, religion and politics, and the sometimes unexpected ways in which Balzac's faith in the twin pillars of Throne and Altar is undercut in his work. Tim Farrant, in turn, reveals the importance of shorter fiction to Balzac's creative aesthetic, focusing especially on the tension between length and brevity that underpins the shape and internal structure of *La Comédie humaine*. Turning then to a discussion of Balzac's artistic afterlife, my own chapter deals with adaptations of his work in film, television and radio before Scott Lee elucidates the profound influence that Balzac has exerted on subsequent generations of writers and theorists. The volume concludes with a two-part epilogue by contemporary French novelists Chantal Chawaf and Éric Jourdan, who reflect on what Balzac means to writers today.

In covering so many different aspects of Balzac's work, this volume engages actively with the vastness of his literary production. One of our key aims here is to present Balzac as a polyphonic writer who sought to harness the myriad discourses – artistic, historical, social, political, scientific, religious and philosophical – that surrounded him during the first half of the nineteenth century. Accordingly, the volume encompasses an array of topics that are integral to Balzac's work and our understanding of him as a writer. These topics include the representation of history; the relationship between Paris and the provinces; money and power; gender and sexuality; monomania and obsessive behaviour; ambition and the figure of the *arriviste*; philosophy and religion; politics and sociology; the system of reappearing characters; art and the plight of the struggling artist; writing and reflexivity; science and the literary applications of natural history; and, as any comprehensive study of Balzac demands, realism and romanticism. While some of these themes are addressed in individual chapters, others recur throughout the volume, offering points of debate and dialogue between contributors.

Not surprisingly, the scale of Balzac's literary output makes it impossible to cover every aspect of his work in detail. We have necessarily found creative ways of broaching this problem. Although we have not included a chapter devoted exclusively to Balzac's theatrical works, for example, discussions of his dramatic texts feature at key junctures in the volume. In analysing the representation of money in *La Comédie humaine*, Allan Pasco draws on the example of *Le Faiseur*, a play that revolves around questions of financial malpractice. Similarly, in his chapter on *Illusions perdues*, Sotirios Paraschas underscores the highly theatrical nature of the novel, which at the level of plot features both literal and figurative performers. Other avenues of

Introduction

exploration – including the Rabelaisian series of *Contes drolatiques* and *Le Livre mystique* containing the philosophical novels *Louis Lambert* and *Séraphîta* – have intentionally been left open for readers who may wish to engage in their own further study. In accordance with the conventions of the *Companion* series, we have included a chronology of Balzac's life, and at the end of the volume a guide to further reading. In order to give readers a clear sense of the dimensions of Balzac's work, we have also provided an overview of the content and structure of *La Comédie humaine*, in which many of his most well-known works are found.

This *Companion* certainly does not purport to offer the final word on Balzac. On the contrary, in presenting a reappraisal of his work, it reflects the vibrant scholarly interest that Balzac continues to generate in France and beyond. In Paris, the Groupe international de recherches balzaciennes (GIRB) and the Groupe d'études balzaciennes (GEB), publisher of the key strategic journal *L'Année balzacienne*, remain highly active in promoting research on Balzac. The Maison de Balzac in Passy, where the novelist lived between 1840 and 1847, serves as a museum, research centre and home to the Société des Amis de Balzac, which publishes its own journal and newsletter, *Le Courrier balzacien*. The Château de Saché, Balzac's beloved retreat in Touraine, provides a similar focal point for research activity. Moreover, scholars continue to extend and redefine the

Figure 1: The Château de Saché in Touraine, where Balzac wrote some of his most celebrated works.

boundaries of Balzac studies. Among recent key developments in the field, Dominique Massonnaud's *Faire vrai: Balzac et l'invention de l'œuvre-monde* (2014) has reignited the debate over the author's realist techniques which so preoccupied the *nouveaux romanciers* in the 1950s. A new edition of Balzac's correspondence began to appear in the Pléiade series in 2006, with a third volume forthcoming. A further new edition of Balzac's theatrical works by Éric Bordas is currently in preparation, as is the third volume of the novelist's *œuvres diverses*. In a major project, a *Dictionnaire Balzac* is nearing completion. Not to be left behind in the digital age, Balzac has also begun to move online with the vocabulary database compiled by Kazuo Kiriu, and the series of electronic editions of key works from *La Comédie humaine* prepared by Andrew Oliver. Finally, in a different academic context, *La Cousine Bette* was included as a set text for the 2015–16 Prépa S, the competitive examination that precedes entry to France's prestigious *Grandes écoles*.

Perhaps the most compelling illustration of this ongoing enthusiasm for Balzac, however, is the influence that he continues to exert on writers today. As Chantal Chawaf and Éric Jourdan emphasise in the epilogue to this volume, Balzac remains an inescapable presence for contemporary novelists, who like their predecessors in the nineteenth century, must contend with his gargantuan legacy. Often this challenge generates an unspoken anxiety of influence in writers as they strive to assert their own originality in the face of Balzac's monumental achievements. As Chawaf and Jourdan both demonstrate, however, there is also pleasure in writing in the aftermath of Balzac that stems from the impossibility of ever getting entirely to grips with him. For novelists today, as for countless readers since the nineteenth century, Balzac's appeal lies precisely in his range, subtlety and infinite complexity.

NOTES

1. K. Marx and F. Engels, *Collected Works*, 50 vols (London: Lawrence & Wishart, 1975–2004), vol. 48, p. 168.
2. G. H. Lewes, 'Balzac and George Sand', *The Foreign Quarterly Review*, 33 (July 1844), 265–298 (p. 273).
3. E. Gaskell, *The Life of Charlotte Brontë*, ed. A. Shelston (Harmondsworth: Penguin, 1975 [1857]), p. 428.
4. K. Marx and F. Engels, *Collected Works*, p. 168.
5. A. Robbe-Grillet, *Pour un nouveau roman* (Paris: Minuit, 1963), p. 31. Unless otherwise stated, all translations of quoted material in French in this introduction are my own.
6. *Ibid.*
7. R. Barthes, *S/Z* (Paris: Seuil, 1970), p. 19.
8. *Ibid.*

I

ELISABETH GERWIN

Balzac: A Portrait of the Novelist as Social Historian and Scientist

Honoré de Balzac's devotion to fine observation and description set the stage for modern fiction. Though Balzac is primarily a novelist, there has been consistent interest in his importance as a social anthropologist and scientific archivist of the early nineteenth century. This reflects what is doubtless one of the most original features of Balzac's writing, namely his conscious mission to document all of contemporary French society, in accordance with the principle of unity that defined his thought. Though it is instructive to distinguish the interwoven strands of narrative construction, historical observation and scientific innovation in his writing, it is also rather un-Balzacian, given that he meant to insist upon their interconnectedness within human modernity. The society Balzac portrayed was the product of these disparate forces as they influenced one another: a growing interest in science (including occult science), for example, was a defining feature of his contemporaries and shaped their reactions to the turmoil of their socio-historical context. Furthermore, historical events were no longer seen as happening at some remove from ordinary life: since 1789 at least, history was increasingly understood as a current event formed by the acts of individuals. For Balzac, the novelist had to be a creative genius with encyclopaedic knowledge, a historian, a scientist, a moralist, a sociologist, a painter and a dramaturge. These disciplines speak to and about each other in the early nineteenth century: science and history merge explicitly in Balzac's writing but also provide a structural underpinning for his thought. In this sense, the birth of the contemporary Western world was being chronicled in *La Comédie humaine*.

Balzac as Novelist: The Realist Visionary

Balzac read and wrote extensively, across many genres. In the spirit of his tumultuous era, he thought constantly about the relation his own generation could or should maintain to the past, whether this past concerned recent events, recorded history or indeed a recently discovered *pre*history whose retreating horizon was being unearthed through the new science of palaeontology. Importantly, however, his insatiable desire to observe and record his own society in action meant that he was never transfixed by nostalgia. Indeed he reserved some of his most pointed criticism for those inclined to reconstruct the past within the present. Even as he engaged with the historical and scientific heritage of the end of the eighteenth century, his main concern was to explore the present, seeking the sources of creative energy that would propel society into the future. It is in this light that we may best understand Balzac's artistic mission to observe and record his reality in living detail, through a cast of characters who often emerge in more than one of the stories forming *La Comédie humaine*. This mission we now call 'realism' and trace from Balzac, though the term itself emerged after his death in 1850.

Balzac's celebrated declaration in his 'Avant-propos' – the 1842 'Author's Introduction' to *La Comédie humaine* – was that 'French Society was to be the historian, I had only to be the secretary' ['La Société française allait être l'historien, je ne devais être que le secrétaire'][1] (CH I 11). This mission statement echoes Balzac's narrative position in texts such as *Facino Cane* (1836), where the narrator claims that by eavesdropping on passers-by 'I could join in their lives ... I would be walking in their tattered shoes'[2] ['je pouvais épouser leur vie ... je marchais les pieds dans leurs souliers percés'] (CH VI 1020); it is a promise of honesty and breadth of scope rather than of objectivity or impartiality. Nor does Balzac exclude fantastical elements, for he sees them as integral to human experience, as formative novels such as *La Peau de chagrin* (1831) reveal. Other writings grouped by Balzac as the *Études philosophiques* directly explore abstract principles – from aesthetic perfection to alchemy – and thus complicate any easy association of Balzac with what the term 'realism' came to mean. Few self-declared realists would write tales of artists such as Frenhofer (*Le Chef-d'œuvre inconnu*, 1831) or Sarrasine (*Sarrasine*, 1830), and scientists such as Balthazar Claës (*La Recherche de l'absolu*, 1834), all pursuing the Absolute and often ending their search in madness. Balzac's psychological curiosity and sagacity adds a dimension to his writing that led to his being read, in the late twentieth century, as a writer of the unconscious before Freud (for example by Roland Barthes in *S/Z*). Thus, as Charles Baudelaire pointed out in *L'Art romantique* (1869), Balzac was more an ingenious visionary than a detached observer of his society. Unlike later realists such as Gustave Flaubert or (more subversively) Alain Robbe-Grillet, he made no authorial claim to a neutral perspective.

Balzac's aesthetic idea and authorial practice were inextricably bound up in his mission to observe and describe his world. Novels and short stories provided the format best suited to his societal portraiture, and Balzac expanded the stylistic terrain being opened by Sand, Hugo and Stendhal. The depth and engagement of his observation, combined with his interest in the motivations behind human actions, account for the particular interest Balzac generated among later social theorists, especially Marxists (Jameson, Lukács, Engels and Marx himself). These readers found in Balzac a realist rendering of class conflict and the rise of Western capitalism. Yet Balzac himself did not have such a focused agenda. Any political bent to his observation was embedded in his ubiquitous critique of the exercise of power, particularly as it had been violently embodied in recent French history. Balzac's frequent and ambiguous references to Napoleon are exemplary of his realist approach. Whether the Emperor is directly personified, evoked by admirers and detractors, or referenced as the backdrop for a story, Napoleon provides a kind of realist allegory for the impact of political power.

Though Balzac was a legitimist and a Catholic, his fiction spares no criticism of contemporary monarchies. Conversely, his admiration for Napoleon was sincere. If, as Annie Becq suggests, the notion of the individual genius was a post-Revolutionary concept,[3] it is such genius and force of will that Balzac idealised in Bonaparte. Yet Balzac's own creative genius countered this, recounting events from the perspective of history's minor players and of random occurrences: 'Chance is the greatest novelist in the world; one has only to study it in order to be fertile' ['Le hasard est le plus grand romancier du monde: pour être fécond, il n'y a qu'à l'étudier'] ('Avant-propos' 137, CH I 11). Any event can produce history, claims Balzac, but only the writer can turn events into a story: 'Many things that are true are supremely boring. Half the skill lies in choosing which of them can become poetic' ['Beaucoup de choses véritables sont souverainement ennuyeuses. Aussi est-ce la moitié du talent que de choisir dans le vrai ce qui peut devenir poétique'] (*Le Message* (1832), CH II 395). No doubt this is what Pierre Barbéris had in mind when he called Balzac the novelist who 'could see and show not so much the appearance as the tensions of the things that are' ['a su voir et faire voir non l'apparence mais les tensions de ce qui est'].[4] Balzac's own genius, inspired by his early neo-gothic influences (E. T. A. Hoffmann, Ann Radcliffe), was to add psychological depth and complexity to his writing, particularly as regards the opacity of human motivations and the inevitable 'absurdity' of historical circumstances.[5] Although a champion of observation, Balzac understood that the novelist is neither record-keeper nor archivist. Indeed, his famous artist Frenhofer could be speaking about future misunderstandings of realism when he exclaims: 'The goal of art is not to copy nature, but to express it!' ['La mission de l'art n'est pas de copier la nature, mais de l'exprimer!'] (CH X 418).

Balzac as Social Historian: Writing a Forgotten History

The turn of the nineteenth century in France was an unprecedented moment of rethinking the meaning and structure of history. The repeated waxing and waning of aristocratic power, the steady rise of the bourgeoisie and the unrest among the labouring poor all combined with global trends (such as industrialisation) to create a sense that history was being forged in new ways and places. Before the earliest texts of *La Comédie humaine*, Balzac aspired to distinguish himself from the earlier Romantics by writing about events that had occurred within living memory. The majority of his tales unfold during his own lifetime, from *Les Chouans* (1829, set in 1799) to *L'Envers de l'histoire contemporaine* (1848). This almost journalistic engagement required a new assessment of what qualified as historical, confounding any modern opposition between accuracy and subjectivity.

Although, in his eulogy for Balzac, Hugo calls *La Comédie humaine* a 'history', and though Baudelaire refers to Balzac in *L'Art romantique* as a 'great historian', Balzac himself underscores his emancipation from official annals: 'I have done better than the historian, I am freer' ['J'ai fait mieux que l'historien, je suis plus libre'] ('Avant-propos' 141, CH I 15). No doubt this is Balzac's way of championing the creativity of novelists who infuse history with poetry. The reigning monarch of historical fiction in Balzac's day was Walter Scott (1771–1832), whom Balzac frequently cites among his greatest and earliest influences, praising him for giving the maligned novel 'the philosophical value of history' ['la valeur philosophique de l'histoire'] ('Avant-propos' 137, CH I 10). In his early twenties, Balzac was inspired by reading Scott's tales of medieval Scotland, and began his own literary trajectory with the unfinished *Histoire de France pittoresque*. Yet, as he matured, Balzac found Scott's various historical settings too episodic, lacking the sense of historical continuity he himself prized, and he sought to align himself with social historians such as Amans-Alexis Monteil (1769–1850). History, for Balzac, should be represented as 'a continuous reality' ['une réalité continue'],[6] recounted by literature comprehensively and artistically in the authentic language of its contemporaries. This is, of course, an almost impossible task, to which not even Balzac could fully adhere. This may explain why he rarely ventures into Scott's territory of the historical novel and, when he does so (*Maître Cornélius* [1831], *Sur Catherine de Médicis* [1842]), conveys historical detail through background characters affected by great events, thereby throwing history itself into doubt: 'historians are privileged liars who write out popular beliefs, the same as most newspapers today merely express the ideas of their readers' ['les historiens sont des menteurs privilégiés qui prêtent leurs plumes aux croyances populaires, absolument comme la plupart des journaux d'aujourd'hui n'expriment que les opinions de leurs lecteurs'] (CH XI 167). Perhaps Balzac is questioning the stable certainty of facts altogether.[7] At the very least, Balzac's relation to history is one of ambivalence and his fictional reporting of historical circumstances is both iconoclastic and critical.[8]

Like Monteil, Balzac exemplifies a growing interest during the post-Revolutionary decades in expanding contemporary historical records to include a broader swathe of society. Balzac believed that a history such as his should look not only behind the scenes of battles but also through the doors and curtains of private existences, bearing witness to what he called the 'history forgotten by so many historians, the history of customs and morals' ['l'histoire oubliée par tant d'historiens, celle des mœurs'] ('Avant-propos' 138; CH I 11). Correspondingly, the *Études de mœurs* is by far the longest of the three 'Studies' which subdivide *La Comédie humaine*. Nor is the task set by the historian of customs and morals a simple one, for from historical fact must be drawn fictional verisimilitude: as he observes in *Les Paysans* (1844): 'the historian of customs and morals obeys more stringent laws than those governing the factual historian, for he must make everything appear probable, even what is true' ['l'historien des mœurs obéit à des lois plus dures que celles qui régissent l'historien des faits, il doit rendre tout probable, même le vrai'] (CH IX 190). Balzac's focus on *mœurs* is concomitant with the importance accorded to the perspective of traditionally undervalued groups, including peasants, the urban poor and women: 'the historian must never forget that his mission is to take everyone into account; the wretched and the wealthy are equal before his pen' ['l'historien ne doit jamais oublier que sa mission est de faire à chacun sa part; le malheureux et le riche sont égaux devant sa plume'] (*Les Paysans* CH IX 65). Such characters, along with the aristocracy with which Balzac was equally enamoured, fill to bursting the pages of the various '*Scènes*' comprising the *Études de mœurs*. Whether Balzac succeeded in conveying historical truth and whether his rather fantastical brand of psychological portraiture gave a just representation of social groups, remain matters for debate. The lasting importance of his choice of subject matter is, however, incontestable.

Within each *Étude*, the various *Scènes* focus the context of Balzac's social history. Balzac intended this structure to provide a taxonomy of society, directly modelled on taxonomies being elaborated in the world of science. In the *Études de mœurs*, two *Scènes* in particular – the *Scènes de la vie de province* and *Scènes de la vie de campagne* – reveal that, in contrast to contemporaries such as Eugène Sue, Balzac reserved a significant place for rural life. Indeed, Balzac is justly regarded as a pioneer of writing about life in provincial towns and in the countryside, particularly because he countered the neo-romantic tendency to idealise this setting after the fashion of George Sand. At the same time, Balzac is a chronicler *par excellence* of nineteenth-century Paris. The texts comprising the *Scènes de la vie parisienne* explore the powers driving the fast-growing city – 'the great modern monster' ['le grand monstre moderne'] (LH I 804) – whether in its back alleys or its elegant salons. The trilogy *Histoire des Treize* (1833–35) provides a comprehensive example of these Parisian scenes: a physiognomy of the streets and neighbourhoods of the capital (*Ferragus*) is followed by an indictment of the Restoration aristocracy holed up in the Faubourg Saint Germain (*La Duchesse de Langeais*), and concluded by a sweeping analysis of the movement of 'gold and pleasure' ['l'or et le plaisir'] through the echelons of society (*La Fille aux yeux d'or*); while the whole trilogy is infused with the intrigue of a *roman noir*.[9]

Such works are far removed from conventional history in both structure and content, and the ever-widening branches of the *Scènes* reveal that Balzac builds his history 'as a web rather than a line' ['en réseau plutôt qu'en ligne'].[10] Conventional annals are critiqued in *Le Colonel Chabert* (1832) as both erroneous and manipulatable, for the false report of Chabert's heroic death, rather than his tragic survival, is upheld by characters who have an interest in aligning personal fate with national regime change. As Chabert learns, official history is resolutely linear, even in the face of factual error. Yet in Balzac's time, the recent discoveries of fossils were suggesting that the dead may indeed come back to rewrite history, welcome or not. Balzac's critique here cannot be seen as arbitrary. In the wake of the July Revolution of 1830, the monarchy was consciously conflating history with nation-building, through teaching history, erecting monuments and founding museums. A famous example was Louis-Philippe's repatriation of the body of Napoleon in October 1840, a show of force designed to definitively subordinate the Empire to the (shaky) July Monarchy. It follows that a linear model of history – plotting history as a constant progression from a necessarily fixed point in the past – is false and even dangerous: as we read in *Sur Catherine de Médicis*: 'We can see, from what is happening in our own time, that history is distorted as soon as it is made' ['Nous pouvons voir, par ce qui se passe de nos jours, que l'histoire se fausse au moment même où elle se fait'] (CH XI 199).

The July Monarchy's retrograde history, like Scott's fragmented history, was anathema to Balzac: for him, the true historian must instead grasp what Castex calls history's dynamism and onward march,[11] and witness how the present can understand the past without becoming bound to it. In terms of the individual, the drive from past to future emerges through the constraining circumstances and the psychological turmoil of characters who strive to determine their own destiny. Balzac expresses this personal history constantly: for example in the humiliation of Lucien de Rubempré returning from Paris to his provincial starting point (*Illusions perdues*, 1837–43), or the desperation of the Comtesse de Dey as she waits to see whether the conscript expected in town is her son in disguise (*Le Réquisitionnaire*, 1831). In terms of the collective, Balzac's interest in *les mœurs* is close to what we might now call social anthropology, or even sociology, though he does not have the strong sociological bent of novelists such as Zola in the latter half of the century. Balzac is not really a demographer when he attributes characteristics to particular streets in Paris, nor a criminologist when he describes the ex-convict Vautrin, because he is more interested in the effects he describes, or in their philosophical and moral causes, than in the material conditions of their possibility. Yet he was immensely interested in the larger socio-historical forces that shaped his society, such as money, class and gender. Insofar as Balzac can be understood to be a frank historian of such forces, each of these deserves brief consideration here.

Concerning money, the changing nature of wealth distribution in post-Revolutionary France is a dominant feature of contemporary history at the opening of the nineteenth century. As Barthes explains in *Le Degré zéro de l'écriture*, Balzac was writing 'at the precise moment when a new economic structure is joined onto an older one, thereby bringing about decisive changes in mentality and consciousness' ['au moment même où deux structures économiques font charnière, entraînant dans leur articulation des changements décisifs de mentalité et de conscience'].[12] According to many critics, money is the principal driving force of society in Balzac's world. The juxtaposed extremes of wealth and poverty were a particularly Parisian phenomenon, as the opening sequence of *La Fille aux yeux d'or* vividly portrays. However, the provinces are the setting for some of the most heartless tales of exerting power through debt, particularly where families collude or fathers financially stifle the next generation (as in *Illusions perdues* or *Eugénie Grandet*, 1833). Money is the motive behind most human cruelty, as the lawyer Derville observes (*Le Colonel Chabert*), and as the usurer Gobseck demonstrates (*Gobseck*, 1830); and personal tragedy can most often be traced back to the kind of crushing debt faced by Balzac's legion of (variously autobiographical) arrivistes and artists.

With questions of wealth come questions of class, and Balzac's contemporaries were living through the most radical dissolution of traditional class structure in France's history. Balzac recorded, even preserved, societal classes on the verge of extinction: the terrifying matriarchal countesses and doddering marquis who had outlived the world for which they had been groomed; but also the imperial soldiers whose loyalty had been discounted by a new regime. Whether they are idealising an outdated model or are forgotten by history, such walking historical examples contrast with the youth and life of the capital. Balzac's societal snapshot also includes the working classes, whose concerns and frank views intrigued him, but whose capacity to evolve from a reactionary mob into a democratic body he clearly doubted after the disastrous turn of post-Revolutionary populist governance from aspiring Republic to civil war and the Reign of Terror. Above all, Balzac examines the dramatic, brilliant and ruthless rise of the bourgeoisie – bureaucrats, merchants, professionals – concerning whom he was famously ambivalent, delighting in their innovation but lambasting the self-interest that motivated their push for progress (the publishing industry being a prime example).

Balzac's treatment of gender both did and did not align with his historical times, as numerous important scholars including Catherine Nesci, Dorothy Kelly and Michael Lucey have shown. He wrote frequently and with sympathetic (if stereotyped) observation from a woman's perspective, maintaining his belief in fundamental differences between men and women, as well as in their equal capacity for intelligence, compassion or cruelty. He insists in his 'Avant-propos' that women are not merely the female of the human species, but must be considered in their own right, and on their own terms. Importantly, Balzac understood that any implied essential difference between men and women is crucially altered by experience, and that this is most often to a woman's detriment. Numerous Balzac heroines exemplify (Eugénie Grandet), or even overtly decry (Antoinette de Langeais) the historically particular difficulties faced by women with respect to education, inheritance and legal rights. While one would be hard-pressed to call Balzac's writing feminist, particularly given the limited outcomes his female characters face, it is interesting that at a time when men's and women's roles were becoming increasingly legally prescribed, Balzac distinguishes what we now call sex and gender. Individuals often have traits that connote masculinity and femininity, and gender affiliation is, in the case of some characters, flexible (Henri de Marsay being a good example), or even fluid to the point of being a function of the desire of the interlocutor (in the case of the angelic Séraphîta).

Finally, it has to be said that there are no important historians, or even archaeologists, in the cast of *La Comédie humaine*: their perspective is reserved for the author and the omniscient narrator. The realist author, like the archeologist, lays bare and analyses the relics underpinning the past, and maps the arbitrariness of the present onto that structure. Yet Balzac never loses sight of the ironic and even dangerous situation of the historian who, with scientific precision, must seek the key to living cultures through examining the dead, and must revive history without, like the heroine of *Adieu* (1830), becoming traumatised and transfixed by the past. The novelist is among those rare historians and even scientists, observers 'who examine human nature without a scalpel, and seek to capture it in the act' ['qui examinent la nature humaine sans scalpel, et veulent la prendre sur le fait'] (*Théorie de la démarche* [1833], CH XII 277). Arguably, human nature itself found its living historian in Honoré de Balzac.

Balzac as Scientist: The Unity of Nature, from Medics to Mesmer

Balzac's enthusiasm for the sciences is legendary: references to scientific names and principles emerge in every stage and context of his writings. Nor do they represent an incidental curiosity, but the evolution of an early analytic interest in a scientific project concerning human behaviour. This youthful ambition serves as a reminder that, for Balzac and his contemporaries, science was understood far less narrowly than it is today. Balzac's interest in science was linked to theories of unity: as he writes in the voice of the eponymous Louis Lambert: 'Science is one. It is impossible to touch upon politics without taking up morals, and morals touch upon all scientific questions' ['La science est une. Il est impossible de toucher à la politique sans s'occuper de morale et la morale touche à toutes les questions scientifiques'] (CH XI 655). The originality of Balzac's engagement with the objectives of science was his desire to apply a scientific method in his writing, by way of analytic observation and deduction. 'The observer is incontestably the greatest genius' ['L'observateur est incontestablement homme de génie au premier chef'] (CH XII 276), he insists in his *Théorie de la démarche*, and attributes this realist skill to thinkers as diverse as Buffon, Lagrange and Mesmer. Yet such analytical insight is rare amongst writers, firstly because the novelist, as 'the observer of morals' ['l'obervateur de la nature morale'], must look beyond the surface of custom to discern what a person 'involuntarily lets slip about his conscience' ['laisse involontairement deviner de sa conscience'] (CH XII 277) and secondly because authors must make their texts enjoyable to read. The writer is faced with the task of adorning science with the beauty of poetic form: 'How to be a great writer and a great observer, Jean-Jacques [Rousseau] and the Bureau of Longitudes, that is the problem; and it is insolvable' ['Être un grand écrivain et un grand observateur, Jean-Jacques et le Bureau des Longitudes, tel est le problème; problème insoluble'] (*ibid.*). Perhaps the problem is indeed 'insolvable', as unattainable as was 'the Enlightenment dream of totalising knowledge'[13] to which Balzac firmly adhered, but which, when pursued actively as the aesthetic or scientific Absolute by Balzacian characters such as Louis Lambert and Balthazar Claës, leads only to madness.

ELISABETH GERWIN

Biology, the Natural Sciences and Medicine

In intellectual circles and in the popular press, the natural sciences had a strong and growing hold on the French imagination at the turn of the nineteenth century, particularly concerning theories of unity. 'After the natural history of Linnaeus and Buffon, and with the work of Lamarck, Cuvier and Geoffroy Saint-Hilaire, biology was emerging as the totalising study of life forms as Balzac came to maturity'; and Balzac saw himself as the collaborator, even the rival of this study.[14] However, Balzac often places the natural sciences in what he sees as their larger context, alongside mysticism, philosophy and indeed literature. For example, he points out that the evolutionary debate between Cuvier and Geoffroy Saint-Hilaire was not new, given that the idea of *unity of composition* had already under different names preoccupied the greatest minds of the last two centuries' ['L'*unité de composition* occupait déjà sous d'autres termes les plus grands esprits des deux siècles précédents'] ('Avant-propos' 134, trans. modified; CH I 7). At the same time, the natural sciences were unquestionably revolutionising the terms and the urgency for exploring this issue of the unity of nature, and Balzac was keen to engage with recent scientific theories. Thus he set out 'to lend scientific truth' to *La Recherche de l'absolu* ['laisser le livre vrai scientifiquement'] (LH I 193) by consulting two chemists of the Académie des sciences, by drawing directly on the theories of the Swedish chemist Berzelius (1779–1848) and even by making its hero Balthazar Claës a fictional student of Antoine Lavoisier (1743–94), the father of modern chemistry. Balzac's challenge, as a novelist, was to avoid the Scylla of scientific imprecision while skirting the Charybdis of stylistic tedium.

While chemists were revealing the world of elements as the invisible building blocks of all matter, physicists such as the Italian Alessandro Volta (1745–1827) were exploring the transfer of tangible energy through electricity. Such unseen forces, whose manifest effects were nothing short of supernatural, could not fail to thrill a spiritualist like Balzac. However, insofar as Balzac saw himself as actively participating in scientific discoveries through his history of social *mœurs*, it is the life science of biology that served as his model and most direct inspiration. As he says, the 'chimera' ['chimère'] that enticed him to formulate *La Comédie humaine* was the idea of 'a comparison between Humanity and Animality' ['une comparaison entre l'Humanité et l'Animalité'] ('Avant-propos' 134; CH I 7). In this domain, too, living energy was being understood to exceed conventional perception, due to the advancement in studying microscopic organisms and the establishing of biological continuity from pre-history to the present. Suddenly, life was perceived to be everywhere, from infinitesimal entities to colossal creatures in an immemorial past, and was being defined in terms of energy and movement rather than of static form. As a result, systems of classification were being redrawn to insist on previously unimagined groupings, through the comparative anatomy of Buffon and Cuvier as well as the emerging evolutionary theories of Lamarck and Geoffroy Saint-Hilaire. To these, Balzac wished to add the social divisions of humanity: 'just as there are Zoological Species, there always have been and always will be Social Species' ['Il a donc existé, il existera donc de tout temps des Espèces Sociales comme il y a des Espèces Zoologiques'] ('Avant-propos' 135; CH I 8). It is no coincidence, therefore, that references to Balzac and science so often invoke the names of two naturalists in particular, Cuvier and Saint-Hilaire. The influence of each scientist on Balzac is worth exploring briefly here.

The statesman and scientist Georges Cuvier (1769–1832) is often called the founder of modern palaeontology. His comparative anatomy, which revolutionised the understanding of fossils, drew on Lamarck's ideas about emerging complexity of life-forms and Linnaeus's system of classification. Balzac refers to Cuvier over thirty times in *La Comédie humaine* alone. Characters attend his lectures, debate his theories and evoke his exemplary genius. Balzac was inspired by Cuvier's deductive method of comparing past artefacts to present appearance and behaviour. In *La Peau de chagrin* the narrator calls Cuvier 'the greatest poet of our century' ['le plus grand poète de notre siècle'] (CH X 75) who lays bare the fossilised layers of the past and toils in the laboratory to demonstrate the interconnectedness of the world: 'When Mr Cuvier beholds the frontal, jaw or thigh bone of some animal, does he not induce a whole creature from it . . . ?' he asks in the *Traité de la vie élégante* (1838), concluding: 'his genius revealed to him the unitary laws of the animal kingdom' ['Quand M. Cuvier aperçoit l'os frontal, maxillaire ou crural de quelque bête, n'en induit-il pas toute une créature . . . ? . . . son génie lui a révélé les lois unitaires de la vie animale'] (CH XII 237). In a letter to Madame Hanska (LH I 804), Balzac compares Cuvier's genius to Napoleon's, and, rather optimistically, to his own. Yet finally Balzac extended the principle of unity of the natural world further than did Cuvier himself, following the transformism outlined by Lamarck and developed by Saint-Hilaire, towards a theory of common origin for animal life.

Étienne Geoffroy Saint-Hilaire (1772–1844) was a brilliant young zoologist when, in 1795, he hired the rising star Cuvier to join the École Centrale du Panthéon and then the Musée d'Histoire naturelle. The long-time colleagues famously parted company during a very public debate in 1830 over an ideological difference that was dividing the scientific community: creationism (*fixisme*) versus evolution. Cuvier was a vitalist, believing that all life originates from a divine energy or spark; this tiered with his creationism, according to which the world was created once, and might admit of extinctions but not of transformative evolution. Saint-Hilaire, however, criticised creationism as wilful ignorance of the inescapable truth that all living creatures share a common point of origin, revealed by what he called their unity of composition, and subsequently evolve according to their environment. Despite his conservative religious and political leanings, Balzac openly sided with Saint-Hilaire. The two met in 1835, and Balzac paid homage to the great scientist by dedicating *Le Père Goriot* (1835) to him. Several years later, he evoked Saint-Hilaire's 'admirable law concerning reciprocal affinity' ['la belle loi du *soi pour soi*'] ('Avant-propos' 135, trans. mod.; CH I 8), a rather complex idea concerning the tendency during growth, and especially during embryonic mutation, of body parts to fuse with reciprocal parts, which Saint-Hilaire saw as a key to unity of composition. However, Balzac makes only eight references to Saint-Hilaire in *La Comédie humaine*, most of which also evoke Cuvier. Although Saint-Hilaire gave compelling voice to Balzac's belief in unity, the first intimations of evolutionary theory seem to have had far less of a hold on his imagination than did the natural history traced back through the emerging fossils of an antediluvian past by Cuvier.

As an applied science that crosses all social boundaries and uses deductive observation as its primary praxis, medicine was an obvious and lifelong source of interest to Balzac. He refers in particular to medical scientists, such as Georg Ernst Stahl (1659–1734) and Paul-Joseph Barthez (1734–1806), who valued living observation over dissection. This distinctly realist approach to diagnosis was upheld by numerous celebrated medical doctors such as Jean-Antoine Chaptal (1756–1832), who reorganised the largest hospitals in Paris after their dissolution in 1793, Pierre Jean George Cabanis (1757–1808), who promoted the method of observation through eliminating variables and Napoleon's doctor Jean-Nicolas Corvisart (1755–1821), a cardiologist who pioneered triage grouping according to symptom. Thus, in *La Maison Nucingen* (1837), Blondet momentarily speaks with Balzac's voice when he declares that the glory of modern medicine is that since 1799 it has passed 'from a state of conjecture to that of a positive science, due to the influence of the great analytical school of Paris' ['de l'état conjectural à l'état de science positive, et ce par l'influence de la grande école analyste de Paris'] (CH VI 342).

This period of transition in medical science is represented across *La Comédie humaine*: Thierry Appelboom counts more than 1,200 references to medicine and sixty-three medical professionals in its pages.[15] It is with good reason that Balzac has in turn generated so much recent interest on the part of historians of medicine. Jacques Borel makes the interesting point that novels such as Balzac's played a reciprocal role in actually shaping medical beliefs of the time.[16] Nevertheless, even in his own day, Balzac was not read as a source of medically accurate information, patently limited as he was to the medical terminology of the previous century, dredged from his father's copy of Panckoucke's *L'Encyclopédie méthodique* (1782–1832). A notable exception to this is Balzac's description of the symptoms of mental illness: for example, later psychiatrists read the sufferings of Louis Lambert as an early and just representation of schizophrenia;[17] and Balzac's insight into the dire impact of the loss of illusions and the lack of love made him a precursor of the emerging medical fields concerned with psychological and emotional ailments.[18]

Balzac's main interest in his detailed descriptions is always moral as well as physical portraiture. Balzac's most important fictional doctor, Horace Bianchon, exemplifies this overarching view, appearing in over thirty texts of *La Comédie humaine*. Bianchon is less showy and politically engaged than other medical characters in Balzac, and less fleshed out than Dr Benassis in *Le Médecin de campagne*. Yet he criss-crosses France throughout its various regime changes, ministering equally to the wealthy and the poor, a virtuous super-ego of French society and a model for the perceptive realist narrator. Balzac's depiction of medics is often sympathetic, and he had great respect for many real doctors including his long-time physician and friend Jean-Baptiste Nacquart (to whom he dedicated *Le Lys dans la vallée* in 1835). However, he was also deeply suspicious of the medical profession as a body, in part because of its dismissal and even ridicule of magnetism and Mesmer. In several texts (*Ursule Mirouët, Le Colonel Chabert*) Balzac denounces the three 'black robes' ['*robes noires*'] (CH III 823) – priests, doctors and lawyers – whom he accuses of disdaining the world they are meant to be serving. He even critiques the inept trio of materialist doctors (parodying famous physicians of the day) who fail to diagnose the magical ailment of Raphaël de Valentin.[19]

Balzac's portrayal of the limitations of science when faced with supernatural forces is nowhere clearer than in *La Peau de chagrin*, as Raphaël's doctors attempt to chemically and physically alter the magical skin that is dwindling away with his life. If Balzac's documenting of the popular reception of science guarantees him a modern readership, the same cannot be said for his fascination with the supernatural, the spiritual and the occult. Yet for this early realist, the tangible effects of intangible forces were of no less consequence in the lives of his characters than were the natural sciences. Nor was Balzac unusual: what seems eccentric today – his interest in magnetism for instance – was in fact his creative participation in debates concerning mysterious forces such as heat and electricity.[20] Balzac was also influenced by his mother's spiritualism and his interest in Swedenborg led him to write his astounding metaphysical novel *Séraphîta* (1835). He believed psychic energy to be a kind of transformative electrical force that was not limited to purely spiritual beings. As an adolescent (and like several of his characters) Balzac wrote a *Théorie de la volonté*, and his continuing obsession with a theory of will emerges, for instance, in the magnetic force of personality he grants to Napoleon or to the arch-criminal Vautrin. In *Ursule Mirouët*, even an elderly medical doctor is shaken from his materialist convictions when his protégée Ursule telepathically communicates to him her private thoughts. Dr Minoret's conversion to magnetism leads him directly to Catholicism – a development that is utterly in keeping with Balzac's own spiritualist convictions.

Thus popular theories, such as magnetism, were as real to many of Balzac's contemporaries as were the emerging domains of science, and Balzac seamlessly moves from praising the advances made by Saint-Hilaire to lauding Mesmer. Balzac in fact believed himself to be possessed of magnetic healing powers, though he worried that, like Mesmer, he would be mocked by serious thinkers. He had an unshakable conviction that below the surface of society lay hidden, structuring forces as substantial as the emerging historical and scientific structures he portrayed in his novels. His interest in the occult seemingly did not extend to freemasonry, though he did found an informal secret society whose members aspired to unite their superior involvement in the arts, publishing, politics and science. He also created fictional fraternities, most famously in the *Histoire des Treize*, where the all-powerful thirteen comrades launch super-human exploits that deploy subversive forces within the historical setting of Restoration France. More generally, Balzac's objective in including mysterious collectives in his *Comédie humaine* was to extend his reach beyond his own context, into the mythical world of occult affinities, and to avoid chaining his imagination too tightly to the tenets of science. The cohabitation in Balzac's prose of the real and the fictional remains consistent and astonishing, and the juxtaposition of natural and supernatural forces provides the most striking example of this blend. If Balzac's descriptions operate on the basis that the best way in which to reveal something is to attempt to hide it,[21] then perhaps his inclusion of the occult becomes a magnificent smokescreen that can be understood as integral to his realist project.

Conclusion

Balzac, the classifier of human society at the opening of the French nineteenth century, remains characteristically, if disconcertingly, unclassifiable. No doubt this is also why he exerts such fascination across the genres and disciplines. The enthusiasm and honesty of Balzac's prolific writing are his response to radical changes to the neo-classical project of mimetic representation – a model that was being overturned by the scientific method of observation, by the recognition of forces exceeding habitual perception, and by the realisation that historical records are not repositories of comprehensive truth. Balzac turns from the static perspective of the historian contemplating a fragmented past, or of the scientist dissecting a cadaver, and seeks instead to participate in the generation of a living archive. Beyond each vivid character, each individual 'stuffed to the very teeth with willpower' ['chargées de volonté jusqu'à la gueule'] as Baudelaire says in *L'Art romantique*, Balzac sees the whole of society moving, like the dinosaur implied by the fossilised bone that is brought to light. And indeed, he urgently saw the need of this society to evolve, or rather to adapt to a radically changed world, to recall the past without repeating it, and harness the creative energy of the younger generation. He was himself an exemplum of this creative vitality: and if he sought to analyse like a doctor, create taxonomies like a scientist and contextualise events like a historian, above all he wrote with the ingenious and passionate eye of the novelist.

NOTES

1. Balzac, 'Preface (Avant-propos) to *The Human Comedy*', trans. P. Morrison in A. Kettle (ed.), *The Nineteenth-Century Novel: Critical Essays and Documents* (London: Heinemann, 1972, 1981), pp. 134–147. Translations of the 'Avant-propos' are from this edition. Translations of other French texts are my own unless otherwise indicated. I have drawn on the early translations of *La Comédie humaine* by G. Saintsbury (among others), generously made available on line through Project Gutenberg.
2. *Facino Cane* in *The Human Comedy: Selected Stories*, trans. L. Asher, C. Cosman and J. Stump, ed. P. Brooks (New York: The New York Review of Books, 2014), p. 4.
3. A. Becq, *Genèse de l'esthétique française moderne* (Paris: Albin Michel, 1994), pp. 6–7.
4. P. Barbéris, 'Préface' to Balzac, *Les Paysans* (Paris: Garnier-Flammarion, 1970), p. 53.
5. P. Barbéris, *Le Monde de Balzac* (Paris: Kimé, [1973] 1999), p. 155.
6. P.-G. Castex, *Horizons romantiques* (Paris: Corti, 1983), p. 157.
7. C. Bernard, *Le Passé recomposé: le roman historique français du dix-neuvième siècle* (Paris: Hachette, 1996), p. 240.
8. N. Mozet and P. Petitier (eds), *Balzac dans l'histoire* (Paris: SEDES, 2001), pp. 7, 15.
9. See O. Heathcote, 'Honoré de Balzac's Vision of Paris' in A.-L. Milne (ed.), *The Cambridge Companion to the Literature of Paris* (Cambridge University Press, 2013), pp. 71–84.

10. Mozet and Petitier, *Balzac dans l'histoire*, p. 12.
11. Castex, *Horizons romantiques*, p. 161.
12. R. Barthes, *Le Degré zéro de l'écriture* (Paris: Seuil, 1972), p. 20; *Writing Degree Zero*, trans. A. Lavers and C. Smith (New York: Noonday Press, 1988), p. 18.
13. A. Thiher, *Fiction Rivals Science: The French Novel from Balzac to Proust* (Columbia and London: Missouri University Press, 2001), p. 39.
14. *Ibid*.
15. T. Appelboom, *Balzac, témoin de la médecine du XIXe siècle* (Bruxelles: Musée de la Médecine et Éditions M.E.O., 2013), p. 11.
16. J. Borel *Médecine et psychiatrie balzaciennes: la science dans le roman* (Paris: Corti, 1971), p. 65.
17. *Ibid.*, p. 102.
18. A.-M. Baron, *Le Fils prodige: l'inconscient de 'La Comédie humaine'* (Paris: Nathan, 1993), p. 237.
19. Appelboom, *Balzac, témoin de la médecine*, pp. 27–32.
20. Thiher, *Fiction Rivals Science*, p. 43.
21. A.-M. Baron, *Balzac occulte: alchimie, magnétisme, sociétés secrètes* (Lausanne: L'Âge d'Homme, 2012), p. 25.

2

MICHAEL TILBY

Balzac's Early Works

Balzac's writings prior to the publication in 1829 of *Le Dernier Chouan*, the first of his novels to be incorporated in *La Comédie humaine*, comprise published and unpublished works, completed compositions and others that he left unfinished. They are also strikingly diverse. They encompass not only works of fiction, but also stage plays, essays, pamphlets and journalism. Some were undertaken in collaboration and raise questions of authorship.

The eight novels Balzac published between 1822 and 1825 under the pseudonyms Lord R'Hoone (a patent anagram of Honoré) and Horace de Saint-Aubin have long exerted a particular fascination as a result of their uncertain status within his overall œuvre and will therefore necessarily form the primary focus of this chapter. Their origins lay in an enterprise directed by one Auguste Lepoitevin de l'Égreville, whose 'petits crétins' ['little morons'], as he called them, helped him produce under the pseudonym Viellerglé (another obvious anagram) novels designed to appeal to patrons of *cabinets de lecture* ['public reading rooms and circulating libraries']. Uncertainty regarding the extent of Balzac's participation in the Viellerglé novels is matched by doubts concerning his sole authorship of the first two R'Hoone titles: *L'Héritière de Birague* and *Jean Louis, ou la fille trouvée*, the title pages of which hint at the involvement of other Viellerglé authors, including Étienne Arago. Such comments as Balzac made on his early fictions were invariably derogatory. He eventually disowned all works not published under his own name. Yet the publication of the two-volume *La Dernière Fée, ou la nouvelle lampe merveilleuse* was soon followed by a revised, three-volume version, and he clearly oversaw the revision by assistants of all but the first two of his early novels and their re-publication in the mid-1830s, with new or truncated titles. The same assistants were responsible for the completion of the previously unpublished *L'Excommunié* and *Dom Gigadas*, which, together with Jules Sandeau's overtly imaginary *Vie et Malheurs de Horace de Saint-Aubin*, formed part of the latter's so-called complete works.

The presence in Balzac's early novels of material appropriated from an eclectic range of contemporary writing has encouraged the view that they are derivative. Initially, they made little impact. Such positive comments as were expressed by reviewers were largely content to highlight R'Hoone's comic characters and Saint-Aubin's merits as a painter of provincial manners. Later critics, aware of the author's true identity, made ironic use of these fictions to undermine his hard-won standing. Their recent scholarly rehabilitation has rightly considered them integral to Balzac's œuvre, while arguably placing too exclusive an emphasis on specific characters and situations later developed in novels of *La Comédie humaine*. Comprehension of their significance in his evolution as a novelist is dependent on examining them as autonomous compositions.

Account needs also to be taken of the fact that Balzac's pseudonymous novels came to an end with the publication of *Wann-Chlore* in 1825 and that it was not until 1829 that he published, under his own name, *Le Dernier Chouan ou la Bretagne en 1800*. The conclusion that he temporarily abandoned his ambitions as a novelist during the latter years of the Restoration in order to devote himself to other forms of hack-writing and to his short-lived acquisition of a printing works is, nevertheless, misleading. His likely authorship of the first volume of the Viellerglé novel *Le Corrupteur*, published in 1827, may well date from earlier in the decade, but cogent arguments have been advanced for his being largely responsible for two novels published by the self-styled 'entrepreneur littéraire' Horace-Napoléon Raisson: *Marie Stuart* in 1827 and *Une blonde*, published in 1833 though probably written five years earlier. In the same period, he devised a series of novels entitled, with an obvious nod to Walter Scott, *Histoire de France pittoresque*, though none of its constituent works was ever completed by him. Two may never have consisted of anything more than the fragments that have survived. It was for this series that both *L'Excommunié* and *Dom Gigadas* were originally intended. The discovery, in the 1980s, of a holograph manuscript of the former, a novel set in Balzac's native Touraine in the early fifteenth century, revealed that he himself wrote almost half of it. The second, which is set in the Camargue during the seventeenth century and which, like other of the young Balzac's fictions, contains echoes of Scott's *Ivanhoe*, possesses far fewer Balzacian characteristics, which suggests that his role was limited chiefly to the provision of an outline. It is clear that *Histoire de France pittoresque* was intended to break with R'Hoone's jocular treatment of the historical novel, though the chapters Balzac completed for *L'Excommunié* include features recycled from the earlier of his pseudonymous novels.

Balzac's published early novels are, nonetheless, but the most prominent strand in a multifarious literary activity spanning the entire decade of the

1820s. This included joint or sole authorship of a brochure on the law of primogeniture, an alleged *Histoire impartiale des Jésuites* and the life story of the public executioner Sanson. He assisted the Duchesse d'Abrantès in the production of her memoirs and gave advice to the criminal-turned-police-chief Vidocq, a partial model for his own infamous Vautrin, with regard to his memoirs. He was joint or sole author of Raisson's *Code des gens honnêtes* and contributed to several other *Codes*. He may also have had more than a printer's hand in some of the *Arts*, or 'how-to' guides, published by Émile-Marco de Saint-Hilaire. As 'H. Balzac', he contributed the biographical preface to an edition of La Fontaine he both published and printed, and printed a first version of his *Physiologie du mariage* for his own private use. In addition to apparent authorship of puffs for his own fiction, his early articles included reviews of Viellerglé and Walter Scott. There is reason to believe that he also contributed anonymously to several irreverent news sheets, including the original *Figaro*, which was briefly acquired by Lepoitevin soon after its creation in 1826.

His earliest ambition was to achieve success as a dramatist and, in particular, to emulate the masterly comedies of Beaumarchais, which explains the frequent references to the latter's plays *Le Barbier de Séville* and *Le Mariage de Figaro* both in his early novels and in those Viellerglé titles in which he almost certainly had a hand. It is significant that several plays by 'Viellerglé-Saint-Alme', in collaboration with Étienne Arago and others, were successfully staged in the years 1823–25. Their advertised genres (a *comédie-vaudeville*, a *comédie* and a *mélodrame*) were amongst those represented by Balzac's own projects. The first was based on the Viellerglé novel *Stanislas, ou La Suite de Michel et Christine*, and it has been suggested that Balzac may have been involved in its composition. In contrast, no play of his own was published or staged in this period. Only two were completed. Of these a five-act verse tragedy, *Cromwell*, the earliest of his literary creations, failed to pass muster with either the academician or the actor invited to appraise it. A *mélodrame* entitled *Le Nègre* was rejected by the Théâtre de la Gaîté. The other projected plays, which included *drames* and an *opéra comique*, remained fragmentary or failed to progress beyond a title or list of characters.

A contrasting early ambition took the form of a desire to achieve status as a philosopher. The family friend Dr Nacquart duly addressed him as 'mon jeune philosophe'. A flavour of the taste for philosophical speculation he acquired during his Oratorian schooling may be gained from his quasi-autobiographical novel initially entitled *Histoire intellectuelle de Louis Lambert*. He attended the Sorbonne lectures of the 'eclectic' philosopher, Victor Cousin (banned in 1820 by the University authorities for his subversive ideas). There survive notes from his reading of Nicolas Malebranche, René Descartes, Baruch Spinoza and Baron d'Holbach, as well as a manuscript essay on the immortality of the soul and the beginnings of a Treatise on Prayer that suggests a retreat from materialism. A desire to combine philosophy and the novel was equally strong, though the works that resulted remained incomplete. The most developed is an epistolary novel set in Touraine, *Sténie ou Les Erreurs philosophiques*, which was inspired by Rousseau's *La Nouvelle Héloïse* and Goethe's *Werther*. The significant fragment known as *Falthurne II*, in order to distinguish it from another of his youthful works, depicts an idealised female figure who constitutes the focus of a reflection on love and religion that seeks to achieve greater poetic and philosophical depth than is possible in *La Dernière Fée*. A further philosophical essay sought to comprehend the phenomenon of 'poetic genius'.

Although the substantial early fragments *Agathise* and *Falthurne*, novels set respectively during the Crusades and prior to the First Crusade, will be shown to possess exceptional interest for an understanding of Balzac's development as a novelist, the compelling starting point for such an enquiry must be the novels that he completed and published, not least because they exhibit greater independence of the stereotype than has often been assumed.

Superficially, the latter conform to Lepoitevin's market-driven prescriptions. The *cabinet de lecture*, which in 1834 Balzac would hold responsible for the demise of French literature, was associated with a particular kind of popular novel most commonly published in two, three, or four duodecimo volumes. The most consistently successful practitioner of the genre was Paul de Kock, whose *Georgette ou la nièce du tabellion* (1821) could be shown to have provided the author(s) of Viellerglé's *Charles Pointel* (also 1821), a novel in which it is increasingly tempting to detect Balzac's hand, with a range of material. Viellerglé compositions offered a staple diet of a contrast between the well-born and the humble in stories that featured strangers whose mysterious identities are revealed so as to allow them to be reunited with long-lost offspring, previously assumed to be orphans or foundlings. The inevitable journeys featured stage coaches and roadside inns, providing a stereotype against which Horace de Saint-Aubin's significantly more original *Annette et le criminel* can be judged. A dose of sexual innuendo was likewise a favoured ingredient. The continuity with such features displayed by Balzac's early fiction is easily demonstrated, but his novels stand out by virtue of incorporating a range of compatible material encountered in such authors of Gothic novels as Mrs Radcliffe and featuring the inveterate clash between good and evil: villains (often Italian), brigands, passwords, hold-ups, kidnapping, imprisonment, poison and rescues, in isolated settings that included forests.

While conforming to the underlying expectations of the genre, the novels of Lord R'Hoone and Horace de Saint-Aubin are striking for their variety of subject and outward form. *L'Héritière de Birague* is set in a fictional château in Burgundy during the regency of Marie de Médicis; its outline plot is derived from the *roman noir*. *Jean Louis*, the action of which revolves around the forest of Sénart before the Revolution, is conceived as a *roman gai* after Pigault-Lebrun. *Clotilde de Lusignan, ou Le Beau Juif* depicts fifteenth-century feudal Provence and makes explicit use of Scott. *Le Vicaire des Ardennes*, the plot of which features the love of two young Creoles who wrongly believe themselves to be brother and sister, is related to the tradition represented by Bernardin de Saint-Pierre's *Paul et Virginie* and Ducray-Duminil's *Lolotte et Fanfan*; its European scenes take place in a fictional village in the Ardennes. *Le Centenaire, ou les Deux Béringheld* is a *roman fantastique* after Maturin's *Melmoth the Wanderer*; set in Touraine, its action begins on the night of '15 June 181 ... ', with more precise dating made possible by the subsequent allusion to Napoleon's Spanish campaign. *La Dernière Fée*, which takes as its starting point a passing Parisian theatrical vogue for Aladdin and makes significant reference to *The Tempest*, assumes the form of a modern fairy story for adults. *Annette et le criminel* straddles Paris and the Rhône Valley and is, in essence, a variation on the theme of the noble bandit, as exemplified in authors as distinct as Schiller and Ducray-Duminil. Its dénouement is likened by Saint-Aubin to the final act of a tragedy. The form of *Wann-Chlore* is less easily assigned to a particular genre. Set in Touraine, it combines a love story that exploits elements from Goethe and Maturin's novel *Women* with the basic compositional technique employed (for rather different effects) by Pigault-Lebrun, while incorporating letters, the hero's memoirs and further borrowings from Laurence Sterne and the German sentimental novelist, August Lafontaine. The philosopher Alain would judge it an unsuccessful novel that, in spite of its recourse to stock theatrical types and practices, would not have made a good stage play either.

Such generic distinctions are, however, less germane than might be assumed. In no instance does Balzac produce exemplary versions of the form he is ostensibly concerned to imitate. It is characteristic of his pseudonymous fictions that they combine, within a single composition, different forms of writing, a phenomenon that is only incidentally a hangover from the collaborative practice of the Viellerglé novels. In the case of *Le Vicaire des Ardennes*, for example, a lengthy attempt at a humorous account of village life centred on the village priest, his *gouvernante*, the schoolmaster and the marquise de Rosann (eventually revealed as the mother of the eponymous curate, whom she had had by a noviciate who has meanwhile risen to be bishop of the diocese) is followed by the surreptitious reading, by the priest and his incurably nosey servant, of the curate's memoir of his early life in the French West Indies, which includes an account of a mutiny led by the eventual pirate Argow as well as that of Joseph's love for his 'sister' Mélanie. (The theme of sibling incest also features in *Sténie*.) This is followed by the marquise's devastating experience of a passionate attraction to the as yet unidentified curate and the kidnapping of Mélanie, whom Argow is determined to have as his wife. Additional examples of peripeteia thwart the latter's designs, causing him to seek vengeance. The conclusion depicts an involved situation, which after offering hope of resolution leads not to marriage but to premature death.

This impression of the hybrid is increased by the way these fictions combine popular forms with examples of writing that imitate (and on occasion plunder) elements of more powerful contemporary products of the creative imagination in a way that distances the composition from both. No attempt is made either to exploit the *cabinet de lecture* formula fully or to fulfil the poetic potential of features deriving from such substantial Romantic writers as Goethe, Schiller, Nodier, Maturin, Thomas Moore and Scott. The innumerable borrowings are redeployed indiscriminately across generic boundaries in the creation of an all-purpose 'adventure story' format that does not develop, for example, any initial specificity of date or location, and is capable of assimilating any number of features of disparate origin. An element of homogeneity is achieved as a result of the compositions being grounded in an essentially comic mode of narration that submits both the already comic (for example the garrulous or eccentric characters of Scott that are affectionately mimicked or the inheritance of a manuscript story by John Melmoth after his uncle's death, which lies behind the humorous preface to *L'Héritière de Birague*) and many of the originally non-comic elements to a process of simplification and exaggeration. Character, theme and plot are subordinated to a delight in narration itself, presented, self-consciously, as a combination of imitation and an opportunity to indulge in an idiom of exaggerated fictionality, an aesthetic that has obvious parallels with Balzac's fellow child of Touraine, the priest-turned-fabulator Rabelais, who, in addition to being a frequent presence in Balzac's work, is evoked in Viellerglé's *Charles Pointel*. Of still greater significance are the frequent references to Sterne's *Tristram Shandy*, the self-conscious practices of which provided him with an explicit model for an early unfinished work entitled *Une heure de ma vie*. A narrator who intervenes to comment on the form of the work he is purveying, and on his own times, is one of the most striking of the unifying features of Balzac's pseudonymous novels. This self-conscious voice also serves as a reminder of the ease with which such practices can be superficially imitated, which is further illustrated by the addresses to the reader to which Paul de Kock, and the Viellerglé authors, have recourse. Sterne's Uncle Toby is also clearly the model for the Pyrrhonist Oncle Barnabé in *Jean Louis*. *Tristram Shandy* likewise encouraged the inclusion of smutty innuendo in, for example, the opening chapter of *La Dernière Fée*.

This hybrid nature is further communicated by the narratorial persona's regular parading of references to a range of literary, philosophical and historical figures or works, a feature that matches the plethora of heterogeneous epigraphs employed by Lord R'Hoone (though not Saint-Aubin). This makes the persona a teasing combination of the simple-minded and the learned, even if the references smack of the schoolroom. Ultimately, this indicates that the compositions are addressed to a more sophisticated reader than the stereotypical patron of the *cabinet de lecture*. They solicit a critical engagement by the reader, though at the risk of being considered to have fallen between various stools. They might nevertheless be seen as a reflection of Balzac's ambivalence towards the underlying format and as an attempt to hold onto his intellectual pretensions, while humorously highlighting their inappropriateness in such a humble context.

In the final analysis, this eccentric combination of self-consciousness and a hybrid mélange of genres and styles may be taken to indicate relative indifference to an effective development of the basic fictional components of character and plot or to the sustaining of fictional illusion. It may indeed be argued that the fictional canvas serves essentially as a pretext for observations relating to the author's extra-fictional concerns, most notably in the realms of art and politics.

Balzac certainly takes every opportunity to parade his interest in painting. The artists recalled include Old Masters such as Correggio, an engraving of a Virgin by whom serves as frontispiece to *Le Vicaire des Ardennes* and who had been evoked in Viellerglé's *Charles Pointel*, but also contemporary painters such as Gérard, Gros and Girodet, and the sculptor Canova. (Guérin's 'Le Retour de Marcus Sextus' is highlighted in *Une heure de ma vie*.) Not all such allusions are identified. The comparison of Argow and his henchman to 'Crime' and 'Remorse', for example, alludes to an allegorical painting by Prud'hon exhibited at the Musée du Luxembourg in 1818. Annette's apostrophe in echo of Marie Stuart: 'Fair land of France, I thus leave you for ever' must surely refer to the four paintings that formed Louis Ducis's 'The arts under the influence of love', which Balzac would have seen at the Salon of 1822. Confirmation exists in the previous comparison of her eyes to 'those a painter has given to Mary Queen of Scots singing with Rizzio', this being another of Ducis's subjects. The painter's scene depicting

Tasso was plausibly the prompt for references to the poet in other of Balzac's early novels. The arguable superiority of painting over literature is rehearsed when Saint-Aubin wishes that a painter had been present to capture Mme de Rosann's expression on first beholding her adult son in *Le Vicaire des Ardennes*.

Balzac's early novels likewise contain numerous hints of their author's political stance, which in contrast to his later attraction to Legitimism, was staunchly Liberal. The title page of *L'Héritière de Birague* sounds an anti-clerical note that is continued in the satire of priests and monks found elsewhere in R'Hoone's compositions, including the unfinished *Agathise*, which betrays its Liberalism through a thinly disguised evocation of the sermons of Frayssinous, court preacher to Louis XVIII. The highlighting in *Le Vicaire des Ardennes* of a broken vow of priestly chastity, and the subsequent cover-up, inevitably attracted a charge of anti-clericalism. The positive effect of a missionary sermon on Argow in *Annette et le criminel* might be seen as a form of authorial repentance.

The mutiny in *Le Vicaire des Ardennes* is carried out in the name of social justice. Argow's boast 'A man with five million is never hanged' is in essence a quotation from Rousseau's *Discours sur l'origine et les fondemens de l'inégalité parmi les hommes*. Social class provides a key focus in *Jean Louis*, with the love interest centring on the contrasting attractions of a village girl and a titled lady. The fairy temptress of *La Dernière Fée* is a fictional duchesse de Sommerset [sic]. Balzac's Republicans are models of probity, as in the case of Jacques Butmel in *Le Centenaire*, who is endowed with a suitably noble Roman physiognomy. It is in that novel, and in *Wann-Chlore*, that the Republican theme is extended through the inclusion of characters named Marianine and Marianne, the figure of Marianne having been adopted by the Revolution of 1789 as the incarnation of 'liberté, égalité et fraternité'. In *Clotilde de Lusignan*, R'Hoone jests that the acquisition of a medieval manor house could easily turn him into the most ultra of ultra-Royalists. The use of the otherwise innocuous phrase *nec plus ultra*, in both *Le Centenaire* and *La Dernière Fée*, inevitably connotes Liberal opposition, as does the recurrence of the word *légitimité* in *Le Vicaire des Ardennes*, where the Mayor is belittled by his obsession with the 'gouvernement légitime' of the restored Bourbon monarchy, and likewise the designation of *opposition* as an instance of 'langage parlementaire'. An unflattering portrait of state preferment during the Restoration is provided by Charles de Servigné's promotion in *Annette et le criminel*. The words *libéral(e)* and *libéralement* in *Clotilde de Lusignan* and *libéralité* in *Le Centenaire* inevitably assume a positive political hue. The former work, which possesses a link to *La Dernière Fée* through its reference to Mélusine and the château de

Lusignan, appropriately includes epigraphs from Voltaire. It may not be a coincidence that Saint-Aubin brought his novels to an end following the Royalist landslide in March 1824.

A comic treatment of monarchy, feudalism and chivalry, which Louis XVIII's Minister the duc de Richelieu had celebrated as emblematic of a virtuous age, and of a 'troubadour' aesthetic that would achieve greater prominence as a trend within contemporary painting, is prominent in *L'Héritière de Birague*. Parodic allusion to the current king through the improbably high dynastic number of Mathieu XLVI is thrown into relief by the cult of the perennially popular Henri IV, first of the Bourbon kings who reigned from 1589 to 1610, on the part of the two principal comic characters. The ironic reference to the centrist, ministerial government is repeated, using the nickname *ventrus* [pot-bellied], in *Jean Louis*. (A manuscript poem in Balzac's hand from this period is entitled, after the *chansonnier* Béranger, 'Le Ventru'.) Most of the early novels include asides to *les ministériels*; in *Annette et le criminel*, Saint-Aubin jokingly asks the reader not to assume that he has become one. If references to *ministres* are especially prominent in *Clotilde de Lusignan*, it is because care is taken to include in the medieval cast the four ministers of Jean II, King of Cyprus. The latter is, with clear reference to present-day France, one of a number of monarchs said to have been deposed 'for the time being'. In some cases, the validity of a non-innocent reading of such references is less easily established, as, for example, in the temptation to see the mentions of [Cardinal] Richelieu and Villani in *L'Héritière de Birague* as veiled references to the current king's successive first ministers in 1821–22: Richelieu and Villèle. Hidden allusions to the revolutionary *carbonaro* movement (of which Étienne Arago, Balzac's fellow writer and collaborator, and, most probably, the controversial philosopher Victor Cousin were members) may, however, be discerned in the presence of honest *charbonniers* in *Jean Louis* and *Le Vicaire des Ardennes*, as well as in the explicit designation of Argow's pirates as *carbonari*. (The former novel can be seen to contain traces of Balzac's attraction to Cousin's philosophy of Eclecticism.) There are references to *charbonnerie* too in the first two Viellerglé novels, *Les Deux Hector* and *Charles Pointel*. Carbonarism had its origins in the initiation rights of the charcoal burners of eastern France who formed brotherhoods of 'bons cousins charbonniers'; there is no shortage of cousins in Balzac's early fiction, starting with R'Hoone and Viellerglé, who in the preface to *L'Héritière de Birague* appear as nephews of 'Dom Rago', while in both *L'Excommunié* and *Dom Gigadas* there are chapters entitled 'Les Deux Cousins'. The inclusion in *Jean Louis* of a Duc de Parthenay recalls the Carbonarist-inspired conspiracy in the midwestern town of that name in February–March 1822.

Lepoitevin was, nevertheless, a declared Bonapartist. His admiration for the Emperor was duly shared by the young Balzac. The animated discussion around loyalty to Argow in *Annette et le criminel* comes, suggestively, in the wake of a reference to Napoleon's Hundred Days. Furthermore, the pirate, who in *Le Vicaire des Ardennes* reminds Joseph of Cromwell, is compared in its sequel to Themistocles, to whom Napoleon had compared himself after Waterloo. The reference to the Greek statesman, previously evoked in *Le Centenaire* in connection with the young Tullius Béringheld's admiration for Greece, is accompanied by one to Jacques-Louis David's painting 'Léonidas aux Thermopyles', which depicted the Spartan king and general on the eve of the Battle of Thermopylae. Together with the Aegean background of *Clotilde de Lusignan* and sundry other mentions of Greece in Balzac's early fiction, it would have signalled a Liberal's support for the Greek campaign for independence. Annette's speech to Argow begging him to escape his pursuers exhorts him to die fighting not on the scaffold but in a battle for an (unspecified) nation's freedom and independence so as to assume the title of popular liberator. It was for less high-minded motives that in *Le Vicaire des Ardennes* he and his pirates had allegedly participated in the defence of Charlestown, but Jean Louis Granivel, who likewise is said to serve the cause of American Independence, is purportedly raised by Washington to the rank of colonel.

There is no doubt that Balzac's early works of fiction are of uneven, not to say limited, artistic worth. Yet it is equally clear that they contain the seeds of features of some of the best known works of *La Comédie humaine* and that the novels he published under his own name do not illustrate a clean break with the past. Continuity is provided, for example, by the deployment, in *La Peau de chagrin*, of a wild ass's skin that shrinks to a degree commensurate with the size of the owner's wish; by the continuity of the adventure story format in *Histoire des Treize*; by the *parenté* between Argow-Maxendi and Vautrin-Collin in the novels of the so-called Vautrin cycle; by Montéjanos's recourse in *La Cousine Bette* to poison in a manner reminiscent of Argow's poisoned dart; or by the treatment of Eugénie Grandet by her cousin Charles, which recalls Annette Gérard's experience at the hands of her cousin also named Charles. Of greater significance for Balzac's mature compositions, however, is the early novels' exemplification of a search for a new kind of composition through an overt engagement with existing genres of fiction that was essentially critical rather than imitative, coupled with their illustration of Balzac's instinctive sense of the need for a mode of expression that could accommodate the multiplicity, diversity and ambivalence that characterised the post-Revolutionary world. Crucial to the evolution of such a narrative language would be the retention of the commitment to the self-conscious practice to which he was attracted in his earliest attempts at fiction. It is, however, the progression in this respect from *Agathise* to *Falthurne* that can be shown to demonstrate this lesson most clearly, in the process revealing that both these incomplete compositions are part of the same quest for form that operates in more modest ways in the early published novels, with which they nonetheless have elements in common. Both works, together with *Clotilde de Lusignan*, which like *Agathise*, re-works features from *Ivanhoe*, purport, for example, to be based on original manuscripts. Enguerry le Mécréant's recourse to violence and torture in R'Hoone's novel may look forward to the modern comic strip, but the differences between his presentation and that of the characters in the two fragments are essentially ones of degree.

Agathise resembles an episodic medieval romance in which narrative alternates with dramatic speeches (rather than dialogue). Its explicitly Rabelaisian dimension is seen in the monk described as 'le grand gros gras Bongarus', an aficionado of Latin tags who nonetheless crudely confuses sacred and profane, and in the way the worm-eaten manuscript recalls the opening chapter of *Gargantua*. The narrative idiom is a pastiche of a conventional naïve and hyperbolic mode duly larded with examples of learned wit. The distillation of the abbé Savonati's manuscript, translated by a schoolmaster who in *Falthurne* acquires the name Matricante, is interrupted by addresses to the reader that comment on the narrative and its origins, thereby conferring on the work a comic self-consciousness in harmony with the overriding impression of pastiche. *Falthurne*, the shorter of the two compositions, is more considered. Its self-consciousness extends to a more far-reaching disowning of the text. The deployment, in the often-lengthy footnotes, of authorial self-consciousness in the service of a pseudo-critical commentary is facilitated by the core narrative's problematic status as translation. Matricante confesses that he knows no Italian and has had to rely on a first draft, in poor French, provided by his nephew, whose sole qualification for the task had been his service as a corporal in Napoleon's Italian campaign. The joint inadequacy of uncle and nephew is compounded by their mutual ignorance, their misguided reasoning, and their criticism of each other's efforts. The end-product of their task is avowedly incomplete and responsibility for its imperfections ambiguously attributable to either the translators or Savonati himself. To that extent, the work is 'unreadable', though one that is teasingly designed also to disarm the potentially critical reader.

The notion of translation generating numerous different versions of the original may stand as a metaphor for Balzac's conception of the literary text itself. It also highlights the extent to which language and writing constituted the young author's fundamental concern. What he carried forward to his conception of *La Comédie humaine* was a sense of the illusory nature of complete or definitive expression. Authentic representation thus demanded an infinite activity of re-writing that subjected all expression to critical questioning. The product of more ambitious goals than those that had presided over his early fictions, the works of *La Comédie humaine* would nonetheless continue to meld a host of conventionally distinct, not to say incompatible, styles and registers in order to thwart premature closure, above all in respect of interpretation or judgment. An overall idiosyncrasy of language and form would likewise continue, albeit in a more sophisticated manner, though this did not spare their author critical disparagement and accusations of hasty and undisciplined writing, thereby denying him the popular success that he envied his contemporary, the popular novelist Eugène Sue, author of *Les Mystères de Paris*. It would, however, be left to the works of *La Comédie humaine* to merge philosophical ideas with less-elevated scenarios rooted in the depiction of material reality, and to accord prominence to lengthy, multifaceted descriptions. The most important element of continuity of all, however, would consist in the retention of a commitment to self-consciousness that highlighted the way the ludic text invites from the reader a simultaneous combination of acceptance and rejection. In other words, underlying all of Balzac's subsequent compositions is to be found, with greater profundity than in the case of his early fictions, a reflection on the novel and, more especially, on the teasing relationship between the fictional and the real.

A Note on Editions

There exists a facsimile edition of Lord R'Hoone and Horace de Saint-Aubin's original eight novels, published by Les Bibliophiles de l'Originale (Paris, 1961–63) and a reprint of the original three-volume edition of *La Dernière Fée*, published by Slatkine (Geneva, 1976). The Éditions Rencontre edition of Balzac's *Romans de jeunesse*, with introductions by R. Chollet (Geneva, 1962–68), reproduces (except in the case of *L'Héritière de Birague* and *Jean-Louis*, which were not published in revised versions) the text of the *Œuvres complètes de Horace de Saint-Aubin* (Paris, Souverain, 1836–37): *Clotilde de Lusignan* therefore becomes *L'Israélite*; *Le Centenaire* becomes *Le Sorcier*; *Annette et le criminel*, *Argow le pirate*; and *Wann-Chlore*, *Jane la pâle*. It includes *L'Excommunié*, but legitimately excludes *Dom Gigadas*. Volume XV (1952) of the Club Français du Livre edition of *L'Œuvre de Balzac*, edited by A. Béguin and J.-A. Ducourneau, contains *Jean-Louis*, *Argow le Pirate* and *Wann-Chlore* [though in the form of the Souverain text of *Jane la pâle*], presented by P.-G. Castex. The two-volume Bouquins edition of Balzac's *Premiers Romans*, edited by A. Lorant (Paris, Robert Laffont, 1990), adopts the text of the original editions of the eight novels previously reproduced in facsimile by Les Bibliophiles de l'Originale. Separate editions exist of *Annette et le criminel* (edited by A. Lorant, Paris, Garnier-Flammarion, 1982) and *Wann-Chlore* (edited by T. Bodin, Paris, Mémoire du Livre, 1999). There are also scholarly editions of two Viellerglé titles: *L'Anonyme, ou Ni père ni mère* (edited by M.-B. Diethelm, Paris, Le Passage, 2003) and *Le Mulâtre* (edited by A. Sol and S. Davies Cordova, Paris, L'Harmattan, 2009), and of *Une blonde* (edited by M.-B. Diethelm, Wimereux, Éditions du Sagittaire, 2013), the three works having originally been published as the work of A. de Viellerglé-Saint-Alme, Aurore Cloteaux and Horace Raisson, respectively. Balzac's melodrama *Le Nègre* has been edited by S. Davies Cordova and A. Sol (Paris, L'Harmattan, 2011) and translated into English with an introduction and notes by M. Cheyne and A. Watts (Liverpool Online Series. Critical Editions of French Texts, 2014: http://www.liv.ac.uk/media/livacuk/modern-languages-and-cultures/liverpoolonline/Le-Negre.pdf). Balzac's remaining *juvenilia* will mostly be found in the two volumes that make up his *Œuvres diverses* in the Bibliothèque de la Pléiade (edited by R. Chollet and R. Guise, Paris, Gallimard, 1990–96).

3

EWA SZYPULA

Balzac's Correspondence

Introduction

Balzac was a prolific letter-writer. His general correspondence comprises three volumes of 1,200 pages each (excluding notes), while his letters to the Polish countess Eveline Hanska alone constitute a two-volume publication amounting in length to a quarter of the size of *La Comédie humaine*. Though frequently exhausted by writing novels, Balzac still took the time to maintain long and extremely detailed correspondences. His published letters are a rich collection, spanning professional correspondence, letters to creditors, acquaintances, friends and family, love letters and replies to admiring readers.

Balzac's correspondence offers precious, and largely untapped, insights into his life and the artistic principles that underpin his work. In France, it has been the object of studies by José-Luis Diaz and Anne-Marie Baron; in England, the letters have received some attention, notably from Owen Heathcote, who recently redefined the Hanska correspondence as a 'paratext' to *La Comédie humaine*.[1] In this chapter, I would like to suggest that Balzac's letters are significant not only as a historical document, or an appendix to his literary work, but primarily because Balzac used them as a space for literary creation. Crucially, they provide another window onto the workings of his creative imagination. Many of his personal letters can be seen as creative exercises in which the novelist is honing his craft; and as we shall see, Balzac employs many of the same literary processes in his letter-writing as in his fiction, using his correspondence as an opportunity for storytelling, invention and self-presentation.

The epistolary form recurs throughout Balzac's fiction – from his first attempt at novel-writing, *Sténie*, to *Mémoires de deux jeunes mariées* (1842) and the long confessional that Félix de Vandenesse addresses to Natalie de Manerville in *Le Lys dans la vallée* (1836). This chapter will look at some instances where Balzac used correspondence as a literary device. Occasionally the line between letters and novels becomes blurred; letters and novels are seen to feed into each other, and his novels acquire a communicative purpose. On one occasion, his page coming to an end, Balzac finished a letter to Eveline Hanska by telling her to read *Pierrette* (1840): 'You will find in here a thousand things which I want to say, but which the paper no longer allows me to express.' ['Vous trouverez ici mille choses que j'ai à vous dire, mais que le papier ne me permet plus d'exprimer.'] (LH I 522, 16 December 1840)[2] We can read this in two ways. One is that his correspondent can begin reading *Pierrette* and so continue her 'conversation' with him; the other is that letters can only express so much, whereas novels can be made to contain additional thoughts, which one may prefer not to spell out clearly in a letter.

Balzac's Correspondence: A Life in Letters

Balzac's earliest surviving letter is to his mother in 1809, apologising for his schoolboy misdemeanours and promising to work hard and to clean his teeth. His letters to his family, which are especially numerous in early adulthood, become rarer as he enters his thirties, and tend to discuss financial matters, with Balzac asking for money or complaining of his pressing financial need.

Balzac kept up correspondence with several illustrious acquaintances – notably the aristocrat and travel writer Marquis de Custine, the poet, dramatist, novelist and critic Théophile Gautier, literary giant Victor Hugo, poet and politician Lamartine, author and librarian Charles Nodier and illustrious female writer George Sand. Yet he also made the time to respond to letters from his female readers, women who wrote to him to praise (and occasionally condemn) his works. His published correspondence is a curious platform for these often anonymous voices, which now command equal attention to those of Lamartine or Sand, the provincial reader metaphorically rubbing shoulders with literary celebrities in its pages.

Balzac's business correspondence ranges from letters relating to his (failed) businesses, his contracts with publishers and the odd subsequent lawsuit. Exchanges with his editors are punctuated by reclamations over unmet deadlines and unfinished manuscripts, with Balzac going mysteriously silent when confronted with a request for either. For example, his correspondence in 1838 with his editor Hippolyte Souverain appears rather one-sided, as Souverain chases belated or unfinished manuscripts in letters which receive no reply. Balzac's various ploys for avoiding creditors – for example, using assumed names and changing addresses – sometimes made him inaccessible to close friends, such as Auguste Borget and Zulma Carraud.

Balzac's barely disguised self-interest is a striking feature of his letters. His correspondence with the family friend Dr Nacquart in the year 1838, for example, alternates between two themes – asking to borrow money, and apologies for being unable to visit. In letters to friends and lovers, Balzac frequently tried to elicit sympathy, making much of the fact that his family had 'mistreated' him, exaggerating their purported role in his business troubles. When he told Madame Hanska 'my mother ruined me in 1827' ['Ma mère m'a ruiné en 1827'] (LH I 625, 20 December 1842), this was certainly untrue. According to Wurmser, Balzac's indebtedness was very much self-inflicted and invoked to enlist support and sympathy for the self-appointed Napoleon of letters.[3]

Balzac seems to have elicited loyalty and dislike in equal measure. Hugo, for example, whose earliest letters to Balzac are extremely formal and perhaps a little patronising, would go on to provide staunch support to Balzac's theatrical aspirations and to his candidature for the Académie française throughout the years. (Balzac later dedicated *Illusions perdues*, written between 1837 and 1843, to Hugo.) Nodier, to whom Balzac dedicated *La Rabouilleuse* (1841–42), likewise impressed him with down-to-earth advice on winning a much-coveted membership of the Académie, and also profoundly influenced him with his fantastical writings. Yet the correspondence also offers examples of Balzac's relentless self-interest, alienating some of those closest to him. Balzac's friendship with the renowned journalist Henri Latouche during the writing of *Les Chouans* (1829) is a case in point. From his letters to Balzac, Latouche emerges as a devoted friend, ready to assist Balzac with anything from publishing his novels to decorating his home or paying for an evening's entertainment. Over time, this important epistolary friendship deteriorated. Balzac's inability to respect promises and deadlines, after Latouche took over the publication of *Les Chouans*, seems to have caused a serious rift, and matters were not helped by the 'similarities' noticed by Latouche between Balzac's work and his own (not least the close resemblance between the title *Les Chouans ou la Bretagne en 1799*, under which Balzac published a revised edition of the novel in 1834, and Latouche's 1829 work *Fragoletta: Naples et Paris en 1799*).

In its range and frequent preoccupation with financial concerns, Balzac's correspondence is comparable to that of his contemporary George Sand, who also managed an extensive personal and business correspondence. However, their correspondences also differ in several crucial ways. Balzac never escaped the worries of his daily existence long enough to have the leisure to write reflectively. In her later years, Sand wrote to Flaubert of the pleasure she took in the smallest of sounds in her environment, or in simply watching the seasons change and spending time with her family.[4]

Balzac's correspondence was to the last filled with business directives, preoccupations with daily concerns and attempts to further his short-term ambitions. Even in the lead-up to his marriage to Eveline Hanska, his so-called intimate letters were filled with 'business', from constant deadlines to hard-pressed finance.

Furthermore, unlike Sand and other literary contemporaries such as Flaubert, who cultivated life-long friendships with male literary friends, Balzac's most important correspondents were women. In his youth, he was mainly writing to his sister, Laure, sharing his hopes of a literary career and trying out his imaginative flights of fancy. In his coming-of-age phase, it was Madame de Berny, his first lover, who became his most significant correspondent and mentor from 1822, and who took on the task of reading and correcting his work. Other significant friendships included the married confidante Zulma Carraud (whose earliest surviving letter to Balzac dates from 1826), the writer George Sand (whom he met in 1831), and the wealthy and single Marquise de Castries (whom Balzac attempted unsuccessfully to seduce in 1832). From 1833, it was largely Madame Hanska with whom Balzac shared his literary ideas.

Balzac was not above suggesting to his female correspondents that each was the only woman in his life, while maintaining several significant letter-writing relationships simultaneously. Not only do these correspondences overlap chronologically; they also occasionally read as rewritten versions of one another. We can read Balzac's letters to the key women in his life as creative exercises, or palimpsestic drafts, the remnants of an earlier correspondence visible in the new. Throughout his life, Balzac appeared to be seeking the ultimate, ideal relationship with a maternal figure who would make up for his disappointing relationship with his own mother.

Epistolary Self-Creation: The Young Balzac

When Balzac was still an impoverished would-be writer trying to pen his versified tragedy, *Cromwell*, in his garret in the rue Lesdiguières, he was already using his letter-writing relationships as part of his process of positive self-creation. When Laure reports to him his parents' fears over his extravagance (prompted by his purchase of two mirrors for his room) Balzac writes that he has done worse: he has engaged a servant.

> M. Nacquart's [servant] is called Tranquil, mine is called Myself. As soon as I am awakened, I ring for Myself and he makes my bed.
> - Myself!
> - What is it, sir?

[Celui de Mr Nacquart se nomme Tranquille, le mien se nomme Moi-même. Lorsque je suis éveillé, je sonne Moi-même et il fait mon lit.
 -Moi-même!
 -Quoi, Monsieur?] (Corr. 1 12–13)

Already in 1818, writing his first letter to his sister from his new Parisian lodgings, Balzac shows an ability to fictionalise himself, humorously rewriting his difficult financial situation into one which suggests his future earning potential. Balzac's self-fashioning narratives really come into their own in his first great love correspondence, which began in 1822, with Laure de Berny – a married woman with grown-up children. Attractive, erudite and exuding maternal tenderness, she inflamed the young Balzac's desires, representing at once the passionate mistress and the loving mother he claims never to have had. His epistolary courtship of her reveals, already at the age of twenty, an ability to use letters as a tool to soften, persuade and convince.

Of Balzac's letters to Madame de Berny, only a few drafts from 1822 remain. The rest of his letters, stored and carefully organised by her in the months before she died, were burnt after her death on her own instruction. Yet from the drafts which remained in Balzac's possession (now published in his *Correspondance*), it is possible to build up a picture of the twenty-year-old Balzac as a skilful letter-writer, carefully crafting his prose. In his earliest (anonymous) letter to her, Balzac represents himself as a chaste and timid youth, who hardly dares to speak the word 'love' (Corr. 1 89). Yet the professed timidity of the letter-writer is at odds with the confident and manipulative tone in which the letter is written. 'Do not think that I am unaware of even the smallest thought which shall cross your mind when reading [this letter]', he writes. 'Initially, you will see in it the subject of the most wonderful mockery' ['Ne croyez donc pas que j'ignore la moindre des pensées que vous aurez en la lisant .... D'abord, vous y verrez la matière d'une des meilleures railleries qui soit au monde'] (Corr. 1 89). He steers her towards the desired reaction – which is 'compassion' and 'generous pity' ['la compassion, la pitié généreuse'] (Corr. 1 91). Not only does the epistolary voice dare 'speak' of love, it goes so far as to pre-empt and indeed script the reaction of the addressee.

Three drafts of another letter, dated 23 March 1822, purportedly show Balzac having recourse to the verses of 'our young poet' ['notre jeune poète'], Chénier; he claims that including them shows his humility (Corr. 1 94). The verses he 'cites' change slightly from draft to draft – thus betraying that they are in fact not by Chénier, but were penned by Balzac himself (Corr. 1 94–98). In another letter to de Berny, he 'cites' the Greek philosopher

Theophrastus (Corr. 1 98–99) on the importance of not judging those who are in love; again, editors have established that these words are Balzac's own invention. Whatever his reasons for this appropriation – whether to give his words more weight, or give himself plausible deniability, should the correspondent reject his advances – it would certainly seem that the future writer of La Comédie humaine was already trying on the 'famous writer' label for size.

Writing to Madame Hanska: 1832

Balzac's relationship with the married twenty-seven-year-old Polish countess Eveline Hanska began when she sent him an anonymous letter in 1832. In it, she criticised him for the representation of women as 'femmes fatales' in his latest work, La Peau de chagrin (1830–31). This letter, which has been lost (see LH 1 5), must have impressed Balzac, for he went so far as to place a personal notice in a newspaper in order to reply. No doubt his curiosity was piqued by the sight of an expensive postmark (she lived in Russian-occupied Poland) and a foreign coat-of-arms. A friendship with a 'Russian or Polish princess' ['princesse russe ou polonaise'] (LH I 13), was clearly highly desirable to an impoverished writer struggling with debt. Thus began an eighteen-year correspondence, ending only with their marriage in 1850 – just months before Balzac's death.

Eveline Hanska, a mother of one, was, it would appear, unhappily married to a much older man; bored and secluded on his remote estate, her chief pleasure was reading the latest available novels. In writing to a French author, she risked compromising herself; she signed her early letters only as 'L'Étrangère', meaning both 'foreigner', and 'stranger' (and later demanded that her signed letters be burnt; hence only three remain today, making the published correspondence very much one-sided). The beginnings of this relationship thus contain hints of a romantic adventure of the sort that Balzac himself might have invented in his novels. Indeed, in his first known letter to her, Balzac suggests that their epistolary exchange belongs to the realm of the 'novelistic' ['romanesque'] (LH 1 8, May 1832).

Most striking about Balzac's first letter is the fact that he does not attempt to find out anything about the Étrangère. He asks no questions about her. Instead, she becomes a project for his creative imagination, 'the object of [his] sweetest dreams' ['l'objet des plus doux rêves'] (LH 1 7, May 1832). He paints a Romantic picture of her as a lonely letter-writer, 'exiled perhaps from the heavens' ['exilé peut-être des cieux'], reaching out to him – a brother – miraculously across immense distances (LH 1 7, May 1832).

The details he does later elicit, he uses to his own ends. When she reveals her name to be Eveline, he tells her he will call her Eve, or Eva, and suggests that they are like the first man and the first woman on earth (thus reinforcing his suggestion of exclusivity, and also deflecting her suspicions as to any rivals she might have): 'Well, my dear Eve, let me shorten your name, it will tell you all the better this way that you are the entire sex to me, the only woman in the whole world' ['Eh bien, ma chère Ève, laissez-moi abréger votre nom, il vous dira mieux ainsi que vous êtes tout le sexe pour moi, la seule femme qu'il y ait dans le monde'] (LH I 53, 9 September 1833).

On occasions when she did not conform to his image of her, his response was 'Poor Eva! We do not know one another at all' ['Pauvre Éva! Nous ne nous connaissons donc pas'] (LH I 85, 6 November 1833). Thus there is a sense that Balzac does not wish to know his correspondent better, for fear of losing the control he had sought to establish over their exchanges. Their correspondence is a playground for his literary imagination.

Objects and Sensuality

Balzac had described correspondence as a 'Proteus', or shape-shifter (CH XI 1095; *Physiologie du mariage*, 1829). He was referring to the fact that a correspondence can take many other forms beyond simple letter-writing: a flower worn in a certain way at a ball, or a poem written on the cover of a book, can also be used to send a message.

The correspondence with Madame Hanska and its beginnings, which took the form of anonymous letters and responses given in newspaper announcements in order to keep the relationship secret, is such a 'Protean' correspondence. It continued to take on different forms; from newspaper announcements it morphed into private letters supplemented by 'dummy' ones [*lettres ostensibles*], penned so that they could be shown to Eveline's family, maintaining Balzac's cover as a family friend. Balzac's fictional writings, too, became requisitioned for the purposes of corresponding with Eveline. His dedication of the novel *Séraphîta* to her, for example, ostensibly innocent, appeals to their secret mutual understanding. Balzac's idea, in 1834, to have the manuscript of *Séraphîta* bound in a piece of grey silk from Eveline's dress, which she wore when they met in Geneva (LH I 136, 15 February 1834), was another instance of the correspondence transcending traditionally defined borders. This symbolic enrobing of his work in a piece of Madame Hanska's clothing illustrates very effectively the kind of interrelationship between objects, works and letters which Balzac apparently had in mind when writing his theory on the 'Protean' nature of correspondence.

Physical objects have a special place in Balzac's love letters. Balzac supplemented the letters with small gifts, such as flower petals he had kissed, and locks of his own hair. In return, he demanded specific items for himself – on one occasion berating Eveline for the disappointing gift of an unscented violet, and suggesting that a white hair ribbon would have been preferable. In the gifts he demands, we can discern an almost fetishistic yearning for some form of physical contact during their necessary separation. His requests to be sent small items worn by Hanska – hair ribbons, scraps of clothing – carry an erotic charge.

In later years, Balzac's letters to Eveline Hanska dwell at length on the collection of objects he received from her, and on their arrangement on and around his writing desk (LH I 798, 2 February 1844). Interestingly, the insistence is on their position in relation to his writing, indicating that in some way their presence aids Balzac's writerly routine. Balzac's relationship and his creative writing process are deliberately conflated in these descriptions of his writing-desk-museum, suggesting that the shrine which purports to be a celebration of Eveline Hanska is at least as much a celebration of Balzac's creativity.

Novels as Correspondence

The correspondence is all the more Protean when we consider that Balzac's novels, too, become gradually drafted into the service of this correspondence. Two novels which contain tributes and messages to Madame Hanska are *Le Médecin de campagne* and *Séraphîta*; the first written before the pair met for the first time in September 1833, the second, after.

Le Médecin de campagne is portrayed in Balzac's letters to Hanska as a tribute to her. Her first name, Eveline, which was a source of fascination and pleasure to him, finds its way into the novel at a key point. 'She will tremble with joy to see that her name was on my mind, that she was present in my thoughts' ['[e]lle frémira de joie, en voyant que son nom m'a occupé, qu'elle était présente à ma pensée'] (LH I 44, 19 July 1833), he wrote in anticipation of her reaction to the novel. 'Did you put the book down at the point when Benassis lets slip the beloved name?' ['Avez-vous posé le livre au moment où Benassis laisse échapper le nom adoré?'] (LH I 55, 9 September 1833).

Yet how does one write a tribute to a woman whom one does not know, and whom one does not wish to risk offending – especially as she had expressed her disapproval of some of his more feisty female heroines? Cautious of ascribing to her any qualities she might not appreciate, Balzac's attempt at creating this fictional tribute to Madame Hanska becomes instead a self-reflective act, a sort of representation of the creative process itself; it is an exercise in what the creative imagination can do when it has almost no information to work from. The result is a somewhat bland figure – one which has either attracted criticism from, or been entirely dismissed by, Balzac scholars unaware of this context.

Yet the fictional Eveline is interesting, precisely because of her 'uninterestingness'. What Balzac explores through this portrayal is the way in which we attach meaning to small, insignificant messages, and how we read volumes of information into the merest of occurrences, in an attempt to understand the elusive Other. Each Eveline – the fictional and the real – is a blank page, which the writer/storyteller fills as best he can; each Eveline remains (at that stage, at least) ungraspable, the male writer being left to his own devices, attempting to clutch at any trace of her.

Similarly, *Séraphîta* (1834–35) owes a great deal to Balzac's personal correspondence. It is highly ironic that the dedication to *Séraphîta* should claim to be 'proof of [Balzac's] respectful affection' ['un témoignage de [ma] respectueuse affection'] (CH XI 727) towards Eveline Hanska, when in fact the whole plot of *Séraphîta* was constructed in order to help justify their love affair.

By the time Balzac wrote *Séraphîta*, he and Eveline had met, fallen in love, added a physical dimension to their relationship and made a promise to marry as soon as her ageing husband should die. As Eveline vacillated between happiness at this new-found love, and guilt over the deception of her husband, Balzac found himself frequently having to alleviate her fears. In writing *Séraphîta*, Balzac had a hidden agenda; he used this novel to reinforce the idea to the wavering Eveline that there is nothing wrong with starting again.

The novel is all about new beginnings. *Séraphîta* is ostensibly the story of an angel, facing a final transformation before ascending to heaven. Through the Buddhist aspects of the story – namely, the overtones of rebirth and reincarnation – Balzac tried to suggest that it is possible to reclaim an earlier sense of identity and re-become a previous self – in the case of himself and Eveline Hanska, young free spirits who have no ties to anyone else. Balzac's discussions of this novel in his letters to Eveline are heavy with the rhetoric of 'first love'; he and Eveline are Adam and Eve; he dreams of kissing her 'virgin lips' ['lèvres vierges'], which have never known love before (LH I 114, January 1834); he suggests that '*Séraphîta* is the two of us, ... let us love in the same way' ['*Séraphîta*, c'est nous deux, ... aimons de la même manière'] – essentially giving her a narrative in which there is a quasi-theological justification for their love affair (LH I 142, 22 February 1834).

Correspondence as a Device in Balzac's Novels

A correspondence in a Balzac novel is rarely a straightforward method of communication. On the contrary, Balzac makes the most of the purported 'failings' of the epistolary medium. Misunderstanding a letter from the beloved, as in *Le Médecin de campagne*, leads to a lifetime of solitude and storytelling for the narrator, who spends the rest of his life musing on his unrequited true love. In *Albert Savarus* (1842), letters are stolen, substituted and deliberately used to break off a relationship between two lovers, with unfortunate consequences for all the characters involved. In *Le Lys dans la vallée*, Félix de Vandenesse describes, in an extended confessional written to his mistress, how he spent his childhood writing letters to his mother which either received no reply, or which at best attracted reproaches from her over his childish style. Ironically, this missive receives the same negative reaction from the mistress as those childhood letters had once received from the mother; thus he is shown to be hopelessly repeating the same pattern of letter-writing met with rejection. Letters filled with honesty are shown to be all the more vulnerable to being judged harshly.

In *Mémoires de deux jeunes mariées*, letters serve as a means for correspondents to undermine one another. Two best friends are shown to be frequently – and, perhaps unwittingly – scoring points. The Parisian socialite, Louise, tells her newly engaged, provincial friend Renée that her dull, provincial marriage will be a living death, and offers to make up for this with tidbits from her own exciting life; Renée, later happily married and a mother, retaliates by telling the childless Louise that a woman without children is a monstrosity (CH 1 346). Through such instances of casual cruelty, the novel explores an aspect of what Balzac had termed the 'fatal power' ['fatale puissance'] of the letter (LH 1 335, 1 October 1836); that is to say, the terrible effect thoughtlessly written letters can have on loved ones, especially if read at an inopportune moment.

Lastly, Balzac's novel *Modeste Mignon* – which was initially Madame Hanska's idea, and which draws on her correspondence – rather than celebrate the love letter, seems instead to undermine its potential for sincere expression. The protagonists, Modeste and Ernest, are shown to read and reread the flirtatious letters they receive, hoping to infer something special from them, or to gain access to the other person's innermost thoughts; they are unaware that the letters in question were carefully constructed so as to reveal absolutely nothing genuine. Both correspondents find themselves deceived; Modeste is particularly enraged to discover that instead of her correspondent being the illustrious poet he pretended to be, he was in fact a perfectly unremarkable secretary, and – worse – one of those suitors 'whom parents like' ['qui plaisent aux parents'] (CH 1 606).

Conversely, the inadequacy of letters as a means for communication often seems to be celebrated in Balzac's novels, rather than bemoaned; if they fail to communicate, they offer consolations in other ways. Primarily, they serve the purpose of helping to create narratives. In real life, it seems that Balzac really did welcome the purported 'failings' of this medium. The distance that separated him from Madame Hanska, for example, was really perceived by him as a blessing, allowing his imagination to weave stories about her undisturbed.

Conclusion

We have seen how the correspondence is an insight into Balzac's creative processes, and an opportunity to see his creative imagination at play. Balzac draws a distinction between the kind of writing needed for his *Comédie humaine*, and the writing of letters to close friends. In writing to his Eveline, he made a point of telling her that he wrote to her either late at night or in the early morning, before starting work. He appreciated this precious moment of letter-writing as an additional breathing space, a moment when his creative faculty could roam free, before that moment when he had to 'become' Balzac the writer:

> You are my debauchery, my happy reveries, the meanderings of my soul! . . . Normally, whenever I have been able to write to you, it is and it always has been in the morning, when I get up, and while I am waiting for my faculties to return to me . . . . You are thus the continuation of my sleep, of my happy time!
>
> [[V]ous, c'est ma débauche, c'est mes rêveries heureuses, c'est les flâneries de mon âme! . . . Ordinairement, quand je puis vous écrire quelques lignes, c'est et ce fut toujours, le matin en me levant, en attendant que mes esprits reviennent . . . . Vous êtes ainsi la continuation de mon sommeil, de mon temps heureux!] (LH I 578, 29 April 1842)

The idea of 'lingering in bed' with the correspondence before going back to his day's work ties in with Balzac's whimsical suggestions throughout that his correspondence is his 'mistress', while his paid writing work is his wedded wife. On several occasions, tearing himself away from his letter to Eveline Hanska, Balzac describes his paid writing work as a bad-tempered spouse, to whom he must dutifully return – much refreshed after the pleasures and distractions offered by the former, and apparently benefitting from this distraction in his dealings with the latter.

Balzac willingly sacrificed some of the time which ought to have belonged to *La Comédie humaine* in order to write to Madame Hanska – only occasionally alluding to the loss of earnings incurred in 'taking this yet another sheet, from the pile of paper destined for work' ['prenant encore cette feuille au tas de papier destiné à la copie'] (LH II 659, 3 August 1847), or to stealing pages from his novels in order to write letters to her (LH II 492, 29 December 1846).

He seems continually aware that every page filled with writing to be sent to Eveline is one which is not being filled with the kind of writing which brings in an income. 'How we have talked! 7 pages! If this was work, it would be worth 700 francs!' – he exclaims wistfully in a letter from December 1846. ['En voilà une causerie! 7 pages! Si c'était de la copie, cela vaudrait 700 francs!'] (LH II 463, 12 December 1846). Money is a theme on which the eternally indebted Balzac unrestrainedly holds forth in his letters to Eveline; complaining of his financial troubles, describing his poverty, thanking her for her occasional financial assistance, and, in the later years of their relationship, attempting to justify large expenses which he saw as necessary for the future home they were to share together one day.

He never did get paid for those letter-pages filled with writing, in which he had invested so much time – though they certainly yielded returns in other ways. As far as we readers are concerned, the fact that today they can be purchased – having been published initially under the attractive title of *Un roman d'amour*, and later as *Lettres à Madame Hanska*, with scholars debating their ambiguous status, and readers dipping into them for pleasure – renders these letter-pages a more than worthwhile investment.

NOTES

1. O. Heathcote, '(Auto-)portrait d'un auteur en courtisane: le travail du sexe et le sexe du travail dans les *Lettres à Mme Hanska*' in R. Le Huenen and A. Oliver (eds), *Paratextes balzaciens: 'La Comédie humaine' en ses marges* (Toronto: Centre d'études du XIXe siècle, 2007), pp. 179–190.
2. All translations into English are my own.
3. A. Wurmser, *La Comédie inhumaine: la signification de l'œuvre et de la vie d'Honoré de Balzac* (Paris: Gallimard, 1965; first published 1964), pp. 65–66.
4. G. Sand, *Correspondance*, ed. G. Lubin, 25 vols (Paris: Garnier, 1964–81), vol. XXI, p. 30.

4

DAVID F. BELL

Fantasy and Reality in *La Peau de chagrin*

'It cannot be denied that to us the great Balzac, save for one or two of his books, makes rather difficult reading', wrote the Spanish philosopher José Ortega y Gasset (1883–1955) in his 1925 'Notes on the Novel'.[1] Indeed, Balzac's 1831 *La Peau de chagrin* is not an easy novel to read, because the narrative is awkwardly constructed and displays a somewhat unfinished quality. It is also marked by a certain hesitation concerning the analytical perspectives the author wishes to adopt in his attempt to represent his historical period. It has nonetheless become one of the most read and discussed works in Balzac's entire corpus in the past thirty years. The frequently republished and refreshed paperback editions of the novel and the numerous critical essays devoted to it by specialists and amateurs alike are testimony to the depth of reader interest. The title itself, which refers to a magical talisman, a wild ass's skin, whose size diminishes with each of the protagonist's wishes as they are fulfilled by its uncanny powers, has become a common expression in French referring to diminishing resources in almost any context.

The difficulties encountered in reading *La Peau de chagrin* should come as no surprise, since the novel is among the earliest texts that would comprise what Balzac ultimately called *La Comédie humaine*. Only thirty-one years old when he composed the novel, Balzac had not yet reached the height of his creative powers, despite the precocious talent displayed in the works he had previously published, several of which were already destined to find their way into the *La Comédie humaine*. The story recounted in *La Peau de chagrin* was at least partially conceived as two separate pieces, each of which stood almost on its own. They were 'pre-published' in three different periodic press venues specialising in serialised fiction (*Le Voleur*, *La Revue de Paris* and *Le Cabinet de lecture*) before the novel appeared in a complete edition in August 1831. Serialisation was quickly becoming the preferred method for publishing prose fiction in the 1830s in France and was exploited successfully by all popular novelists of the period. Balzac was later to become very adept at articulating and tying together the serialised pieces of his publications in order to give them a compositional and conceptual wholeness as novels, standing on their own merits in volume format after they had appeared as serials. The serialised parts of *La Peau de chagrin* were only very minimally revised when they were brought together into a single-volume format, however, and the novel made its way into the future editions of *La Comédie humaine* in largely original form.

Balzac's readers have frequently highlighted two opposing interpretive perspectives recurring regularly in works included in Balzac's *Comédie humaine*. *La Peau de chagrin* is an early and exemplary novel of the series precisely because it foregrounds this on-going opposition in Balzac's approach. On the one hand, the novelist can be seen as the iconic nineteenth-century realist writer, whose work is therefore a rich source for historians who study his period. On this account, the accuracy of his descriptions produces a characteristic portrait of the Restoration and the July Monarchy as he explores the psychological and social motives of the citizens of post-Revolutionary France. Marxist critics such as Georg Lukács and Pierre Barbéris have interpreted his work within this framework. On the other hand, Balzac's novels display a persistent fascination with the fantastic, with narratives whose elements exceed the familiar structures of everyday life, suggesting hidden mysterious or supernatural forces. In 1859, Charles Baudelaire's (1821–67) comment on Balzac as visionary showed the poet to be an early champion of this approach: 'I have often been surprised that Balzac's great glory was that people thought of him as an observer; it always seemed to me that his main merit was to have been a visionary' ['J'ai mainte fois été étonné que la grande gloire de Balzac fût de passer pour un observateur; il m'avait toujours semblé que son principal mérite était d'être visionnaire'].[2] Balzac's debt to E. T. A. Hoffmann (1776–1822), generally considered one of the principal modern creators of fictions of the fantastic, is well documented by Balzac readers such as Maurice Bardèche, José-Luis Diaz, or Isabelle Charpateau. In fact, in the 1831 preface to *La Peau de chagrin*, Balzac specifically mentions Hoffmann, as well as Charles Maturin's *Melmoth the Wanderer* (1820), a Gothic romantic novel familiar to the French reading public of Balzac's period. Other Balzac stories, *L'Élixir de longue vie* (1830) or *La Recherche de l'absolu* (1834), for example, both of which were incorporated into *La Comédie humaine*, clearly connect to the contemporary cultural fad for the fantastic tale, and they demonstrate Balzac's knowledge of characteristic examples of this literary genre. Published during the early gestation of the conceptual project that would become *La Comédie humaine*, *La Peau de chagrin* is marked by these conflicting perspectives. Is the intention of the novelist to critique Restoration and July Monarchy society in a faithful historical description, or is it to create a fantastic tale? Ultimately, Balzac decides not to decide in *La Peau de chagrin*, and this is perhaps a key to understanding why the novel continues to fascinate modern scholars and critics.

A closer look at characteristic sequences in the novel can help to make these preliminary points more concrete. Part one of the novel, 'Le Talisman', begins with a description of a young man entering into a gaming house located in the Palais Royal at the centre of Paris. Balzac wastes no time invoking the codes of the fantastic tale, describing the entrance into the room as a *pact* with a demonic power. The cloakroom attendant asks the young man to hand in his hat, and this request immediately evokes something more ominous than an everyday transaction: 'When you enter a gambling house, the first thing the law does is to deprive you of your hat. Is this as it were a parable from the Gospel or a providential warning? Or is it not rather a way of concluding an infernal pact with you by exacting a sort of pledge?' (21)[3] ['Quand vous entrez dans une maison de jeu, la loi commence par vous dépouiller de votre chapeau. Est-ce une parabole évangélique et providentielle? N'est-ce pas plutôt une manière de conclure un contrat infernal avec vous en exigeant je ne sais quel gage?'] (CH x 57). The pact motif will return later in a crucial scene when Raphaël de Valentin comes into possession of the wild ass's skin. Crossing the threshold into the gaming house strangely resembles a passage into a hellish underworld, which sucks the very life out of its inhabitants. The cloakroom attendant's 'haggard white face' soon makes of him 'the very incarnation of the gaming table', a 'dreary-looking Cerberus' (22) ['la longue face blanche', 'le JEU incarné'; 'ce triste Cerbère'] (CH x 58). The opening sequence of the novel is easily readable in two interpretive registers: it can be seen as an accurate description of the appearances of the gamblers in an enclosed and airless space, fascinated by the flow of the game, but Raphaël's entrance is simultaneously a rite of passage into a space of perdition peopled by strange, almost inhuman creatures.

Attention must also be given to the notion of the threshold in this scene, to the *liminal* character of the entry into the gaming house (from the Latin *limin-, limen*, meaning 'threshold'). Liminal moments are highly characteristic of the fantastic tale, because the passage across a threshold is always a moment of uncertainty and interpretive complexity. Once someone has actually entered into a new space, an interpretative framework for events is quickly established, and a more stable system of reference reduces the potential for misinterpretation or strangeness. The opening narrative sequence emphasises this moment of liminality because thresholds will be a theme throughout the entire first part of the novel. Since Raphaël is contemplating suicide, he is constantly in a liminal psychological state, between life and death, as he wanders aimlessly in the streets of Paris after having gambled away his last coin: 'He was plodding along as in the middle of a desert, elbowed by men he did not see, attentive, through the hubbub of the crowd, to one voice only – that of death' (28) ['Il marchait comme au milieu d'un désert, coudoyé par des hommes qu'il ne voyait pas, n'écoutant à travers les clameurs populaires qu'une seule voix, celle de la mort'] (CH x 64). The sensations in the street are indistinct noise and provide no anchoring point that might end what has become a prolonged moment of oscillation between this life and the next.

   The fantastic stylistic register employed in the first pages of *La Peau de chagrin* is much more than simply an example of the superficial literary influence of the fantastic tale; rather, it is a concerted effort by Balzac to use a now-familiar literary tradition for his own purposes. The extraordinarily perceptive author's preface that accompanied the 1831 edition of *La Peau de chagrin* addresses a fundamental aesthetic question faced by novelists who want to situate their fictions in the first thirty-five years of the nineteenth century: how does one create an aesthetically beautiful literary object when the contemporary world one wants to depict is perceived as universally drab, no longer buoyed by the histrionics of the Napoleonic adventure? This is how Balzac puts it: 'The world asks us to produce beautiful paintings? Where are we to find models? Your cheap clothing, your failed revolutions, your bourgeois windbags, your dead religion, your extinct powers, your kings on pension, are they really so poetic that we have to transfigure them for you?' (my translation) ['Le monde nous demande de belles peintures? où en seraient les types? Vos habits mesquins, vos révolutions manquées, vos bourgeois discoureurs, votre religion morte, vos pouvoirs éteints, vos rois en demi-solde, sont-ils donc si poétiques qu'il faille vous les transfigurer?'] (CH x 55). Balzac's appeal to a fantastic mode in the description of the scene in the gaming house is a form of *captatio benevolentiae*, a rhetorical ploy designed to garner the sympathy and attention of readers and plunge them immediately into the tale. The monotonous dreariness of a starkly realistic description will not suffice. Fantasy is an aesthetic necessity in order to 'transfigure', as Balzac puts it, a world that would otherwise be an impossible subject for a writer of his time.

   Balzac's reflection on the aesthetic techniques necessary for a novelist of his day is echoed and amplified by a graphic on the dedication page of the novel, a reproduction of the famous meandering line that Trim, Toby's manservant, traces with his walking stick in volume 9, chapter IV of Laurence Sterne's *Tristram Shandy* (1759–67). Trim describes with a flourish of his cane an idea that can only be traced in a spatial figure, and not expressed in language, namely, what it might mean to be celibate and therefore free of the demands of marriage.[4] But also, one might gloss, what it would mean to subvert causal chains by narrative caprice, thereby escaping the snare of a social and cultural reality offering no hope for transcendence. The serendipity of potential narrative openings leading to unexpected results, at the whim of the narrator, brings fantasy and the fantastic into play. Balzac, who was a reader of Sterne (mentioned several other times in the body of the novel [29, 39, 229 CH x 65, 74, 242]), takes as a motto of *La Peau de chagrin* to expect the unexpected in the unfolding of the story.

Raphaël de Valentin enters the gaming house to wager his last gold coin in an attempt to avoid complete financial and social ruin. At the centre of the episode is an appeal to chance. Bereft of the will and the means to succeed in his Parisian life, the young man abandons his fate to the game. The other gamblers in the room read his intentions clearly: the outcome of the game will decide between life and death. To replace the fate of the gods with the chance of the game is, in essence, to re-introduce fate in another form and to endow the gambling scene with a mysterious dimension that goes beyond the banality of the moment. Moreover, it reduces the system of capitalist exchange, which is at the heart of the social system Raphaël confronts, to the nudity of the money form, a naked gold coin, which Raphaël throws onto the green cloth of the card table, where it rolls onto the black and becomes his wager. At the heart of Balzac's project in *La Comédie humaine* is an analysis of capitalism (before the term became the key concept of Marxist enquiry), the economic system that allows the rise of the bourgeoisie after the Revolution. The gaming table isolates a key element at the centre of that system, money, which is detached from the circulation it normally facilitates and exposed as a fetish object, a quasi-fantastic thing quite suggestive of the strangeness of the gaming house. Many pages later, in the second part of the novel, the reader will learn that this wager echoes a scene occurring much earlier when Raphaël was only twenty. He surreptitiously borrowed money from his father's purse during an evening reception in order to place a bet at a card table and win enough cash to gain a modicum of independence from his overbearing parent (95–96, CH x 124–125). This early naïve fascination with the workings of chance and with the fetishistic nature of gold coins placed on the card table presages the desperate gesture recounted in the first pages of the novel.

The loss of his last gold coin casts Raphaël out into the street to pursue an itinerary whose potential destination is suicide. His experience at the threshold is prolonged as he crosses the Seine on the Pont des Arts, contemplating the act of throwing himself into the river. Bridges are paradigmatically liminal, passages at an edge that link two opposing banks, in *La Peau de chagrin* two related spaces: on the Right Bank the gaming house, on the Left

Bank the antiques shop, scene of the second major sequence in the novel. Raphaël's entrance into the shop reiterates the characteristic suspension between states and spaces that marked the entrance into the gaming house. He moves decisively through the door, but his physical state immediately betrays him: '[H]is dizziness came back, and he continued to perceive things in strange colours or starting into slight movement' (33) ['Il retomba bientôt dans ses vertiges, et continua d'apercevoir les choses sous d'étranges couleurs, ou animées d'un léger mouvement'] (CH x 68). Raphaël's inner turmoil is expressed through an alteration of his own perceptual mechanisms.

The famous sequence that depicts Raphaël wandering through the disparate collection of objects in the curiosity shop turns into a meditation on human history, during which temporal periods are jumbled, juxtaposed without logic, and all sense of order is lost. The absence of stability provoked by entering the shop mimics quite precisely the first stage in traditional initiation rites, and the parallel is extended when a slow progress towards enlightenment ensues. Moving from room to room, Raphaël espies increasingly valuable objects. Ultimately 'a number of paintings by Poussin, a sublime statue by Michelangelo ... Rembrandts and Murillos, some Valasquez canvases' can be found in an inner sanctum of the curiosity shop (39) ['plusieurs tableaux de Poussin, une sublime statue de Michel-Ange ... des Rembrandt, des Murillo, des Velasquez'] (CH x 73–74). Weakened by lack of food and sleep (another archetypal element of initiation rituals), Raphaël faints, whereupon his guide, the antique dealer, arrives: 'From then on there occurred a certain lapse of time during which he had no clear perception of terrestrial things. ... Suddenly ... he saw, shining in the darkness, an orb of glowing red, and in the centre of it was a little old man, erect, turning the beam of a lamp upon him' (43) ['Il s'écoula, dès ce moment, un certain laps de temps pendant lequel il n'eut aucune perception claire des choses terrestres. ... Tout à coup ... il voyait briller au sein des ténèbres une sphère rougeâtre dont le centre était occupé par un petit vieillard qui se tenait debout et dirigeait sur lui la clarté d'une lampe'] (CH x 77). The whole sequence is a compendium of many of the elements that define the fantastic fictional genre: a space transformed from ordinary into extraordinary, set off from the banality of the street outside; liminal psychological conditions, fainting and/or sleep, for example, accompanied by a dream state; and an indefinably strange new fictional character, the antique dealer, who immediately takes on the appearance of a mage or sorcerer.

The narrator straightaway chides both his protagonist and the reader after drawing them into the mystery of the scene just described, precisely for their willingness to presume a fantastic dimension to Raphaël's experience. On the contrary, 'This vision was taking place in Paris, on the Quai Voltaire, in the nineteenth century, at a time and place which should surely rule out the possibility of magic' (45) ['Cette vision avait lieu dans Paris, sur le quai Voltaire, au dix-neuvième siècle, temps et lieu où la magie devait être impossible'] (CH x 79). The modern, post-Enlightenment dimension of Balzac's thought comes to the fore. Despite having spent much time in these early sequences of the novel establishing a tone that suggests we are entering into a strange, fantastic warp in the fabric of modernity, Balzac puts us in doubt about what we have just read. Raphaël himself recovers from his state of torpor, returning to a reality he understands: 'He became himself once more, saw that the old man was merely a creature of flesh and blood, fully alive and in no way phantasmagorical' (46) ['[Il] redevint homme, reconnut dans le vieillard une créature de chair, bien vivante, nullement fantasmagorique'] (CH x 79). Oscillation between the rational and the fantastic sets the stage for the pact whereby Raphaël comes into possession of the talisman.

After the antique dealer realises that Raphaël does not have the capacity to buy any of the treasures in the store, he steers the young man towards the wild ass's skin. The skin is engraved in Arabic with a sentence describing its power to grant the holder's wishes and its quality of shrinking with every wish until it disappears, implicitly signifying the death of its owner.[5] The graphic illustration in Arabic script, accompanied by a translation in the form of an inverted pyramid (in two dimensions), signifies the slow disappearance of the skin through the process of wish fulfilment and echoes the earlier use of a graphic image illustrating the wobbly movement of Trim's cane on the dedication page of the novel. The two most powerful forces in the narrative, the meandering of chance and the draining of will and energy through the process of wish fulfilment promised by the wild ass's skin, are beyond language, requiring graphic illustrations, possible within the typographical conventions of printing, but exceeding the linear, articulated language of the fiction in which they appear. Playing with typography on the printed page is another practice that connects Balzac to *Tristram Shandy*. Crucial as well is the fact that the skin escapes the boundaries of capitalist exchange, which were at the heart of the gambling scene, and thereby belongs to another universe – perhaps governed by the anthropology of the gift, since the antique dealer asks nothing in return for it? In any case, it exceeds the constraints of monetised social interaction and is also deeply exotic (produced in the 'Levant', according to the antique dealer), and thus perhaps it is truly a fantastic object. Raphaël receives the wild ass's skin from the old man for nothing more than the dispensing of a lesson on its powers and dangers.

What is this lesson? 'Man exhausts himself by two acts, instinctively accomplished, which dry up the sources of his existence. Two words express all the forms that these two causes of death can assume: will and power' (52) ['L'homme s'épuise par deux actes instinctivement accomplis qui tarissent les sources de son existence. Deux verbes expriment toutes les formes que prennent ces deux causes de mort: VOULOIR et POUVOIR'] (CH x 85). Because Raphaël has recovered his Enlightenment scepticism, he is unable to heed the warnings of his interlocutor and asks: 'Is there any man in the world so simple-minded as to believe in such stories?' (49) ['Existe-t-il au monde un homme assez simple pour croire à cette chimère?'] (CH x 82). And shortly thereafter: 'Is it a hoax?' (51) ['Est-ce une plaisanterie?'] (CH x 85). The old man's highly dramatised explanation of what the wild ass's skin is and does cannot fit the framework that now governs Raphaël's perspective on the scene. Consequently, the young man impetuously accepts the gift of the talisman by making a wish for a 'dinner of royal splendour' (54) ['un dîner royalement splendide'] (CH x 87), whereupon the second pact in the story, this time even more clearly Faustian, is signed: '[R]ash young fool. You have signed the pact, and there is no more to say. From now on, your desires will be scrupulously satisfied, but at the expense of your life' (55) ['[J]eune étourdi. Vous avez signé le pacte, tout est dit. Maintenant vos volontés seront scrupuleusement satisfaites, mais aux dépens de votre vie'] (CH x 88).

Raphaël facetiously expects a fairy-tale-like response to his wish for a feast, a magical transformation of the shop scene into a royal feast, but the old man mocks him and indicates instead that 'the chain of events in [his] new existence' (55) ['[les] événements de votre nouvelle existence'] (CH x 88) will reveal itself in due course. This is a crucial remark, because it provides the reader with the precise formula for all subsequent moments of wish fulfilment, pinpointing the manner in which an ambiguous duality will repeatedly reside at the heart of these events: each time a wish is realised it will be through a mechanism that fits seamlessly into the chain of everyday events, as the antique dealer puts it so aptly. And because this is so, a happily fulfilled wish can always be viewed either as a normal outcome (and therefore uninterestingly humdrum) or as the intervention of some fantastic force, which effectively steers everyday life towards a particular event. To the arsenal of structural mechanisms that allow for the appearance of the fantastic, which, as we saw, already includes the notion of liminality, we can now add a second notion, something like a chance intersection of causal chains.

The old man turns the wild ass's skin over to Raphaël, who, annoyed by the mocking tone of the parting remarks and the repeated warnings about the road upon which he is about to embark, utters a second wish: the antique dealer will fall in love with a dancer (55, CH x 88). This wish will be duly fulfilled much later at the beginning of the third section, 'L'Agonie', when

Raphaël espies the old man, whose appearance is now 'a striking analogy with the hypothetical face of Goethe's Mephistopheles' (207) ['cette homme [offrait] de frappantes ressemblances avec la tête idéale que les peintres ont donnée au Méphistophélès de Goethe'] (CH x 222), arm-in-arm with the dancer Euphrasie in the foyer of the Théâtre Favart (the old man is wearing grotesquely exaggerated makeup to mask his age). The first test of the antique dealer's description of how wishes will be fulfilled happens more instantaneously, however. Raphaël exits from the antique shop only to encounter a group of his friends who have been searching for him. They are headed to a festive dinner to celebrate the founding of a newspaper. The 'royal dinner' desired earlier will indeed take place, and Raphaël is 'less astonished at the accomplishment of his wishes than surprised at the natural way events were linked together in a logical chain. Although he found it impossible to believe in the intervention of magic, he was lost in wonderment at the changes and chances of human destiny' (59) ['moins étonné de l'accomplissement de ses souhaits que surpris de la manière naturelle par laquelle les événements s'enchaînaient. Quoiqu'il lui fût impossible de croire à une influence magique, il admirait les hasards de la destinée humaine'] (CH x 92). Is this a chance occurrence (normal human destiny), or is it instead the magical intervention of the wild ass's skin? The operational mode that the fantastic will take in the rest of Balzac's story is on display in this passage.

Raphaël accompanies his friends back across a bridge, the Pont des Arts once again, clearly a key liminal place in the novel, and his itinerary leads towards the third and last space featured in the first part of *La Peau de chagrin*, namely, the lavish dwelling of the financier Taillefer, where a feast to celebrate the founding of a newspaper ultimately transforms into an orgy. Evening dinners that become orgies are not unusual in Balzac's novels, because the space of the orgy, like that of Parisian theatres, for example, is where social mixing occurs, distinctions of class become confused, and participants can interact with almost anyone (such dinners figure prominently in *Illusions perdues* [1843], for example). In *La Peau de chagrin*, the chaotic loss of stable categories during the orgy is closely related to the experience created by wandering through the disparate objects in juxtaposition within the antiques store. Both sequences are disorienting and bring Raphaël de Valentin to crucial moments of decision. As the wine and champagne served during the dinner increasingly work their effects on the company of revellers, clarity of thought disappears in a cacophony of opposing opinions and an incapacity to make sense of them, 'this medley of words in which paradoxes of dubious lucidity and truths in grotesque garb clashed amid shouts' (66, translation slightly modified) ['cette mêlée de paroles où les paradoxes douteusement lumineux, les vérités grotesquement habillées se heurtèrent à travers les cris'] (CH x 98). The tangled and disordered conceptual muddle created by the orgy mirrors the philosophical confusion Balzac saw as a characteristic of the historical period represented in *La Comédie humaine*. This is fertile ground for appeals to the fantastic as an explanatory paradigm that might somehow master the cacophony of 'Milton's Pandemonium', as the narrator describes the scene in *La Peau de chagrin* (87, CH x 117).

It happens that Raphaël de Valentin's youthful pursuit of fame in Paris was originally devoted to philosophical reflections attempting precisely to synthesise and make sense of the fundamental elements of human existence. Speaking to Émile Blondet in the second section of *La Peau de chagrin*, entitled 'La Femme sans cœur', Raphaël makes reference to the volume he wrote on this subject: 'You alone, my dear Emile ... admired my *Theory of the Will*. ... This treatise, if I am not mistaken, will complete the researches of Mesmer, Lavatar, Gall and Bichat' (111) ['Toi seul, mon cher Émile, ... admiras ma *Théorie de la volonté*.... Cette œuvre, si je ne me trompe, complètera les travaux de Mesmer, de Lavater, de Gall, de Bichat'] (CH x 138). The wild ass's skin was presented by the antique dealer as the distilled essence of will and power, and we discover here that it is also a response to a veritable intellectual quest begun by Raphaël when he imagined and realised a synthetic treatise on the nature of will, extending the theories of four emblematic thinkers of the late eighteenth and early nineteenth centuries. One of the predecessors mentioned here, Franz Anton Mesmer (1734–1815), is a key figure in Balzac's conceptualisation of *La Peau de chagrin*, and his influence on Balzac is a major source of the ideas that give form to the fantastic as a structuring force in the novel. Robert Darnton's *Mesmerism and the End of the Enlightenment in France* is a wonderfully succinct history of Mesmer's influence in France, and Mesmer's inspiration in Balzac's writings has been well documented by critics such as Margaret Hayword and, more recently, Göran Blix. Blix summarises Mesmer's theory elegantly:

> [It] was the theory of a universal fluid, a sort of primordial form of energy, which permeated all matter, travelled easily, and could act at a distance ... For Balzac, Mesmer's discovery served as a simple unifying explanation of a series of still largely mysterious phenomena: electricity, magnetism, light and heat. What especially seduced him was the analogy between these material forms of energy and the moral world of spirit; in Balzac's psychology, the mind was fuelled by willpower, or by a finite quantity of *volonté*, which constituted the vital force allotted to each individual.[6]

Balzac's fascination with mesmerism is indisputable, and it is therefore important to understand the broader significance of the mesmerist movement, whose effects tarried on the social and scientific scene in France for a century or more. It has been argued that the intervention of the French scientific establishment just before the Revolution to quash mesmerist circles in France was no less than a defining moment when French scientists chose to impose and defend a rationalist, abstract, mathematical model of science. Enlightenment French science, with d'Alembert (1717–83) often considered to be the leading figure, elected consciously to circumscribe the natural phenomena science could address, to study only those which could be subject to abstract, mathematical laboratory modelling. Any phenomena not susceptible to approach by these methods were deemed uninteresting, or quite simply pre-scientific. Mesmer's magnetic fluid, his postulations that all humans were subject to it and bound to each other through it – as well as the manner in which such principles translated easily from the domain of still-mysterious physical phenomena in nature (light, heat, electricity) into the moral and spiritual domain of human society (human relations, broadly speaking) – were pronounced non-scientific and thereafter became an affront to Enlightenment reason. Both Darnton and Isabelle Stengers have convincingly read the arc of the mesmerist moment in these terms. Whether one argues that Balzac interpreted and employed Mesmer's thought correctly, incorrectly or incompletely, mesmerist inspiration permeates *La Peau de chagrin* in the form of the prolonged reflection about the circulation of will, power and energy, which crystallises around the wild ass's skin and its interventions into Raphaël de Valentin's fate. The foreignness of these sorts of mysterious forces and of the implicit theory behind them is a major source of the sense of fantasy and mystery modern readers experience while making their way through the novel, because such forces challenge the rationalist, scientific minds of moderns.

In the second section of the novel, Raphaël's unsuccessful attempt to make a name for himself as a philosopher of will is followed by a frenzied effort to advance socially, a period of his life mentored by a Parisian dandy, Eugène de Rastignac, whose description of how a young Parisian man should conduct himself is summarised by what he calls 'the *Rake's system*', 'le *Système dissipationnel*' (173, CH X 192): to spend and delay repayment (whether it be physical energy or money), hoping that something will intervene to prevent an otherwise inevitable collapse into a morass of exhaustion and indebtedness. The notion of social and economic dissipation clearly parallels the logic of the wild ass's skin, since such a trajectory empties its practitioner of financial, spiritual and physical vitality, and, if followed logically to its end, can only result in death. This part of Raphaël's career is also defined by his pursuit of Countess Fœdora, one of the most desirable women in the circles he frequents. Simultaneously, Pauline, the daughter of Raphaël's landlady, takes care of him, and her attentions and feelings for the young man remain if not unrecognised, then certainly not reciprocated.

The contrast between the two women is one of the central narrative tensions in the novel's second section, imparting a clear note of Romanticism to the story. The fantastic dimensions of the preceding sequences are more muted in 'La Femme sans cœur', but they do not disappear entirely. Fœdora quickly reveals that she has no inner depth, desire or even feeling. In fact, one might surmise that Fœdora is less a woman than an enigmatic hieroglyph. When Raphaël decides to court her, Rastignac tells him as much: 'This woman is really an enigma' (124) [*'Cette femme n'est-elle pas une énigme?'*] (CH x 149). In a strange but suggestive way, Fœdora is an analogue of the wild ass's skin. She progressively drains her suitor, Raphaël, of his energy and will to live, just as the series of wish fulfilments produced by the wild ass's skin lead its owner inevitably towards death. One might even postulate that within the mesmerist framework of magnetic fluid and energy flow, Fœdora is something of an anomaly: she absorbs energy and emits nothing in return – comparable to a black hole in a galactic system. The ravaging effects of Raphaël's pursuit of Fœdora are what bring him to the suicidal moment in the gaming house described in the first pages of the novel: he sees 'the bright, mocking phantom of Fœdora' (171) ['le fantôme brillant et moqueur de Fœdora'] (CH x 190) everywhere; she 'had passed on to me the leprosy of her vanity' (184) ['m'avait communiqué la lèpre de sa vanité'] (CH x 202). The ghoulish suggestion of contamination by a ghost is worthy of the Gothic novels read by Balzac's contemporaries, hinting perhaps that Fœdora is in some sense a figment of Raphaël's own deranged imagination and suggesting that the wild ass's skin is not as foreign to his state of being as might have appeared when he first encountered it in the antiques shop. Simultaneously, however, the second part of the novel can easily be read as a detailed description of what young men disaffected by post-Revolutionary anomie saw as a road to social success: maintain a veneer of gentility in the face of threatening poverty and marry a rich woman before the façade frays too visibly. Balzac continues to cultivate an uneasy, undecidable balance between fantasy and reality, a hallmark of *La Peau de chagrin*.

The encounter with Émile and other friends outside the antiques shop and the ensuing dinner/orgy is a first wish fulfilment that leads Raphaël to tell his story to Émile and ultimately sends him into a state of frenzy, whereupon he makes a further wish: to receive an annual income of two hundred thousand francs. As the revellers, who have fallen into drunken sleep in Taillefer's dwelling, awake the next morning and prepare to face the day, Cardot, a notary among the previous evening's company, arrives with a sheaf of papers: '[Y]ou would appear to be the sole heir of Major O'Flaherty, late of

Calcutta, who died in August 1828' (190–191) ['[V]ous êtes seul et unique héritier du major O'Flaherty, décédé en août 1828, à Calcutta.'] (CH x 208)[7] This event is simultaneously an uncanny variation on the antique dealer's prediction that the 'chain of events' of Raphaël's life would fulfil wishes straightforwardly and also a variation on the recognition scenes so common in melodramatic novels and theatre in Balzac's period. Raphaël and Émile, who had measured the wild ass's skin prior to this scene, discover that it has shrunk ever so slightly, confirming the earlier prediction. Melodrama, Gothic novel, fantastic fantasy and realist exercise: all of these narrative strands converge to describe Balzac's method in *La Peau de chagrin*.

In the novel's third part, 'L'Agonie', the reader finds Raphaël de Valentin living reclusively, removed from worldly temptations that might induce him to utter a wish. He ventures out to the theatre one evening, however, and reunites with Pauline. A clearly expressed wish that she love him precipitates the now inevitable descent towards Raphaël's demise: 'I wish to be loved by Pauline!' he cries out the next morning, thus sealing his own fate (212) ['Je veux être aimé de Pauline'] (CH x 227). Pauline's positive energy is a foil to Fœdora's ghoulish coldness, but her reappearance cannot counteract the relentless effects of the wild ass's skin. The brief idyll with Pauline is an attempt to escape the power of the talisman, but it inevitably returns, now considerably shrunken. Its reappearance gives rise to a curious sequence in the novel, once again highlighting the conflict between reality and fantasy at the heart of Balzac's story. Raphaël visits three scientific experts to see whether they can stretch the wild ass's skin and halt its seemingly inevitable diminution: a zoologist, a specialist in mechanics and a chemist (medical doctors will be added to the list later in the story). It would be easy to read the description of these consultations simply as Balzac's cheap attempt to caricature the science of his day, since the experts turn out to be resolutely pedantic and are entirely thwarted in their attempts to act effectively on the talisman.

A more suggestive perspective might actually be at stake, however. Earlier we indicated that the mesmerist movement in France was suppressed by a rationalist science bent upon redefining nature as a domain responding only to a carefully limited set of questions, those framed by mathematical abstraction through experimental modelling. Lost in this historical turn towards rationalist abstraction were dimensions of complexity in nature that do not easily lend themselves to such simplifications. What if we were to consider that Balzac is making a more fundamental point here, inviting us to *wonder*? As Isabelle Stengers explains: 'To wonder is a word for which, as a French speaker, I envy English speakers. It means both to be surprised and to entertain questions. It thus may refer to [a] double operation ... being affected, troubled, surprised, but also being forced to think and question'.[8]

At stake here is the suggestion that the wild ass's skin may not be a wholly fantastic object, but, rather, an invitation to wonder, to think past the limitations of a restrictive view of nature imposed by a rationalist consensus severely limiting the types of phenomena actively investigated. Such an approach to interpreting the visits to scientists in the third section of *La Peau de chagrin* suggests that the wild ass's skin challenges Enlightenment science, and this defiance arises assuredly from Balzac's continued fascination with mesmerism. Balzac might not simply be opposing the pre-scientific (or non-scientific) to the scientific, or, to put it another way, a fantastic reading to a realist reading of *La Peau de chagrin*. He might actually be making an important statement about how the concept of nature had been constrained by the science of his period. The wild ass's skin would thus become an exemplary allegorical object, richly constructed and unapproachable in normative ways, a cypher of a complex nature requiring analysis through a potential 'third way', somewhere between the non-scientific and the scientific narrowly defined. It would be an object of wonder in the sense suggested here and not simply an inexplicably strange and fantastic entity: an invitation to be surprised and to question in the face of a seemingly inexplicable phenomenon.

In fact, Balzac invites us explicitly to read the story allegorically when the narrator enters into dialogue with an exemplary reader in the two-page epilogue added to the end of the novel. An unidentified interlocutor asks the narrator what happened to Fœdora following Raphaël's death: 'She's to be found everywhere. She is, if you like, Society' (285) ['elle est partout, c'est, si vous voulez, la Société'] (CH x 294). Moreover, as the novel advances, the fantastic elements of the tale are progressively less emphasised until finally, in the third and final section, a series of commentaries on science and, more broadly, on society as a whole, come to dominate. A literary enterprise that had all the earmarks of a fantastic tale à la Hoffmann at the outset, when it oscillated between a fantastic and a realist perspective on the meaning of the events it described, *La Peau de chagrin* ultimately takes a more abstract and reflective turn in its final pages and puts into doubt an interpretation that would see it as a simple exercise in the fantastic literary genre. 'Oriental tale? Fantastic story? Realist novel? Scene from Parisian life? A gigantic peal of laughter or an intimate drawing room tragedy?' asks Françoise Gaillard. She answers, '*La Peau de chagrin* is all of that and more, because it is all of that *at the same time*'.[9]

NOTES

1. O. Gasset, 'Notes on the Novel' in M. McKeon (ed.), *Theory of the Novel: A Historical Approach* (Baltimore: The Johns Hopkins University Press, 2000), pp. 294–316 (p. 295).

2. C. Baudelaire, 'Théophile Gautier' in *Œuvres complètes*, ed. Y.-G. Le Dantec and C. Pichois (Paris: Gallimard, 1961), p. 692 (my translation).
3. H. de Balzac, *The Wild Ass's Skin*, trans. H. J. Hunt (London and New York: Penguin, 1977). English translations will be taken from this edition.
4. 'A thousand of my father's most subtle syllogisms could not have said more for celibacy' (p. 490).
5. Balzac neglected to correct the proofs of the novel, where he erroneously described the language as Sanskrit. Subsequent editions of the novel retain this error for the purpose of remaining faithful to Balzac's original editions of the work.
6. G. Blix, 'The Occult Roots of Realism: Balzac, Mesmer and Second Sight', *Studies in Eighteenth-Century Culture*, 36 (2007), 261–280 (p. 265).
7. A fortune unexpectedly arriving from India or the Americas is a repeated motif in Balzac and is one means through which the colonial question often creeps into *La Comédie humaine* at the margins.
8. I. Stengers, 'Wondering about Materialism' in L. Bryant, N. Srnicek and G. Harman (eds), *The Speculative Turn: Continental Materialism and Realism* (Melbourne: re.press, 2011), pp. 368–380 (p. 374).
9. F. Gaillard, 'H. de Balzac, *La Peau de Chagrin*, éd. M. Ambrière', *Romantisme*, 13.40 (1983), 166–167 (p. 167).

5

ALLAN H. PASCO

Balzac, Money and the Pursuit of Power

For Balzac, the love of money is the root of life in society, and he was perfectly correct to insist on its importance throughout *La Comédie humaine*. Certainly, no thoughtful person could consider his tumultuous, industrial/commercial age without grappling with the effects of the media of exchange. In *La Maison Nucingen* (1838), Blondet, Finot, Couture and Bixiou settle back to discuss 'the omnipotence, the omniscience, the omniexpediency of money' ['l'omnipotence, l'omniscience, l'omniconvenance de l'argent'] (CH VI 331). Land continued to have importance in many of the functions that it served before the Revolution, such as in justifying a title or in gaining a position of importance (CH VII 763), but it was rapidly becoming little more than one component of capital, a factor of exchange or value, like gold or precious stones, or paintings, or money, or, indeed, a person. For Nucingen, his wife Delphine is 'an indispensable *thing*' ['*une chose* indispensable'] (emphasis in original, CH VI 333), an attitude that Mercadet seems to share: 'my wife still does as she wishes with [Méricourt], and that is what reassures me' ['ma femme fait encore de lui ce qu'elle veut, et c'est ce qui me rassure'].[1] Similarly, Maxime de Trailles impudently tells Gobseck: 'I defy you to find a more handsome *capital* than this one in Paris' ['je vous défie de trouver à Paris un plus beau *capital* que celui-ci'], as he spins on his stylish heels (emphasis in original, CH II 986). After all, a capital exchange is involved in selling oneself or one's wife or the slave trade, in which Charles Grandet dabbles. Whether human or material, capital was the impulsion for the most important movements of Balzac's society. Gobseck declares himself '*papa*', that is, *father* or *pope* (emphasis in original, CH II 991). He saw himself as the symbolic leader of the religion of Mammon, or material wealth, that had taken over bourgeois society.

    Balzac's account of the way an elite private bank gains its enormous financial power, *La Maison Nucingen*, stands at the conceptual centre of *La Comédie humaine*; so, likewise, capital rests at the heart of the society he portrays. Money, in whatever form, was power. 'My eyes', explains

Gobseck, whose name carries the etymological sense of 'god of the sack', 'are like those of God. I see into hearts ... I am sufficiently rich to buy the consciences of those who motivate ministers ... Is that not Power? ... Is not life a machine whose movement is impelled by money?' ['Mon regard est comme celui de Dieu, je vois dans les cœurs ... Je suis assez riche pour acheter les consciences de ceux qui font mouvoir les ministres ... N'est-ce pas le Pouvoir? ... La vie n'est-elle pas une machine à laquelle l'argent imprime le mouvement?'] (CH II 976).

Money has both inherent real value, as with gold, and the idea of that value, as with fiat currency, without any backing but governmental decree. Still, it is perhaps only in periods of crisis that its potential problems come to the fore. The British predicament prior to the Great Recoinage of 1696 provides an excellent example. Even when seriously clipped, or filed, or scraped, the British coin of the realm continued to have the value accorded it by law, though merchants might refuse coins that had been significantly tampered with, thus diminished in weight. This right of refusal might be withdrawn, as was the case of the French revolutionary currency, the *assignat*, after the legislature declared it was a valid means of fulfilling financial obligations. The Revolutionary *assignat* was fiat money; it had value only because of governmental decree and required public confidence. As people lost faith in the true worth of the Revolutionary notes, they became ever more worthless. Speculators used the discrepancy between real and declared value as a means of enhancing their own wealth, by using *assignats* to buy confiscated land and pay taxes in *assignats*, while dealing only in gold for other purposes, in short, by speculating on *assignats* and gold. Balzac was well aware of such practices (e.g. CH VI 51). When a significant disparity between real and ideational values occurs, of course, people at the low end of society eventually suffer, for they have little ability to choose the medium for valuing their services. The inflation inevitably resulting from an excess of fiat money leaves workers, clerks, widows and orphans with little recourse. The rich wallow in gold and other tangible items, while the poor struggle along with banknotes that rapidly lose value.

Balzac's express determination to offer an exact and indeed complete description of the July Monarchy was by no means the only attempt to come to terms with the confusion resulting from the Revolution of 1789 and its aftermath. During this period, extraordinary minds like Balzac's contemporary, Henri de Saint-Simon, and, eventually, Auguste Comte, who was credited with founding sociology, carried on the eighteenth-century work of such *philosophes* as Félix Vicq-d'Azyr, Pierre Jean George Cabanis, Marie François Xavier Bichat and Nicolas de Condorcet, with the goal of finding and describing the underlying idea of this febrile society. Such thinkers were convinced that there was a generative idea behind what they saw around them. They thought it could be used to predict the future, and they sensed a widespread need both to understand what was occurring and to grasp what was coming. Saint-Simon stated repeatedly that the general concept governing his society would be based on the belief that the universe is governed by one single, immutable law.[2]

Balzac shared Saint-Simon's view and his implicit goal: '[S]hould I not study the reasons or the reason for social effects, surprise the hidden meaning in the enormous assemblage of patterns, passions and events?' ['ne devais-je pas étudier les raisons ou la raison de ces effets sociaux, surprendre le sens caché dans cet immense assemblage de figures, de passions et d'événements?'] (CH I 11). Indeed, in regard to *La Comédie humaine*, he considered his characters ideas (CH XII 775). As these character-ideas passed through his creations, touching on other characters and ideas, they represented great social forces (CH VII 763). The interweaving of fictional lives, ideas and movements formed a true *textus* or text that created an ambitious portrait of Balzac's day. Auguste Comte eventually termed the study of such forces or relationships 'sociology'.

It is clear that Balzac was not alone in recognising that the singularity of the quest was a simplification, for there were many currents creating a new social, material and even spiritual world. Today, we see that this age was in transition, as it fashioned a new paradigm for the whole of society. The most important concept serving as the nucleus of this impulsive social force was 'idea'. George Berkeley and John Locke had insisted on an ideational reality. The works of both were translated into French from early in the eighteenth century and had considerable impact on those theorists, philosophers and *philosophes* who struggled with the need for understanding.

Unquestionably, Balzac knew that we can never know the substance of reality. We only grasp its idea. But in doing so, he showed that it is possible to conceive of the *raison d'être* of economics, fiat versus 'hard' money, the opposition between Paris and the provinces, the reality of love and marriage, art and journalism, creation and imitation, class structure and the dissolution of families, to mention but those that are the most clearly emphasised. He called the source of such concepts a *'generative idea'* [*'idée mère'*].[3] He perceived not only that society was constructed on the three major pillars of family, church and state, but he also evolved a method for portraying both the details and the overriding structures. As he explained in *La Revue parisienne*, ideas and images are not the same thing. Ideas may exist in images, and images may occur in ideas. Still, they are different, as different as 'movement and daydream' ['le mouvement et la rêverie'] (RP, 214). It is a matter of whichever dominates. 'All images reflect an idea or more precisely

69

a *sentiment* which is a collection of ideas, and an idea does not always end up as an image' ['Toute image répond à une idée ou plus exactement à un *sentiment* qui est une collection d'idées, et l'idée n'aboutit pas toujours à une image'] (RP, 214; italics in original). Balzac's conception of image parallels modern understandings, that is, *an image is a complex of (remembered) sensations*. It allowed him to deploy a very complicated but satisfying view of such major factors as money. He could see the glittering core of this transitional society, where peasants, clerks and labourers were moving into the middle class, where former aristocrats were struggling to regain their remembered power, where the fragmented regions of France were coming together into a 'great nation' through increased travel, commerce and communication.

Georg Lukács claimed that Balzac's treatment of his present as though it were history was an important innovation, as was his consciousness of 'the rapidly growing forces of Capitalism'.[4] Balzac's genius was, however, in emphasising money as the primal force in this new society, while it changed before his eyes from a land-based to a capitalistic society. As Victoria E. Thompson has summarised, 'The definitive rejection of the estates-based model of the Old Regime gave rise to a search for new models of the social hierarchy. Envisioning society as a market offered a new means of imagining the social order, one in which individuals and groups would be assigned a place according to their relationship to money rather than by their birth or their relationship to the king.'[5] With rare exceptions, not even love, much less ethics and family values, could prevail against money. Readers watch as Balzac's villains crush one character after another in their generally successful efforts to corner the money and the ensuing power. André Wurmser is not far off when he says, 'Balzac's novels would not take place if the question of money were not posed' ['Les romans de Balzac n'auraient pas lieu si la question d'argent ne se posait pas'].[6] Balzac phrased it somewhat differently: '[F]ortune is always the driving force behind the plots that develop, the plans that are formed, the schemes that are hatched!' ['Et toujours la fortune est le mobile des intrigues qui s'élaborent, des plans qui se forment, des trames qui s'ourdissent!'] (CH II 1002).

Eugénie Grandet (1833) perhaps most clearly demonstrates the power of money, especially in regard to love. Before opening the pages of *Eugénie Grandet*, readers of *La Comédie humaine* have already seen love betrayed for the sake of art in *Le Chef-d'œuvre inconnu* (1831). Poussin was willing to sacrifice his mistress's love for a chance to see Frenhofer's 'masterpiece'. The title character of *Eugénie Grandet* is the perfect example of a young woman who is ready to give herself to love. Born in 1796 (CH III 1031), on her birthday in 1819, she is well on the road to becoming an old maid. By law she has little choice in the matter, since her father's express permission is required for her to wed. When a handsome cousin arrives, she is ready to fall in love and commit herself. The gift of her devotion is symbolised by that of the gold she has collected, and she becomes Charles's 'fiancée'. Papa Grandet makes his disapproval known both before and after he learns that his daughter has given the young man her store of gold, and Charles is sent away.

As a miser, controlled by his passion for gold, Félix Grandet makes a marriage of love impossible for his daughter. Neighbours think that one day he will arrange something, and though he eventually trains Eugénie to handle his enormous fortune, her loveless marriage comes only after his death. Dominated by one passion, he hovers not over Eugénie or his wife but over his gold. On learning that Eugénie no longer has any of the precious metal, he locks her up on bread and water, as though she herself had no further value. Acutely cognisant of the worth of things and of those aspects of his society that will allow him to increase his hoard, he fails to recognise the value of the relationships that depend on family, love and trust. Furthermore, his unmitigated lust for gold causes his wife's death and his daughter's loveless life.

Off in the new world, Cousin Charles stoops to any means of building his fortune, including becoming a slaver. He returns hardened, ignorant of his cousin's enormous wealth and unwilling to maintain his commitment to her. Still, even though he is now an acolyte in the gold cult, he is not completely dishonourable, and he converts Eugénie's gift of gold from a free gift, as it was meant, into a debt, and he returns her money with interest before marrying someone else. Abandoned, Eugénie turns to the religion of her youth, the Church, and becomes a secular bride of Christ. Although she marries, the marriage remains unconsummated.

As the novel follows the lives and attitudes of Félix, Eugénie and Charles, Balzac takes every opportunity to demonstrate how fortunes are made legitimately, if not ethically. The first rule was expressed by Lousteau in *La Muse du département* (1843): '[W]e are in a period when success requires being without debt [and] having a fortune, wives and children' ['nous sommes dans une époque où pour parvenir il faut être sans dettes, avoir une fortune, femme et enfants.'] (CH IV 740). Thomas Piketty simplifies and argues that an inheritance was required for a comfortable life.[7] Certainly, some parts of *La Comédie humaine* would make one accept this scholarly summation unhesitatingly. Inheritance, for example, becomes one of the most important keys to the unity of the *Scènes de la vie de province*. Balzac's vision was more inclusive, however. Without a large amount of property of whatever kind that could be invested to provide income, a comfortable life was impossible. Class mattered little. Neither the antiquity of one's lineage nor the neighbourhood of one's abode were differentiating features. The Minoret's bourgeois family dates back five hundred years, for example (CH III 845), while the snobbish Madame de Portenduère lives on rue des Bourgeois (CH III 865). It was money, the very middle-class standard of success, that mattered. Not even the Portenduère name carries weight in Paris (CH III 877). This was a society where 'money was the linchpin, the unique means, the unique motive' ['l'argent était le pivot, l'unique moyen, l'unique mobile'] (*ibid.*).

By the beginning of the novel *Eugénie Grandet*, Félix Grandet's position had already changed. Before the Revolution of 1789, he was a master cooper, thus able to make a good living. His ability to read, write and keep accounts additionally gave him the tools to begin to make his fortune and become a member of the middle class. In this society committed to money, 'Monsieur Grandet then obtained a new title of nobility ... he became *the top taxpayer* in the district' ['M. Grandet obtint alors le nouveau titre de noblesse ... il devint *le plus imposé* de l'arrondissement'] (italics in original) (CH III 1032). His marriage to a rich timber merchant's daughter added a substantial dowry and several inheritances to his funds, ready to invest in revolutionary confiscations and multiply his fortune. Though in effect his wife's property, these funds came under his control as husband. Rather than wasting the modest fortune on a comfortable lifestyle, he lived in penury and bought land and gold, both of which he exploited skilfully.

One of the most important concepts of Balzac's financial world is that of *speculation*, a word that had only recently in 1776, according to the Robert dictionary, taken on the meaning of financial exploitation of future market fluctuation. *L'Illustre Gaudissart* illustrates how seemingly ordinary trust in the future continuation of the present can become gambling. Gaudissart sells periodicals and insurance. Those who purchase subscriptions believe that the money paid guarantees the receipt of magazines or papers, just as those who purchase insurance trust they will be compensated for possible future loss. Today, with the frequent bankruptcy of newspapers and magazines and the financial shenanigans of insurance companies who contort themselves to avoid payment, we might well understand how such 'investment' could be considered speculation. Certainly, Gaudissart's customers have no guarantee, other than the travelling salesman's assurance, that the periodical will continue to arrive and future losses be recompensed. Subscribers trust that there is a substantial reality behind the promise.

In *La Cousine Bette* (1846), Valérie Marneffe becomes the queen of speculation. Crevel taught her about stock market speculation, but her horizons have already been enlarged, perhaps by her husband who indulges in the 'the vilest of speculations' ['la plus ignoble des spéculations'] by sending her to beg for his promotion (CH VII 297). She is already speculating on her lovers. As she depletes Hulot's funds, the wealthy investor Crevel is in the offing. Eventually, when she becomes pregnant, the unborn child serves as a speculation that she successfully attributes to four lovers. She is, of course, not alone. The speculation that is transforming the face of Paris (CH VII 437) is expanding as well to the provinces.

While Gaudissart seems ignorant of the financial reliability of his backers, Grandet has long ago submitted to the god of money, and knows precisely when he skirts the law. It is not exactly illegal to assure his neighbours that he will not sell his crop, but rather cooperate with them to force the price higher. It is still not illegal when he takes advantage of the new, higher price resulting from the restricted sales, and forsakes his colleagues to sell his wine, thus saturating the market and leaving them at the mercy of the buyers. The law might not call it fraud, but it is certainly unethical. Grandet is, of course, a law unto himself. Another religion has come to fill the gaps left by the Revolutionary depredations on the Catholic Church, and Grandet represents this new faith. 'Was not Money in all its power the single modern god in which people believe?' ['N'était-ce pas le seul dieu modern auquel on ait foi'] (CH III 1052). Grandet's name is, of course, an anagram of *d'argent* or *of money*.[8] Although the novelist refers to the Catholic Church in other of his works, in none does he so clearly set it in opposition to that of Mammon, the god of material wealth.

Grandet acquired the region's best vineyards, an old abbey and several farms for 40,000 francs. The French scholar Pierre-Georges Castex tells of a similar purchase of some 600,000 francs for property officially appraised at more than twice that sum.[9] Grandet's deal is so much better than one must question the narrator's statement that the sale was 'legally if not legitimately' acceptable ['légalement, sinon légitimement'] (CH III 1030). Although the date of his purchase is not completely clear, it is possible that Grandet paid partially in the much-devalued Revolutionary *assignats*, since as early as 1792 inflation had seriously eroded the legal tender, perhaps by as much as half.[10] More important, however, the 200 double-louis (8,000 francs) that Grandet's father-in-law gave the 'ferocious republican' overseeing the sale of the confiscated *national assets* (CH III 1030–1031) was clearly a bribe and explains the astonishingly low purchase price. Neither Grandet nor his god is above fraud.

Not all of Grandet's accumulation is so obviously tainted. As mayor, it is perhaps not surprising that his desire to better his district caused him to oversee the construction of new roads which happened to lead to his own property. And the lack of natural light in all his structures was, like that of his neighbours, a simple desire to avoid the taxes imposed according to the number of windows and doors (CH III 1652 note 4). He is also an astute businessman. The miser pays close attention to minutiae with his fine calculations of everything from bread and heat to the best use of his land for income. Later, we learn that his investment of a hundred thousand pounds of annuities at 80 francs has risen to 115. Grandet's further wealth came from exploiting his wife's inheritances, by supplying wine to the republican armies and by undeviating economy. The progression from the somewhat less than respectful 'Old' (*père*) Grandet to *Monsieur* Grandet during the Empire further marks his successful rise into the bourgeoisie. Furthermore, Grandet now owns one of the houses in the upper part of Saumur that formerly belonged to the local aristocracy. Indeed, the bourgeoisie became the ruling force in the July Monarchy, if not before.

There are several coups in the course of *Eugénie Grandet*. Perhaps the most notable is Grandet's sale of his gold. As the miser recognises, virtually everything has value, from the poplar trees that he will not replant in *Eugénie Grandet* to human beings that Vautrin plans to buy in *Le Père Goriot*. Time itself is worth money, and the fictional Grandet exploits his neighbours' in pursuit of arranging Charles's affairs, so that he does not have to travel himself to Paris. However much gold may be considered a conservative investment, in the novel and in life, its value can vary widely. Grandet assumes that he can speculate profitably on the precious metal. Thus Grandet and Nanon load up his gold in the middle of the night and take it to Angers where he sells it profitably, before investing the proceeds in government annuities (CH III 1120–1121).

Grandet's major coup is, however, manœuvring his dead brother's debt through Parisian financiers, so as to erase it, 'without it costing either his nephew or himself a penny' ['sans qu'il en coûtat un sou ni à son neveu ni à lui'] (CH III 1105). Bankruptcy is considered dishonourable, so he first arranges for a receivership under Keller and des Grassins, making Guillaume Grandet's creditors believe that his wealthy, provincial brother will pay (CH III 1142). Charles's inheritance is inventoried, and the debtors have even more reason for optimism as a result. They happily tuck the debt away, until some nine months after the receivership, when the two bankers in charge sell various items and pay 47 per cent of what is owed. As Monsieur Grandet previously predicted, the payment cost neither him nor his nephew. The creditors begin to clamour for the remainder. They are told to recognise in writing what they have already been paid, and then all the rest of the debt is bundled in one account. Not only is it easier to settle with a group than with individuals, appearances work for the debtor. The total of the final settlement amount seems more generous than the much smaller sums that actually go to the individual creditors. With repeated delays and empty promises, optimism fades, and it is possible to pick up the debt on the market for pennies. Grandet is then able to settle his brother's debts very advantageously with what is left in his brother's estate, without having to declare bankruptcy.

Nucingen's story is similar. He sells his bank stock when it is high and buys it back when it is low. Still, it is a complex version of a more elaborate fraud. The banker's two earlier receiverships worked out very well for his debtors, since he paid off with stock that, contrary to the banker's expectations, became very profitable. It was said to be impossible to do poorly in any of Nucingen's enterprises. But even after profitably manipulating these initial receiverships, Nucingen, '[t]his elephant of Finance' ['[c]et éléphant de la Finance'] (CH VI 339), still needs to multiply the five million of his capital by two- or three-fold. Another 'failure' is required. Balzac's story, *La Maison Nucingen*, recounts the banker's very successful, third liquidation, however much it left a number of his admirers in significant distress. The shorn sheep have lost their humanity and are to the speculators in charge of the fraud no more than numbers. They are easily ignored.

The theory behind a successful failure for a major private bank is much the same as that for Guillaume Grandet's individual account in the hands of his brother Félix, though the means differ. Grandet tempers the debt with time, until the creditors no longer believe that he will pay. The Nucingen scheme of *César Birotteau*, as explained in *La Maison Nucingen*, is more elaborate. The banker uses Claparon, who recommends, 'Shear the public, speculate' ['Tondez le public, entrez dans la Spéculation'] (CH VI 241). César is, of course, in the process of being shorn. His notary, Roguin, has fled, leaving Birotteau with enormous losses. While there is nothing wrong with investing in future fluctuations of a market, Nucingen's convoluted legal swindle took years to arrange and would be difficult to prosecute. Rumours fostered by the banker were the force motivating his stock's movement. When Nucingen leaves for Belgium, people begin to wonder whether his bank will be able to meet its financial obligations. The fact that his wife is demanding a legal separation suggests that she has lost faith in him. Will he pay off his obligations with a promising stock as he did before? Those that sell this time on rumoured doubts and buy on more positive rumours, and those that turn in their stock for Claparon's Potemken village lose everything in *César Birotteau*, for Claparon is a straw man. After ten years of preparation, Nucingen and du Tillet have created the Claparon bank that seems financially solid, though it is not. No one, not even Nucingen's closest allies understand exactly what he is doing (CH VI 370). Those who are unknowingly deceived played the role required to make the banker extraordinarily rich, thus what Claparon calls 'the Napoléon of finance' ['le Napoléon de la finance'] (CH VI 241).

Borrowing money was less regulated under the July Monarchy, but the basic mechanism was much the same as today. Victurnien d'Esgrignon's debt caused by his luxurious lifestyle is largely unsecured; Anastasie de Restaud's is guaranteed by her husband's diamonds. In both cases, the promissory notes can be sold, usually at a discount depending on the time that would pass until the debt is due and the chance that it will be satisfied. When Victurnien cannot repay the money drawn on du Croisier's account, especially when withdrawn by a fraudulent letter, he faces jail; Mme de Restaud only faces the loss of the diamonds and what her husband will make of her adultery. As *Gobseck* demonstrates, rumour can affect small debts as well as large. The miser's colleagues sold the notes signed by Maxime de Trailles at a large discount to Gobseck, for they had heard and believed that the dandy would never pay. When Gobseck manages to have the debt paid in full, by exchanging the discounted notes with Maxime at full value, he has exploited rumour (CH II 990–991). Much as it is today, debt like invested money may pay dividends and may increase or decrease in value. Investments may be conservative or foolhardy, and the invested money may be loaned out again. Loans may be bundled or divided and paid in full or in part. They are, in short, 'fungible' and may at any point be discounted or sold. Fraud occurs only when the notes are presented as something of value when they are not.

Balzac illustrated pointedly and repeatedly across *La Cousine Bette* and *César Birotteau* – indeed, across the entire *Comédie humaine* – that there was little that he did not understand about capital and the way it could be used or leveraged. Prospectuses could serve, much as rumour, to enhance the real or pretended value. Wurmser has shown at length in his *Comédie inhumaine* that César Birotteau's *Cephalic Oil* could not possibly grow or even preserve hair as advertised. The perfumer's reputation for probity comes from elsewhere in regard to his obsessive desire to pay off all his debt and not in relation to the promises made on the prospectuses. Sophisticated financiers know better than to believe prospectuses. When Goulard recognises Mercadet's deceptions, he says, 'He lies like a prospectus; but in business, that is done' ['Il ment comme un prospectus; mais, en affaires, cela se fait'] (*Le Faiseur*, p. 217).

César is virtuous to a degree, but perhaps only in comparison with other businessmen. In respect to uncompromised virtue, César Birotteau (and a significant number of other characters of *La Comédie humaine*) has sold out in this society to success; that is, to the successful accumulation of money and power. His prospectus is simply false, designed to attract vain, balding men to a potion that will stop their hair falling out. The money is very real, the potion a fraud, though at the time an unindictable fraud. While César's speculation in land collapses, his speculative prospectuses succeed royally, largely thanks to Gaudissart and César's future son-in-law, Anselme Popinot, and he is able to retire his debt and re-enter into honourable membership of the stock market.

Balzac insisted on the nefarious effects of passion, and we are able to watch the pathetic results of the univocal commitment to money as Gobseck and Grandet end protecting a pile of ashes or attempting to grab the priest's gleaming cross. Simultaneously, the novelist insists on the significance of love, love that unfortunately leads sometimes to ruin. As pointed out previously, Balzac was frequently accused of concentrating on vice rather than virtue. Though he defended himself on several occasions with vigour, it remains true that virtue presents a 'difficult literary problem that consists in making a virtuous person attractive' ['le difficile problème littéraire qui consiste à rendre intéressant un personage vertueux'] (CH 1 18). While the virtuous do exist in Balzac's pages, few become what one might call living characters.

Two notable exceptions occur in *Le Faiseur* (1848). Not only does the play illustrate once again the novelist's understanding of the financial manipulations that were all too common in both his day and ours, it offers marvellous examples of virtuous, long-lived, sacrificial love. Having once lent substantial sums of money to Godeau, in the expectation of gaining significant profit, Mercadet has arrived at the nadir of his career. Godeau has not returned, and Mercadet, the financial manipulator, is broke, shorn, encircled by snarling creditors. At the beginning of the play, his only remaining speculation is to marry his daughter, Julie, to someone who can bring sufficient funds to the marriage to pay off his substantial debts.

There are many impediments to the proposed marriage. The most important problem resides in the daughter herself. Although ever more children in this period were being allowed to marry as they wished, fathers still had the legal right to impose their will. Julie has found the man of her dreams in Minard. Although the young man is church-mouse poor, he loves Julie for herself and is willing to take her even after discovering that her father has only the appearance of wealth, an illusion that is about to disappear as Mercadet is dragged off to debtor's prison. The second problem slowly manifests itself. The elegant suitor Monsieur Michonnin de la Brive is a second Mercadet and broke. Both father and his daughter's suitor hope to gouge the other.

Balzac uses Mercadet to illustrate legitimate and illegitimate credit. Mercadet argues, 'Finally, what is dishonourable about owing money? Is there a country in Europe that does not have debts? ... Life, Madame, is a perpetual loan!' ['Enfin, qu'y a-t-il de déshonorant à devoir? Est-il un seul état en Europe qui n'ait des dettes? ... La vie, Madame, est un emprunt perpétuel!'] (*Le Faiseur* 139–140). One of the reasons that nations continued to experiment with fiat money was that it was simply impossible to have enough metallic money to encourage innovation and trade, and one of the justifications for giving Napoleon some credit for reviving the French economy was his establishment of the National Bank of France in 1800. France had been suffering from illiquidity. There was simply not enough money. On the one hand, the French National Bank encouraged provincials to dig up their hidden gold and deposit it in the national coffers, thus making it available for loans – Balzac's narrator points out that Paris never thinks of the provinces except to ask for money (CH IV 652) – and, on the other hand, the national and international market needed a source of sufficient currency and new credit instruments to stimulate both national and international trade.

There is nothing wrong with having debt; there is nothing wrong with having credit. Madame Mercadet is perfectly correct to say, 'Debts do not dishonour anyone when they are in the open' ['les dettes ne déshonorent personne quand on les avoue'] (*Le Faiseur* 219). When the pendulum begins to swing in the other direction towards the dishonourable and illegal, however, is when Mercadet imitates Nucingen by exploiting rumours he has planted as a means to profit. Just as Nucingen is guilty of 'putting himself above the laws of probity' ['se mettre au-dessus des lois de la probité'] by speculating on the positive and negative rumours he himself inspired (CH VI 339), so too Mercadet. He engineers the fall of Basse-Indre stock, thus providing the opportunity of significant profit when positive news inevitably comes out (*Le Faiseur* 161). He likewise hopes to reignite the story of Godeau's return by hiring a carriage to come into his courtyard in the middle of the night and disguising Michonnin to play the role of his absent debtor.

The joke is, of course, that Godeau has indeed come back. In respect to the play and its characters, that solves many problems. The creditors are paid, interest and fees included. The Mercadets are able to help young Michonnin by allowing him unlimited time to redeem his notes, so that if he has reformed from the scamp he has long been, he can settle down and conduct a business that runs according to good practices. We can hope that Michonnin and the others follow Madame Mercadet's advice: 'amass money by work and faithfulness, not by tricks ... Patience, wisdom, frugality are three domestic virtues that conserve everything that they give' ['amasser l'argent par le travail et par la loyauté, non par des ruses ... La patience, la sagesse, l'économie, sont trois vertus domestiques qui conservent tout ce qu'elles donnent'] (*Le Faiseur* 220). Nicest of all, Julie's true love, Minard, the illegitimate child of Godeau, is recognised as a son and thus becomes a millionaire with a promising future. Finally, the joyous outcome of faithful affection in both Julie and Madame Mercadet provides another example of virtue rewarded. Mercadet himself has changed. He is so exhausted from the constant pressure of speculation that he will retire to the country and become an honest farmer. Honourable Madame Mercadet has been rewarded on all fronts, a fitting accompaniment for the *deus ex machina* of Godeau's return with the 'incalcuttable' wealth of India that he rains on all fronts.

Despite Madame Mercadet's sermon praising financial virtue and the play's conclusion that would please the cruellest (or most virtuous) of public prosecutors, the terminal events of *Le Faiseur* look all too unrealistic and contrived, but they nonetheless bear a serious lesson based on one of Balzac's most perceptive insights into the world of the July Monarchy. Society had not changed. As Gobseck said some years before, 'Gold is the spirituality of your current societies' ['L'or est le spiritualisme de vos sociétés actuelles'] (CH II 976). Crevel later leaves the miser's 'idealism' aside for cruel realism as he lectures Adeline: 'Everyone puts their money to work and fiddles with it as best they can. You are wrong, my angel, if you believe that it is King Louis-Philippe who reigns ... [A]bove the Charter, there is the holy, the venerated, the solid, amiable, gracious, beautiful, noble, young, all-powerful five cent coin' ['Tout le monde fait valoir son argent et le tripote de son mieux. Vous vous abusez, cher ange, si vous croyez que c'est le roi Louis-Philippe qui règne ... au-dessus de la Charte, il y a la sainte, la vénérée, la solide, l'aimable, la gracieuse, la belle, la noble, la jeune, la toute-puissante pièce de cent sous!'] (CH VII 325).

Recent works by Thomas Piketty and Karl Gunnar Persson make well documented arguments that the general economy of the July Monarchy had reached a period of very low growth in which individuals had little or no chance of making a personal fortune without inheriting or otherwise stumbling across a substantial sum of funds.[11] The importance Balzac places on inheritance leaves no doubt that he understood this reality. While these necessary riches may originate from theft, as in *L'Auberge rouge*, or from legitimate earnings, as in *Eugénie Grandet* or *Le Faiseur*, most often such funds come from an inheritance. Whatever the source, today's historians would agree with Balzac: power and a comfortable lifestyle required the backing of a major influx of wealth. From beginning to end of *La Comédie humaine*, much of the action originates from the need of a fortune, a fortune that plays a significant role in the vision of the July Monarchy that Balzac presents.

NOTES

1. *Le Faiseur* (1848) in M. Bardèche (ed.), *Œuvres complètes de Balzac*, 24 vols (Paris: Club de l'Honnête Homme, 1968–71), vol. XX, p. 146. Unless otherwise indicated, all the translations are my own.
2. H. de Saint-Simon, *Mémoire de la science de l'homme* (1813) in P. Enfantin (ed.), *Science de l'homme*, 2e partie (Paris: Victor Masson, 1858), pp. 368–369.
3. Balzac, 'Études sur M. Beyle (Frédéric Stendalh [sic])', *La Revue parisienne*, 25 septembre 1840 in M. Bardèche (ed.), vol. XXIV, p. 253. Emphasis in the original. Further references to this work will be preceded by RP.
4. G. Lukács, *The Historical Novel* (London: Merlin, 1962), p. 84.
5. V. E. Thompson, *The Virtuous Marketplace: Women and Men, Money and Politics in Paris, 1830–1870* (Baltimore: Johns Hopkins University Press, 2000), p. 6.
6. A. Wurmser, *La Comédie inhumaine* (Paris: Gallimard, 1964), p. 102.
7. T. Piketty, *Capital in the Twenty-First Century*, trans. A. Goldhammer (Cambridge, MA: Harvard University Press, 2014), pp. 239–241, 401–429.
8. H. Levin, *The Gates of Horn: A Study of Five French Realists* (New York: Oxford University Press, 1963), p. 192.
9. P.-G. Castex, 'Aux sources d'*Eugénie Grandet*: légende et réalité', *Revue d'histoire littéraire de la France*, 64.1 (1964), 73–94 (p. 88). Precision about these sums is impossible, as Castex and N. Mozet's Introduction to the novel make clear (CH III 1010–1011). The constitution of Grandet's fortune is however realistically possible.
10. A. D. White, *Fiat Money Inflation in France* (New York: Appleton-Century, 1933), pp. 13, 34.
11. K. G. Persson puts economic growth in 1780–1830 at 'only slightly higher than in the pre-industrial period': *An Economic History of Europe: Knowledge, Institutions, and Growth, 600 to the Present* (New York: Cambridge University Press, 2010), p. 95. Piketty echoes this conclusion in his *Capital*, pp. 4, 7, but especially in chapters 7 and 11.

6

ARMINE KOTIN MORTIMER

Le Père Goriot: *Arrivisme* and the Parisian Morality Tale

A Young Man in Paris

Le Père Goriot may well be the best-known title of *La Comédie humaine*. At the 'nerve centre' of the entire work,[1] this is 'a novel of intersection, a roundabout, from which "the broad avenues that Balzac drew in his forest of people branch out"'['un roman carrefour, un rond-point, d'où "partent les grandes avenues que Balzac a tracées dans sa forêt d'hommes"'].[2] Readers have, moreover, described it as the very model of the *Comédie humaine* novel: 'The critics all agree in seeing *Le Père Goriot* as an archetype of the Balzacian novel. Rightfully so' [Tous les commentateurs s'accordent pour voir dans *Le Père Goriot* un archétype du roman balzacien. C'est à juste titre].[3] Most importantly, Balzac's feverish composition of *Le Père Goriot* coincided with the moment, in October 1834, when he was beginning to formulate the scope and structure of *La Comédie humaine* with its basis in a study of human behaviour and social types (LH I 204). Archetype or model, nerve centre or intersection, even 'keystone',[4] the novel focuses the themes of the *Études de mœurs*, in which Balzac elaborated the social history of manners.

This is also the novel in which Balzac lit upon the brilliant and unique plan to reuse characters from his other novels while building an entire society. Reappearing characters thus acquire unexpected depth and breadth. Eugène de Rastignac, young impoverished nobleman recently 'risen' to Paris from his remote provincial home, appears in twenty-four other novels and short stories of *La Comédie humaine*. Rastignac first appeared, in the order of composition, in Balzac's 1830 novel *La Peau de chagrin*, in which he is nine to twelve years older than at his arrival in Paris. In effect, *Le Père Goriot*, which takes place between November 1819 and February 1820, retroactively gives him an origin. Writing the preface to *Une fille d'Ève* in 1839, Balzac somewhat facetiously outlines the young man's life as an example of how readers will eventually recompose the portraits of his characters from the elements disseminated throughout *La Comédie humaine* (CH II 265–266).

The Maison Vauquer where Rastignac resides is a run-down boarding house situated in a dismal, forgotten corner of Paris between the Latin Quarter and the Faubourg Saint-Marceau, at the bottom of an incline of symbolic import: 'in the subterranean region of the social ladder', as Juliette Frølich has put it.[5] Its residents form a microcosm of society, with class distinctions based in significant measure on wealth – or lack thereof. True to his methodology, Balzac details each of these characters' histories in a supple design that establishes the state of affairs from which their dramas will unfold, and the interactions among these dramas weave the plot as the stories are told in sequence and in alternation. The *pension*, the fortuitous locus of each individual story, fosters relations among the characters that otherwise would not obtain. Goriot, though once a wealthy bourgeois industrialist, now lives in straitened circumstances; his passion for his two daughters will make him destitute and cause his death. Rastignac becomes involved in the life of this tortured father. The extrovert but secretive Vautrin, an object of curiosity for Rastignac, serves his fellow criminals as banker and pursues his dealings in the city. In their different ways, 'father' Goriot and 'papa' Vautrin both become symbolic fathers for Rastignac as he seeks to rise above his initial status as an impecunious student.

Eugène de Rastignac's desire to succeed and his actions in view of this ambition make him a central figure in the motif of *arrivisme* as Balzac illustrated it. There are dozens of novels in *La Comédie humaine* in which the author focuses attention on a young man's development – his beginnings in life, his progress, successes or failures (for instance, *Le Cabinet des Antiques; Z. Marcas; Albert Savarus; Les Employés*). Balzac makes a significant investment in Rastignac as a focal figure in *La Comédie humaine*. Born the same year as his creator, he is identified as a 'sosie' or double by Pierre Citron.[6] In portraying Rastignac's *arrivisme*, Balzac is suggestively portraying his own ambitions. This theme is quite often treated with irony, whether the story is given as a *drame* as in this case or when we see comedy, as in *Un début dans la vie*. Vautrin indicates the magnitude of this concept of ambitious youth seeking a brilliant future by telling Rastignac that he is one of fifty thousand young men in his position trying to solve the problem of a rapid fortune (CH III 139).

But Rastignac does not 'arrive' in *Le Père Goriot*; he is only just setting out:

a young man who had come to Paris from near Angoulême to study law ...
Eugène de Rastignac, as he was called, was one of those young men shaped by

misfortune for hard work, who at an early age understand the hopes their families place in them and prepare a fine destiny for themselves by calculating the impact of their studies and adapting them in advance to the future movements of society so as to be among the first to pump it.

[un jeune homme venu des environs d'Angoulême à Paris pour y faire son droit ... Eugène de Rastignac, ainsi se nommait-il, était un de ces jeunes gens façonnés au travail par le malheur, qui comprennent dès le jeune âge les espérances que leurs parents placent en eux, et qui se préparent une belle destinée en calculant déjà la portée de leurs études, et les adaptant par avance au mouvement futur de la société, pour être les premiers à la pressurer.]

(CH III 56)

At the other end of the novel, the young nobleman defies Paris – society, the 'beau monde' he seeks to penetrate – with these famous words propelled from the Père Lachaise cemetery (and quoted far too often): 'À nous deux maintenant!' François Proulx notes how Barrès disliked 'Rastignac's overdone, over-quoted exclamation' and that he denounced 'the phrase's degradation, through overuse, to the status of a cliché that cannot be cited "sérieusement" without incurring ridicule'.[7] The code of the 'childhood of a great man' is saturated when Rastignac sheds the last of his young man's tears into Goriot's grave. His 'belle destinée' will be in other books.

How Rastignac will position himself to achieve that future is the matter addressed in this Parisian morality tale. His escape from the Pension Vauquer will be both literal and figurative. At an elegant dinner with Mme de Beauséant, he is appalled at the contrast with his bourgeois *pension*: 'he was so profoundly horrified by it that he swore to himself that he would move out in the month of January, as much to find a proper dwelling as to flee Vautrin' ['il en eut une si profonde horreur qu'il se jura de la quitter au mois de janvier, autant pour se mettre dans une maison propre que pour fuir Vautrin'] (CH III 151). Between his original condition and his literal escape, he undergoes an education with more than one preceptor. He has considered the troubling alternative between *obedience* and *revolt*, two of the great 'expressions of society' (CH III 262) formulated for him by Vautrin; but his final position, in this novel, rejects these extremes and chooses *struggle*, and that sets the pattern for the character during the rest of his existence in *La Comédie humaine*. By the end of this novel, his education will have progressed to the point where he knows what struggling means and he will succeed; he will have learned what Kanes calls 'the methodology of social conquest'.[8] His figurative escape ensues.

From the start, Balzac anchors his story in Paris not only to set the action but also to address potential readers. Would his story mean anything outside Paris, he pretends to wonder on the first page (CH III 49). Paris has its own rules: 'When one knows Paris, one believes nothing of what is said there and says nothing of what is done there' ['Quand on connaît Paris, on ne croit à rien de ce qui s'y dit, et l'on ne dit rien de ce qui s'y fait'] (CH III 175). Ninety-two uses of the word 'Paris' and thirty-two of 'Parisien(ne)' constantly remind us that this morality tale would be irrelevant anywhere in the provinces and most likely difficult to understand for a provincial reader. It is useful for Balzac the 'Great Explicator' to claim that he knows about 'unheard-of', 'forgotten' corners of Paris. 'Traverse it, describe it – whatever care you may take to traverse it, to describe it; however numerous and interested may be the explorers of this sea, it will always be possible to find a virgin location there, an unknown lair, flowers, pearls, monsters, something unheard-of, forgotten by literary divers' ['Parcourez-le, décrivez-le: quelque soin que vous mettiez à le parcourir, à le décrire; quelque nombreux et intéressés que soient les explorateurs de cette mer, il s'y rencontrera toujours un lieu vierge, un antre inconnu, des fleurs, des perles, des monstres, quelque chose d'inouï, oublié par les plongeurs littéraires'] (CH III 59). Among those Parisian curiosities that other 'literary divers' have missed is the city's devious power to inspire desire and burn its inhabitants with passion.

It is Paris that turns Rastignac into the social type of the *arriviste*. As Balzac put it in the 'Avant-propos': 'Doesn't Society mould Man into as many different men as there are varieties in zoology according to the milieus in which his action unfolds?' ['La Société ne fait-elle pas de l'homme, suivant les milieux où son action se déploie, autant d'hommes différents qu'il y a de variétés en zoologie?'] (CH I 8). When Rastignac arrives in Paris, he does not yet know what he wants. As Franco Moretti has pointed out: 'it is Paris itself, that immense showcase of new social wealth, that will teach [him] what it means to desire – to desire everything, at every moment, starting with the countless "necessary trifles" that will remain forever mysterious to [the people he] left behind in the provinces'.[9] The Paris that Rastignac discovers when he ventures out of the *pension* is a place of luxury – like Mme de Beauséant's elegant, red-carpeted, gold-banistered staircase – and the domain of that remarkable creature known as 'la Parisienne', starting with Anastasie de Restaud admired at the first ball Rastignac attends. The events that determine his destiny occur in distinct parts of the city, until he is no longer in need of the *pension*, the site of his call to duty.

But the city is a bottomless ocean hiding many unavowable secrets (CH III 59). It is an ocean of mud [*boue*] (CH III 262), impossible to navigate on foot without encountering the many rivers of that very special Parisian mud whose conglomeration of revolting ingredients threatens the health and safety of those who go out into the city, particularly if they are reduced to travelling on foot like Rastignac. In pages inspiring relentless disgust, Allan

H. Pasco has detailed those infamous components of *la boue de Paris*: industrial waste, household garbage, dishwater, offal from butcher shops, dung from horses and other animals and of course human wastes, composing 'a fetid, black, sticky substance that would occasionally eat through clothing'.[10] Black streams ran down the edges or the middles of the streets or formed stagnant pools; carts carrying away the hazardous mess dropped residues throughout the city. The stench was unliveable.

While horribly material, *boue* is also compellingly symbolic. As Pasco notes: '*Boue* stands as much for the vile, for shame, for failure as it does for sludge';[11] it marks Rastignac's moments of poverty and failure, like his first visit to the Restaud family, not to mention his very obvious *naïveté*. He needs to avoid getting splashed with the horrendous mixture when he leaves the *pension* to enter the parts of Paris where the old and new aristocracies reside (the Faubourg Saint-Germain for the nobles by birth, the Chausée d'Antin for the new 'nobility' of money). Rastignac's attempts to keep clean during peregrinations through the city readily symbolise his need to keep his moral compass while navigating *le beau monde*. Vautrin warns that in the struggle to arrive, virtuous genius may be buried under the *boue* of corruption: 'I challenge you to take two steps in Paris without encountering its infernal schemes' ['Je vous défie de faire deux pas dans Paris sans rencontrer des manigances infernales'] (CH III 140).

When Paris is not described as a bottomless ocean, it is a New World forest peopled by 'twenty species of savages, the Illinois, the Huron, living on the products of the different kinds of society's hunts' ['vingt espèces de peuplades sauvages, les Illinois, les Hurons, qui vivent du produit que donnent les différentes chasses sociales'] (CH III 143). Infernal Parisian schemers and American savages go together in Balzac's imagination. Vautrin also offers the most cynical advice, which, if followed, challenges morality: 'There are no principles, only events; there are no laws, only circumstances. The superior man espouses events and circumstances so as to control them' ['Il n'y a pas de principes, il n'y a que des événements; il n'y a pas de lois, il n'y a que des circonstances: l'homme supérieur épouse les événements et les circonstances pour les conduire'] (CH III 144). The lesson is not lost on Rastignac. When he launches his famous challenge to Paris at the end of the novel, he is perhaps unconsciously echoing Vautrin, who had cried "À nous deux!" (CH III 137), in trying to win Rastignac over to his views. These moral challenges posed by the city confront the ambitious *arriviste*.

The Balzacian *Arriviste* and his Destiny

The *Lexique des termes littéraires* defines '*Arriviste*' as 'a person who wants to succeed at any price by any means. The novel of education often presents *arrivistes*.' The Petit Robert dictionary is more categorical: an *arriviste* is 'devoid of scruples'. Priscilla P. Clark observes, 'The many *arrivistes* of the *Comédie humaine* welcome the present and adamantly refuse to be bound by the past or to accept their lot in life. Desire determines their lives, not duty, and because desire can never be satisfied, the ambitions that agitate the *Comédie humaine* generate a world of uncommon mobility.'[12]

As the very model of the ambitious young man in *La Comédie humaine*, Eugène de Rastignac undergoes a moral education that ends with the end of *Le Père Goriot*. He is insistently identified as an 'étudiant' – 130 uses of the word applied to him in 241 pages – thus reinforcing a sense of *Le Père Goriot* as a novel of *education* or of *instruction* (*Bildungsroman* versus *Erziehungsroman*). In Clark's view, *Bildungsroman* would not be the appropriate term for *Le Père Goriot*, which is rather an *Erziehungsroman* or novel of instruction.[13] Balzac's use of a descriptor in lieu of a name is a constant in *La Comédie humaine*; it serves to form the *type*: in this case, the naïve provincial identified as a student who will learn how to succeed in the city. Scenes from Fénelon's 1699 *Les Aventures de Télémaque* depicted on the wallpaper in the living room of the *pension* also allude to the genre of the novel of instruction. Written to tutor the duc de Bourgogne, grandson of Louis XIV, Fénelon's book portrays Mentor instructing the prince in his duties.

There are moments when Rastignac is a student in the 'ways of the world' (to use Moretti's phrase), learning from experiences, encounters and events; society is his teacher, as when the gaffes he makes with Mme de Restaud and Mme de Beauséant cause him to reflect on what can and cannot be said in social contexts. In other moments, he is being instructed like a schoolboy; his teachers are then primarily Vautrin and Mme de Beauséant. Vautrin makes pressing offers: 'Ah, if you were willing to become my student, I would put everything within your grasp' ['Ah! si vous vouliez devenir mon élève, je vous ferais arriver à tout'] (CH III 185).

But when Rastignac escapes from the *pension*, his education is finishing and his obedience to duty well under control. Goriot is dying and Mme de Beauséant is leaving Paris for good; the 'belles âmes' do not last in this world, he reflects. And his other instructor, Vautrin, has been hauled off by the police. 'His education was coming to an end' ['Son éducation s'achevait'] (CH III 268). From the Père Lachaise cemetery, Rastignac envisions not his continuing education but the route he will take in his life as an adult; at a physical and moral height, he perceives his future as the future of one who has arrived. As Rose Fortassier writes in her introduction to the novel: 'That Rastignac should know himself only after Goriot is dead and buried is natural and profoundly truthful' ['Il est naturel et d'une profonde vérité

Le Père Goriot: Arrivisme and the Parisian Morality Tale

que Rastignac ne se connaisse qu'une fois Goriot mort et enterré'] (CH III 24). To the extent that Balzac portrays Rastignac as a student, and gives him mentors or instructors, the tack he takes recalls the structures of novels of instruction. But Rastignac would not be the hero that he is, through many pages of *La Comédie humaine*, without the innate personal qualities Balzac endows him with, including his ability to determine his own moral stance, as Balzac will portray him after *Le Père Goriot*.

The ending of *Le Père Goriot*, anticipating Eugène de Rastignac's long future destiny, spawned other narratives of *La Comédie humaine*. Rastignac will quickly become one of the notable young men of Paris, acquainted with aristocrats of both sexes and invited to their *raouts*, seen with Delphine de Nucingen in the theatre elegantly dressed, called on to advise other young men on matters of haberdashery, debt and duelling. When Rastignac's name appears in *Le Contrat de mariage* in a long letter from de Marsay loaded with the cynicisms typical of that character, he is described as 'that little Rastignac, a rascal who's beginning to make his mark' ['le petit Rastignac, un drôle qui commence à percer'] (CH III 645). This is now approximately seven years after *Le Père Goriot*, but the same de Marsay, in *Illusions perdues*, had described him, again 'le petit Rastignac', as launched like a kite – therefore flying high – in 1821 (CH V 280), so Eugène has quickly implemented his challenge to Paris. Still in *Illusions perdues*, around 1822, he is the most famous of the Parisian high-livers, the epitome of fashion, the wittiest roué, the leader of the pack. (But Balzac added his name at a late date.) Two years later, in *Splendeurs et misères des courtisanes*, Rastignac guides the weaker Lucien de Rubempré through some of the difficulties of his Parisian existence. He will also advise, often cynically, other young men who turn to him and whom he may corrupt, such as Raphaël de Valentin (*La Peau de chagrin*), Calyste du Guénic (*Béatrix*), Savinien de Portenduère (*Ursule Mirouët*) and Victurnien d'Esgrignon (*Le Cabinet des antiques*).

His most important reappearance after *Le Père Goriot* is in *La Maison Nucingen*. This retrospective narration provides the necessary link between that impecunious student of 1820 perched on the lip of his *arrivisme* above the city and the 1845 Count, *pair de France*, Justice Minister, member of the Jockey Club and possessor of three hundred thousand *livres de rente*. As the banker Nucingen's somewhat naïve and quite passive accomplice, around 1826 or 1827, he will gain enough money to proceed on the path from which lack of funds held him back during *Le Père Goriot*.

A year later, as he appears in *L'Interdiction*, he possesses his inherited title of Baron and twenty thousand *livres de rente* – and debts. Here his ambition makes him consider the marquise d'Espard a fine conquest, although he is still faithful to Delphine: 'a society woman brings you everything, she is the diamond with which a man cuts all the windows when he doesn't have the golden key with which all the doors are opened' ['une femme du monde mène à tout, elle est le diamant avec lequel un homme coupe toutes les vitres, quand il n'a pas la clef d'or avec laquelle s'ouvrent toutes les portes.'] (CH III 425)

As to the development of his character, in 1829–33 he appears in *La Peau de chagrin* (once again, the earliest appearance of Rastignac in terms of the order of composition) as the promoter of a 'dissipation system' he would teach to Raphaël de Valentin, described as 'the morality of the comedy performed every day in society' ['la moralité de la comédie qui se joue tous les jours dans le monde'] (CH X 145). In 1833, in *Une fille d'Ève*, he is 'arrivé'. In 1838, he is married to Delphine de Nucingen's daughter Augusta. Finally, by 1845, he has reached the pinnacle of his career in life and in *La Comédie humaine*.

In short, through his struggle with society, Rastignac will master the codes of Parisian life, obtain money and high positions and attain high noble rank. He is an enviable success, in contrast to other young provincial aristocrats such as Lucien de Rubempré (weaknesses and failures leading to suicide); Victurnien d'Esgrignon (guilty of a forgery to pay Diane de Maufrigneuse's expenses); Calyste du Guénic (only saved from moral downfall by Félicité des Touches); and even perhaps Félix de Vandenesse (arguably learning lessons too late from Henriette de Mortsauf).[14]

Rastignac's *arriviste* character also extends beyond the pages of Balzac's books, and this takes the form of explicit references and implicit allusions. Early in Flaubert's 1869 novel *L'Éducation sentimentale*, the protagonist Frédéric Moreau has just returned to his provincial home after obtaining his *baccalauréat* in Paris. During a late-night stroll, he and his friend Charles Deslauriers speak of their uncertain futures with melancholy and regret. The slightly older Deslauriers combats Frédéric's discouragement by recommending he become the lover of Mme Dambreuse, the wife of a wealthy neighbour: 'there is nothing so useful as frequenting a wealthy home! Since you own a black suit and white gloves, put them to use! You need to be a part of that society ... A man with millions, think about it! Get him to like you, and his wife too. Become her lover!' [rien n'est utile comme de fréquenter une maison riche! Puisque tu as un habit noir et des gants blancs, profites-en! Il faut que tu ailles dans ce monde-là! ... Un homme à millions, pense donc! Arrange-toi pour lui plaire et à sa femme aussi. Deviens son amant!'][15] It's a plan straight out of *La Comédie humaine*, including the specific reference to the clothing needed to succeed in high society and the value placed on wealth. When Frédéric protests, Deslauriers simply says, 'It's classical, what I'm telling you, don't you think? Remember Rastignac in *La Comédie humaine*! You will succeed, I'm sure of it!' ['Mais je te dis là des choses classiques, il me semble? Rappelle-toi Rastignac dans *La Comédie humaine*! Tu réussiras, j'en suis sûr!']¹⁶ The 'tu réussiras!' visibly echoes Rastignac's 'je réussirai!' in *Le Père Goriot* (CH III 122). Noteworthy is the consistency of the woman's role in a young man's advancement. But this scene is only the beginning of Frédéric's education, and as Peter Brooks details, Flaubert writes *against* the Balzacian novel of desire and ambition; he deconstructs 'the contents of education and the sentiments'.¹⁷

Maupassant's *Bel-Ami* cynically portrays an *arriviste*, Georges Duroy, who begins as a man of no means and of lowly birth, looking much like the lowlife of popular novels, and who climbs irresistibly to high social standing, ably assisted by his unbridled sex drive. In the final pages, the impecunious brute has turned into Baron Georges Du Roy de Cantel, editor of an influential newspaper, decorated with the *légion d'honneur*, respected and rich. As two attendees at his wedding observe about Du Roy, 'the future belongs to the clever' ['l'avenir est aux malins'] and 'He's set for life' ['Sa vie est faite'].¹⁸ Several women boost him up the ladder. Towards the end, the *arriviste* realises that marrying the rich daughter of the proprietor of the newspaper would be a way to play the game for higher rewards: 'With the little Suzanne for stakes, what a fine position he could have won' ['Quelle belle partie il aurait pu gagner avec la petite Suzanne pour enjeu'].¹⁹ In the final scene, stepping out of the Madeleine church with his bride on his arm, he eyes the Chambre des Députés next door and imagines himself there: 'a single jump would take him from the entrance of the Madeleine to the entrance of the Palais-Bourbon' ['il allait faire un bond du portique de la Madeleine au portique du Palais-Bourbon'].²⁰ This vision of his next advancement, coming in the last sentence of the penultimate paragraph like Rastignac's 'À nous deux maintenant!' has, according to Louis Forestier, been compared by almost all commentators to Rastignac's final act of defiance.²¹

Beyond these two important examples, there are many cases of ambitious young men in Zola's *Rougon-Macquart* series and even in Gide's *Les Fauxmonnayeurs*, where Bernard's struggles distantly recall those of Rastignac. Interestingly, however, certain writers in the late nineteenth century felt Balzac's influence as a negative force. Rastignac represented a model to reject or avoid in the novels of instruction by Barrès and others, as analysed in François Proulx's study of the dangers of reading for young men in the late nineteenth and early twentieth centuries. Proulx mentions an article by a young Barrès, 'La Contagion des Rastignac', which

> is likewise reminiscent of Bourget's *Essais* in its use of a medical lexicon to describe the deleterious effect of the 'enfiévrant romancier' on rising

generations since the middle of the century. Balzac's ambitious and amoral heroes, Barrès writes, have become dangerous models for young men from the provinces who dream of emulating their social and amorous triumphs; these impressionable young readers confuse the possibilities afforded by fiction with prospects for their own life.[22]

Clearly before the end of the nineteenth century, many considered the model of the *arriviste* a dangerously immoral element, as indeed definitions of the word tend to affirm. But does the *arrivisme* of this Parisian morality tale oblige us to consider Rastignac as immoral?

Rastignac Escapes

Writing in 1835, with several works behind him and *Le Père Goriot* about to appear, Balzac found it necessary to defend himself against charges of immorality in a preface famous for a kind of balance sheet of the 'good' and the 'bad' characters in his past and future novels – and since men seem to be immune from such objections by Balzac's reading public, all the characters listed are women. The author of sarcasms about the relations between husband and wife in the *Physiologie du mariage* recaptures the witty tone of that work while pretending to satisfy the upright women who object to his portrayals of adulteresses. For, as he writes in that March 1835 preface: 'vice is more apparent, it abounds', whereas 'virtue offers only excessively tenuous lines to the brush' ['le vice a plus d'apparence, il foisonne; ... la vertu n'offre au pinceau que des lignes d'une excessive ténuité'] (CH III 45). This, then, is the problem for the writer who would like to interest his readers: he must portray what some will call immorality.

Taught by both Vautrin and Mme de Beauséant, Rastignac understands that they are making the same point in different styles, but there is more to be said about this distribution of the instructor roles. Mme de Beauséant teaches skills pertinent to social life, instructing Rastignac in how to rise and succeed according to social measures, whereas Vautrin is blunt, brutal and goal-oriented, focused on money and power. Mme de Beauséant at the Théâtre des Italiens chastises the young man for staring at Delphine de Nucingen in a loge opposite: 'You will succeed at nothing if you throw yourself upon others like that' ['Vous ne réussirez à rien, si vous vous jetez ainsi à la tête des gens'] (CH III 153). Vautrin's message concerns 'the morals – or rather the anti-morals of the period' [la morale – ou plutôt l'anti-morale de l'époque'] as Françoise van Rossum-Guyon puts it.[23] And the student perceives the nuances that distinguish Mme de Beauséant's instruction from Vautrin's. As for 'father' Goriot himself, the young hero finds in him if not a model, at

Le Père Goriot: *Arrivisme* and the Parisian Morality Tale

least an inducement to 'work nobly like a saint' ['travailler noblement, saintement'] (CH III 146) (an illusion he loses a page later (CH III 147)).

If Goriot symbolises obedience (at least before the epiphany that occurs during his death agony) and Vautrin exemplifies revolt, Mme de Beauséant stands as an unwitting model of struggle – but before *Le Père Goriot* ends, she will have lost, as recapitulated in one of Balzac's most compelling novellas, *La Femme abandonnée*. She is a suitable mentor for Rastignac because she is herself in a struggle against the infamous, cruel world and she provides 'the teachings that the anger of a rejected woman had torn from [her]' ['les enseignements que la colère d'une femme abandonnée avaient arrachés à madame de Beauséant'] (CH III 118). It is she who pithily formulates the composition of society, in terms similar to Vautrin's, as 'an assemblage of dupes and scoundrels. Do not join in with either of them' ['une réunion de dupes et de fripons. Ne soyez ni parmi les uns ni parmi les autres'] (CH III 117), and she begs to be left alone because 'We women too must fight our battles' ['Nous autres femmes, nous avons aussi nos batailles à livrer'] (*ibid.*). Dupes obey; scoundrels revolt; but heroes and the occasional heroic woman struggle.

The *natural* qualities Rastignac possesses project his later successes in the *social* world, in spite of his early *naïveté*. He has audacity, courage and drive; he learns fast and is capable of formulating the process as a kind of rule. He is not put off by hurdles nor hampered by his evident mistakes. His natural pride prompts him to jealousy and jealousy to emulation. His southern origins, of which Balzac frequently reminds the reader by calling him 'le Méridional', have a role in these natural abilities, as if it is only Paris that teaches the need to dissimulate to reach social standards. He behaves like a southerner, for example, in spontaneously expressing his annoyance at the interruption of a servant, for which Mme de Beauséant scolds him (CH III 109). In spite of such *naïveté*, Rastignac surprises the reader by learning on his own, without external guidance; for instance, he is enough of a 'genius' to figure out the real barbs disguised by the affectionate language spoken between Mme de Beauséant and Mme de Langeais; and he interprets his cousin's gestures because he has 'promptly' become a good observer. The perceptive Ajuda-Pinto says Eugène will 'break the bank' ['faire sauter la banque'] and, mixing his metaphors, that he is 'supple like an eel' ['souple comme une anguille'] and will go far (CH III 157). Rastignac thus possesses inherent qualities that cannot be taxed with immorality.

Nevertheless, some readers describe him as corrupt in letting his ambition guide his course in life while covering his corruption with apparent *naïveté*, passivity and laziness. To a degree, one may see the character as having internalised some of Vautrin's lessons, as if the temptations put before him by the 'sphinx' were a necessary ingredient in his later struggle. No revolt – but he will espouse the 'circumstances' of which Vautrin spoke, the better to control his destiny, and that includes, most pertinently, his monetary ambitions. Struggle includes elements of revolt – the fight against established powers like the haughty gatekeepers of social status represented by a Maxime de Trailles. But struggle also includes obedience to the rules of society. One can however question that 'material wealth, power and recognition' must be taken as *corrupt* values. Those are Marianne Hirsch's terms to describe 'the corrupt values of a society that fosters the unnatural parent-child relationships of Magwitch and Estella, of Goriot and his daughters' which 'invade the realm of the individual and contaminate all that he could oppose to such values'.[24]

The narrator's reflection on his character's thinking is of utmost importance in placing the *arriviste* student on a moral continuum. In a page-and-a-half passage during which Rastignac walks back to the *pension* after an evening with Mme de Beauséant, he muses about Delphine, to whom he has just been introduced, while simultaneously the familiar Balzacian narrator comments on Rastignac. It is in this passage that the student conceives the idea of becoming rich with Nucingen's help. Already he realises that attaching himself to Delphine will allow him to 'pick up an immediate fortune' ['ramasser tout d'un coup une fortune'] (CH III 158). These vague ideas floating on the horizon of Rastignac's conscience, says the narrator, would not emerge pure from its fires, but 'by a series of transactions of this kind, men arrive at this relaxed morality that the present time professes' ['Les hommes arrivent, par une suite de transactions de ce genre, à cette morale relâchée que professe l'époque actuelle'] (*ibid.*). Defending his novels, as he did regularly, against those who would object that characters are not 'rectangular' and perfectly honest like Molière's Alceste or Scott's Jeanie Deans, Balzac insinuates that 'the opposite sort of work, the portrayal of the sinuosities through which a man of the world, an ambitious man, propels his conscience while attempting to steer around evil in order to arrive at his goals while maintaining appearances, would be neither less attractive nor less dramatic' ['l'œuvre opposée, la peinture des sinuosités dans lesquelles un homme du monde, un ambitieux fait rouler sa conscience, en essayant de côtoyer le mal, afin d'arriver à son but en gardant les apparences, ne serait-elle ni moins belle, ni moins dramatique'] (*ibid.*).

The intriguing concepts of 'relaxed morality' and 'sinuosities', explicitly connected to the words designating ambition and *arrivisme* (in the form of the verb), neatly reflect the moral conundrum that faces the reader of *Le Père*

Goriot. These terms express the morality of the day, and the appropriate one for anyone who would arrive. We admire Rastignac. Why? If we recall his moral strivings as a student in *Le Père Goriot*, perhaps we may forgive later actions. In serving as a son to Goriot, Rastignac acts according to a moral imperative, unlike the two daughters, even though his behaviour with Goriot does little for his ambitions. Furthermore, nothing shows that Rastignac will have lost this capacity for compassion once Goriot is dead

It is, I propose, a mistake to judge Rastignac and the moral compass of the novel by any sort of external measure. One should judge its morality according to the values inherent in the novel and in the rest of *La Comédie humaine*, from which it cannot be separated. 'Parisian law', or 'the law of Paris', with its 'sinuosities' and its 'relaxed morality', conveniently takes the place of the law Rastignac purports to study at college. Circumstances and situations excuse actions that can be considered to lack probity and virtue. Moreover, what Balzac calls the 'present constitution' (CH III 174) of society, which forces women to commit errors (meaning extra-marital affairs), broadens the view of Parisian society as open to such corruption. Anyone who has the courage to struggle with Paris deserves admiration.

If this novel can be considered a model of realism and an archetype of the *Comédie humaine* novel, it is in considerable measure because of its portrayal of these issues of mores and morality, of 'human feelings, social crises, evil and good, the whole hodgepodge of civilisation' ['les sentiments humains, les crises sociales, le mal et le bien, tout le pêle-mêle de la civilisation'] (Preface of May 1835, CH III 47). *Le Père Goriot* may be a morality tale, and certainly one may accuse Goriot's daughters of immorality, but its highest value for Balzac does not lie in a chastisement of immorality. Its value is expressed in the key words '*All is true*' (CH III 50).

The 'truth' of Balzac's narrative lies in the portrayal of a hero in a new mould, as Flaubert, Maupassant, and several other later writers clearly understood. Eugène de Rastignac is a hero for the society Balzac knew; anything less would not deserve this '*All is true*' designation. Without being a dupe, Rastignac is obedient to the extent that he recognises and follows social rules, even though in later novels he has moved far from the innocence of his origins. But there is more than one sort of innocence: it can be opposed to knowledge or to guilt, and Rastignac is in a position of knowledge at the end of *Le Père Goriot*, not guilt.

Thus, in the value structure of *La Comédie humaine*, Rastignac is not an immoral character. His challenge to society comes not from the outside, as a struggle against society, but from *within* the social system, as will be confirmed by his ultimate destiny as Justice Minister (a title that may nevertheless ring ironic). The *arriviste* questions only 'his place in the structures, not the structures themselves' ['sa place dans les structures, non les structures mêmes'], Jean d'Ormesson observes,[25] and this is true of Rastignac. In such internal terms, then, Rastignac escapes corruption. To say he is immoral or corrupt is to apply a grid of values that tend towards the absolute, whereas the novel's values are relative. Ronnie Butler comments that Balzac's viewpoint is one that 'favours individual struggle within society, whose laws and values must be recognised and acted upon to ensure the successful pursuit of ambition'.[26] Or is it simply that there is nothing so successful as success? Mme de Beauséant has it thus: 'In Paris, success is all. It's the key to power' ['À Paris, le succès est tout, c'est la clef du pouvoir'] (CH III 117). David Ellison has astutely noticed how Rastignac's position uncannily anticipates the Nietzschean transvaluation of all values; Rastignac prefigures the *Übermensch*, 'one who has uncovered the origins of moral values and has undertaken to transvalue them according to how they enhance or prove detrimental to one's goals'.[27] Rastignac illustrates a kind of morality that will stand for the rest of the world of social behaviour – *les mœurs* – invented in *La Comédie humaine*.

In sum, Rastignac's experiences in this novel culminate in the challenge he addresses to Paris and its society at the end, a challenge he will take on successfully. 'I shall succeed!' was the cry – ambition in a nutshell, and Balzac shows us his successes in later narratives, in money, in love, and in power.[28] Rastignac will weather unscathed all the social conditions he confronts. The justification of this future result lies in *Le Père Goriot* with its ending in the moment when Rastignac accepts the concept of *lutte*. That moment can be considered the consolidation of a reassuring myth of the unity of the hero in his social situation. Even without knowing his destiny in other narratives, the reader has the right to believe that Rastignac is ready to confront his future.

NOTES

1. F. Marceau, 'Préface', *Le Père Goriot* (Paris: Gallimard, 'Folio', 1971), p. 9. All translations are mine.
2. S.-A. Picon quoting Mauriac, Dossier in *Le Père Goriot* (Paris: Folio-Plus classique, 2011), p. 357.
3. A. Michel, *Le Réel et la beauté dans le roman balzacien* (Paris: Champion, 2001), p. 136.
4. M. Kanes, *'Père Goriot'. Anatomy of a Troubled World* (New York: Twayne, 1983), p. 9.
5. J. Frølich, 'Étudiants voyageurs dans l'espace balzacien' in N. Mozet and P. Petitier (eds), *Balzac voyageur: parcours, déplacements, mutations* (Tours: Université François Rabelais, 2004), pp. 223–236 (p. 233).

6. P. Citron, *Dans Balzac* (Paris: Seuil, 1986), p. 177.
7. F. Proulx, '"À nous deux", Balzac: Barrès's *Les Déracinés* and the Ghosts of *La Comédie humaine*', *Nineteenth-Century French Studies*, 42.3–4 (2014), 235–249 (p. 241).
8. Kanes, '*Père Goriot*', p. 31.
9. F. Moretti, *The Way of the World: The 'Bildungsroman' in European Culture*, trans. A. J. Sbragia (London: Verso, 1987), p. 166.
10. A. H. Pasco, *Sick Heroes. French Society and Literature in the Romantic Age, 1750–1850* (University of Exeter Press, 1997), p. 24.
11. *Ibid.*, p. 26.
12. P. Clark, 'The Metamorphoses of Mentor: Fénelon to Balzac', *Romanic Review*, 75 (1984), pp. 200–215 (p. 201).
13. *Ibid.*, p. 206.
14. Clark calls Lucien and Victurnien 'failed counterparts' of Rastignac (*ibid.*, p. 213).
15. G. Flaubert, *L'Éducation sentimentale* (Paris: Garnier-Flammarion, 1969), p. 52.
16. *Ibid.*
17. P. Brooks, *Reading for the Plot: Design and Intention in Narrative* (New York: Vintage Books, 1985), p. 215.
18. G. de Maupassant, *Bel-Ami* in L. Forestier (ed.), *Romans* (Paris: Gallimard, 'Pléiade', 1987), p. 475.
19. *Ibid.*, p. 440.
20. *Ibid.*, p. 480.
21. *Ibid.*, p. 1430.
22. F. Proulx, *Victims of the Book: Reading Anxieties in the French Novel of Formation, 1880–1914* (Unpubl. doctoral dissertation, Harvard, 2010), p. 215. Barrès's article appeared in *Le Voltaire* on 28 June 1887.
23. F. van Rossum-Guyon, *Balzac: la littérature réfléchie. Discours et autoreprésentations* (Montreal: Département d'Études françaises, 'Paragraphes', 2002), p. 70.
24. M. Hirsch, 'The Novel of Formation as Genre: between Great Expectations and Lost Illusions', *Genre*, 12 (1979), 291–311 (p. 308).
25. J. d'Ormesson, 'Arrivisme, snobisme, dandysme', *Revue de métaphysique et de morale*, 68.4 (1963), 443–59 (p. 447).
26. R. Butler, 'The Realist Novel as "Roman d'éducation": Ideological Debate and Social Action in *Le Père Goriot* and *Germinal*', *Nineteenth-Century French Studies*, 12.1–2 (1983–1984), 68–77 (p. 74).
27. D. R. Ellison, 'Moral Complexity in *Le Père Goriot*: Balzac between Kant and Nietzsche' in M. Ginsburg (ed.), *Approaches to Teaching Balzac's 'Old Goriot'* (New York: MLA, 2000), pp. 72–80 (p. 76).
28. A. R. Pugh writes: 'In 1844 the translator Edward S. Gould told American readers that: "The reader may believe that Eugène returned to the Maison Vauquer thoroughly cured of his fancy for Parisian high-life and female patronage; and that, in due time, he married Victorine and took up his abode in the provinces." Even if the text of *Le Père Goriot* were the only evidence, this would be a peculiar conclusion to draw ("vraiment grotesque" is Malcolm Jones' description). In 1957, E. C. Hobart argued that Rastignac left the Père

Lachaise as a missionary. One would have thought, however, that the analysis of Rastignac throughout the novel left one in no doubt about his moral vulnerability, and that there were enough hints to suggest that he became a typical playboy – a pocket edition of de Marsay, in fact, whose mistress he takes when de Marsay has won a princess.' (*Balzac's Recurring Characters* (London: Duckworth, 1974), pp. 84–85)

7

SOTIRIOS PARASCHAS

Illusions perdues: Writers, Artists and the Reflexive Novel

When *Illusions perdues* was first published, it was seen as one of these novels 'which one does not regret failing to read, which are published today only to disappear and be completely forgotten the next day' ['qu'on n'a nul regret de ne pas lire, qui paraissent aujourd'hui pour disparaître le lendemain dans un immense oubli'].[1] What Balzac presented as a study of the (highly questionable) morals of journalists was seen by reviewers as an unjust and biased, almost defamatory, attack on their profession. Despite this almost unanimously hostile reception, *Illusions perdues* became an emblematic nineteenth-century novel. The theme of the young man from the provinces who tries to make his way in Paris (with varying degrees of success) recurs in a number of novels spanning the nineteenth century, from Stendhal's *Le Rouge et le noir* (1830) and Balzac's own *Le Père Goriot* (1834–35), to Flaubert's *L'Éducation sentimentale* (1869) and Zola's *Pot-Bouille* (1882).

However, what sets *Illusions perdues* apart from all these novels is that the main character, Lucien de Rubempré, is not only an (inexperienced) *arriviste* but also a talented poet who arrives in Paris determined to prove his genius, achieve fame and acquire an aristocratic title. This very fact grants a unique place to the novel also in the context of Balzac's own œuvre, since geniuses and *arrivistes* rarely mix in *La Comédie humaine*. The former, who appear primarily in the *Études philosophiques*, whether they are artists (the composer Gambara in the eponymous tale or the painter Frenhofer in *Le Chef-d'œuvre inconnu*), scientists (Balthazar Claës in *La Recherche de l'absolu*) or thinkers (the titular character of *Louis Lambert*) are exclusively dedicated to their work to the point of being oblivious to society, success and the material world. Lucien is not a real genius, even if he is described as such by characters who wish to flatter him, such as Mme de Bargeton (CH V 174, 210), the woman who falls in love with him and takes him to Paris.

The narrator, however, is consistently ironic towards Lucien's intellectual aspirations and moral qualities: while he expresses his sympathy for Lucien's vicissitudes and recognises his unquestionable talent as a poet, he refuses to grant him the status of a truly exceptional author. Instead, Lucien is implicitly juxtaposed to characters who conform to the type of genius depicted in the *Études philosophiques*. In the first and the third parts of the novel, this role is assumed by Lucien's friend and brother-in-law, David Séchard, a printer and inventor who finds a way of manufacturing cheap paper at the cost of his family's financial ruin. More importantly, in the second part of the novel, Lucien meets the *Cénacle*, a group of exceptional young men who take the penniless Lucien under their wing, after he has been abandoned by Mme de Bargeton.

The *Cénacle* is described as an ideal society of geniuses, whose members represent all domains of intellectual activity, and are led by the writer Daniel d'Arthez: refusing to compromise their gifts, they live in self-imposed poverty, concentrate on their work and wait patiently for the recognition of their talents. Lucien abandons this way of life very soon, when he meets a new mentor, Étienne Lousteau, who introduces him to the world of journalism, which is anathema to the *Cénacle*. The contrast between Lucien and the members of the *Cénacle* is immediately evident in their physical appearance: whereas Lucien's most notable characteristic is his remarkable beauty, the members of the *Cénacle* 'bore on their forehead the stamp of a particular genius' ['portaient au front ... le sceau d'un génie spécial'] (CH V 315), and d'Arthez exhibits 'the indefinable symptoms of superiority' ['les indicibles symptômes de la supériorité'] (CH V 309). While d'Arthez recognises the signs of genius in Lucien, he points out the main difference that sets him apart from the *Cénacle*: he lacks the determination, or 'the will-power' ['la volonté'] and 'the angelic patience' ['la patience angélique'] of genius (CH V 311).

If d'Arthez is willing to see Lucien as a potential genius when they first meet, Lucien's trajectory forces d'Arthez to deny him the very quality of a poet, in his letter to Lucien's sister, Ève, in the third part of the novel: 'Lucien has poetry in him but is no real poet. He's a dreamer, not a thinker; he makes a great to-do but is not creative' ['Lucien est un homme de poésie et non un poète, il rêve et ne pense pas, il s'agite et ne crée pas'] (CH V 578). Indeed, Lucien produces nothing new during the course of his Parisian career: his collection of poems, *Les Marguerites*, and his historical novel, *L'Archer de Charles IX*, have already been written when the narrative begins and Lucien only revises them for a brief period of time, after he has been abandoned by Mme de Bargeton.

However, the question of whether Lucien is a genius or a mere poet proves to be of somewhat secondary importance in the novel: by emphasising that Lucien does not produce, d'Arthez does not merely stress the unbridgeable gap between the work ethic of Lucien and the *Cénacle* but also points out a peculiarity in a novel whose protagonist is an author. Unlike other works about artists by Balzac, which not only detail the process of the creation of a work of art, but also make it the main focus of the narrative (such as *Gambara* or *Le Chef-d'œuvre inconnu*), *Illusions perdues* pays little attention to the art of writing. Instead, what is primarily of interest in the novel is not the creation but the *business* of literature: *Illusions perdues* is not so much a novel about writing as it is a novel about authorship as a profession and about the commodification of literature, as well as the main facilitator of this commodification, journalism. In this context, the second part of the novel, *Un grand homme de province à Paris*, which focuses on Lucien's short-lived literary career in Paris, before he is forced to return to Angoulême, alternates between Lucien's (melo)dramatic rise and fall and what one of the first reviewers of the novel called 'a satirical review of the Parisian book trade' ['[une] revue satirique de la librairie parisienne'].[2]

On the one hand, Balzac introduces Lucien (and the reader) to the world of the book trade by depicting a series of types of publisher. The satirical tone is reinforced by the headings of the chapters of the second part of the novel which enumerate these 'variétés de libraire'. Lucien, a wide-eyed Candide whose illusions and *naïveté* are never exhausted, serves this satirical purpose well. On the other hand, however, the prevailing tone of the novel is melodramatic: Lucien becomes an influential and much-feared journalist in the course of a day, by the end of which he has a job and a mistress (Coralie, an actress who falls instantly in love with him), he has written a review for a play 'which started a revolution in journalism by the revelation of a new and original style' ['qui fit révolution dans le journalisme par la révélation d'une manière neuve et originale'] (CH V 399) and has started exacting his revenge on Mme de Bargeton. His downfall is equally sudden: in the course of what the narrator calls Lucien's 'fatal week' ['fatale semaine'] (CH V 526), he is immersed in debt, loses his job (after he has been manipulated by his enemies into changing his political allegiances), is wounded in a duel with one of his former friends from the *Cénacle*, Michel Chrestien, and witnesses Coralie's death.

Lucien's story is in many ways the opposite of the drama of the Romantic genius, emblematically illustrated by Alfred de Vigny in his 1835 play, *Chatterton*, whose protagonist is explicitly (and ironically) compared to Lucien in *Illusions perdues*: the latter is described as 'a Chatterton without that ferocious hatred for social eminence which had prompted the English poet to lampoon his benefactors' ['un Chatterton ... sans la haine féroce contre les grandeurs sociales qui poussa le poète anglais à écrire des pamphlets contre ses bienfaiteurs'] (CH V 164). For the Romantics, Thomas Chatterton, the eighteen-year-old English poet who had committed suicide in 1770, had become a symbol of the inability of the unappreciated genius to survive in a materialistic society. In Vigny's play, Chatterton ends his life because he is unwilling to commodify his talent: he decides 'to throw off his mask and be himself until the end' ['de ne [s]e point masquer et d'être [s]oi-même jusqu'à la fin'], rather than play a role and 'animate miserable puppets or become one himself and trade on this mockery' ['faire jouer de misérables poupées, ou l'être soi-même et faire trafic de cette singerie'].[3] By contrast, Lucien's drama is that of the man of letters who commodifies his gift and writes precisely in order to survive. In doing so, he resembles Chatterton's 'misérable poupée', especially since his career (and the depiction of authorship and journalism in the novel) is presented as being inextricably intertwined with the theatre and the profession of the actor.

On a first level, the role of the theatre and of actors in *Illusions perdues* is integral to the plot. On the one hand, theatre was a source of fascination for nineteenth-century authors: most nineteenth-century novelists either fostered dramatic aspirations in their youth or tried to embark on a parallel career as playwrights – in the case of Balzac, both. Lucien, in this sense, is no exception and feels the attraction of the stage, 'the first love of all poetic spirits' ['ce premier amour de tous les esprits poétiques'], as soon as he arrives in Paris. Even in the midst of his poverty, Lucien 'had no strength to resist the seductions of theatre-bills' ['se trouva sans force contre les séductions des affiches de spectacle'] (CH V 299). On the other hand, one of the sources of revenue for journalists, such as Lousteau, is the benefits they draw from reviewing plays, both by bartering a good review or threatening with a negative one and by selling their share of free tickets.

However, the link between authorship, journalism and acting in the novel is not only a matter of the circumstances of the plot but is also based on deeper affinities which are revealing about the way in which Balzac chose to depict the professionalisation of authorship. *Illusions perdues* does not focus on the art of acting but on what goes on backstage: Lucien is introduced at the same time to the workings of the book trade and of the theatre industry. Lousteau takes Lucien first to the 'librairies des nouveautés' at the Galeries de Bois, where he is disillusioned after witnessing the shady dealings of publishers, authors and journalists. On the same day, they attend the premiere of a play at the Panorama-Dramatique and when Lucien is invited backstage, he experiences a similar disillusionment: 'all this array of ludicrous, dismal, dirty, hideous and tawdry objects was so unlike what Lucien had seen from out front that his astonishment was unbounded' ['cet ensemble de choses bouffonnes, tristes, sales, affreuses, éclatantes, ressemblait si peu à ce que Lucien avait vu de sa place au théâtre, que son étonnement fut sans bornes'] (CH V 373).

This parallelism between Lucien's initiation to the worlds of the book trade and the theatre is not accidental. The novel establishes a systematic metaphorical equivalence between authorship and the theatre: 'literary life has its backstage area. Success, whether filched or merited, is what the pit applauds; the revolting tricks and dodges, the supernumeraries in their grease-paint, the hired clappers, the call-boys and scene-shifters, that's what it's not allowed to see' ['[l]a vie littéraire a ses coulisses. Les succès surpris ou mérités, voilà ce qu'applaudit et voit le parterre; les moyens, toujours hideux, les comparses enluminés, les claqueurs et les garçons de service, voilà ce que recèlent les coulisses'] (CH V 342). Indeed, *Illusions perdues* is a novel about the backstage of both worlds.[4]

The metaphor of the theatre appears in *Illusions perdues* even before Lucien has stepped into the Opera or the Panorama-Dramatique. Already in the first part of the novel, Lucien is in search of an environment suitable for the demonstration of his talents, which is usually described in theatrical terms: high society or Paris are seen as 'le théâtre' in which he will excel (CH V 174, 215, 249). In the second part of the novel, Lucien discovers that every aspect of life in Paris is a stage: 'here, indeed, all is spectacle, matter for comparison and instruction' ['[i]ci, vraiment, tout est spectacle, comparaison et instruction'] (CH V 294).

This is especially true of the profession of authorship whose performative aspects are constantly emphasised in *Illusions perdues*. Literature is not associated with performance only when Lucien is shown to read his works to an audience (Mme de Bargeton's guests, d'Arthez or Lousteau), but the notion of performance extends beyond literature to include the idea of the author as a performer in society. At the beginning of the novel, Lucien abandons his plebeian last name (Chardon) and appropriates his mother's aristocratic maiden name, de Rubempré, which is little more than a pseudonym, given that he has no legal right to it. When he visits the Opera with Mme de Bargeton, he discovers that the real spectacle is not the one represented on the stage but the one taking place in the boxes and that, in order to perform his role as an aristocratic poet, he must look the part and, for instance, be dressed accordingly: the narrator stresses that 'the question of costume, moreover, is one of enormous importance for those who wish to appear to have what they do not have' ['[l]a question du costume est d'ailleurs énorme chez ceux qui veulent paraître avoir ce qu'ils n'ont pas'] (CH V 269). The narrator's comment implies that the association of authorship with performance stresses the inauthentic, deceptive aspects of both.

However, the idea of performance, of pretending to be someone else and espousing multiple points of view is not an exclusively negative, insincere practice in *Illusions perdues* but is also presented as a fundamental principle of artistic creation: 'everything is bilateral in the domain of thought. Ideas are two-sided. Janus is the tutelary deity of criticism and the symbol of genius' ['Tout est bilatéral dans le domaine de la pensée. Les idées sont binaires. Janus est le mythe de la critique et le symbole du génie'] (CH V 457). At first sight, this idea seems to be an apology of sophism, since it is not only voiced by Émile Blondet[5] (another journalist who mentors Lucien) but is also meant to help Lucien write a praising review of Nathan's novel, which would contradict his earlier, unfavourable review of the same work. In explaining it, Blondet argues that this duality enables authors to distance themselves from their works and depict contradictory characters and views in an equally convincing fashion: 'What puts Molière and Corneille in a category apart is their ability to make Alceste say yes and Philinte say no, and likewise with Corneille's Octave and Cinna' ['Ce qui met Molière et Corneille hors ligne, n'est-ce pas la faculté de faire dire *oui* à Alceste, et *non* à Philinte, à Octave et à Cinna?'] (CH V 457). Coralie agrees with Blondet and makes the theatrical implications of this idea explicit: '"Write reviews", said Coralie. "Get some fun out of it! Shall I not myself be posing this evening as an Andalusian, wearing gypsy costume tomorrow and trousers another day?"' ['Fais de la critique, dit Coralie, amuse-toi! Est-ce que je ne suis pas ce soir en Andalouse, demain ne me mettrai-je pas en bohémienne, un autre jour en homme?'] (CH V 461). Blondet and Coralie equate the very acts of writing and acting, rather than their external circumstances.

Indeed, the novel presents genius, the man of letters, the journalist and the actor as occupying different positions in a spectrum which ranges from the ability to distance oneself from one's own work to mere duplicity – with d'Arthez and Lucien placed at the two ends of this spectrum. On one end, d'Arthez is not merely able to distance himself from his work and adopt an opposing view but has the generosity of spirit to revise and make more effective the devastating review of his own novel that Lucien is forced to write (CH V 528–31). On the other end, Lucien is characterised by an inability to hold opposing opinions at the same time: he does not merely write what Lousteau and Blondet dictate to him in his contradictory reviews of Nathan's novel but he is also convinced by their arguments in both cases. Lucien's inability to participate in this duality reveals not only that he cannot lay claim to genius but that he cannot engage in the sophism that the novel presents as a necessary skill for a journalist.

If duality is associated with genius and his ability to view his work objectively or create diverse characters, duplicity, the other end of the spectrum, is inextricably linked with another pervasive metaphor in *Illusions perdues*, namely prostitution, which provides another *tertium comparationis* for authorship, journalism and the theatre. Coralie's concluding argument, when trying to convince Lucien to write his palinode on Nathan's novel, does not simply reveal the theatrical nature of authorship but also the association of both acting and writing with prostitution: 'Do as I do: make faces at them for their money, and let's live happily' ['Fais comme moi, donne-leur des grimaces pour leur argent, et vivons heureux'] (CH V 461).

Prostitution casts its shadow on authorship, journalism and the theatre in multiple ways in the novel. The book trade is at first associated with prostitution on the grounds of their co-existence in the same space, the Galeries de Bois, 'le temple de la prostitution' (CH V 360). In the world of the theatre, actresses are depicted as either having been prostitutes (Coralie was sold by her mother to de Marsay when she was fifteen years old) or live as *femmes entretenues* (Coralie is kept by Camusot, while Florine, Lousteau's mistress, by Matifat).

These circumstantial links are transformed into structural similarities: Michel Chrestien describes journalism as 'the decision to barter away one's soul, intellect and thought' ['le parti pris de trafiquer de son âme, de son esprit et de sa pensée'] (CH V 328) – echoing one of Balzac's early characters, Victor Morillon, who, in the 'Avertissement du "Gars"' (1828), refers to publication as 'the prostitution of thought' ['la prostitution de la pensée'] (CH VIII 1669). Lucien himself, when witnessing Nathan's dealings with the journalists in Dauriat's bookshop, notices the equivalence between prostitution and the book trade:

> Our great man from the provinces learnt some terrible truths from the sight of an eminent poet prostituting the Muse to a journalist and thereby debasing Art, just as Woman was debased and prostituted in these squalid galleries. Money! That was the answer to every riddle.
>
> [À l'aspect d'un poète éminent y prostituant la muse à un journaliste, y humiliant l'Art, comme la Femme était humiliée, prostituée sous ces galeries ignobles, le grand homme de province recevait des enseignements terribles. L'argent! était le mot de toute énigme.] (CH V 365)

In the same spirit, Lousteau presents an elaborate analogy between different kinds of authors and prostitutes:

> Dame Reputation, whom so many men lust after, is almost always a crowned prostitute. Yes indeed, in relation to the lower kinds of literature, she figures as the needy whore who stands shivering at street corners; in relation to second-rate literature, she's the kept woman who has come straight from the brothels of journalism – and I am one of her pimps; in relation to successful literature, she's the flashy, insolent courtesan with furnished apartments; she pays her taxes, is at home to eminent people and is kind or cruel to them by turns.

> [Cette réputation tant désirée est presque toujours une prostituée couronnée. Oui, pour les basses œuvres de la littérature, elle représente la pauvre fille qui gèle au coin des bornes; pour la littérature secondaire, c'est la femme entretenue qui sort des mauvais lieux du journalisme, et à qui je sers de souteneur; pour la littérature heureuse, c'est la brillante courtisane insolente, qui a des meubles, paye des contributions à l'État, reçoit les grands seigneurs, les traite et les maltraite.] (CH V 345)

In this context, prostitution does not merely allude to the commodification of literature and 'la prostitution de la pensée' but also to the commodification of the author himself. Lucien is gradually described as a commodity or a prostitute – a quality subtly announced in his very first description in the novel:

> Anyone looking at his feet would have been tempted to take him for a girl in disguise, the more so because, like most men of subtle, not to say astute mind, he had a woman's shapely hips. This is usually reliable as a clue to character, and was so in Lucien's case, for his restless turn of mind often brought him, when he came to analyse the present state of society, to adopt the depravity of outlook characteristic of diplomats, who believe that any means however shameful they may be, are justified by success.
>
> [À voir ses pieds, un homme aurait été d'autant plus tenté de le prendre pour une jeune fille déguisée, que, semblable à la plupart des hommes fins, pour ne pas dire astucieux, il avait les hanches conformées comme celles d'une femme. Cet indice, rarement trompeur, était vrai chez Lucien, que la pente de son esprit remuant amenait souvent, quand il analysait l'état actuel de la société, sur le terrain de la dépravation particulière aux diplomates qui croient que le succès est la justification de tous les moyens, quelque honteux qu'ils soient.]
> (CH V 145–146)

This description does not merely emphasise Lucien's feminine beauty but stresses his opportunism and his willingness to use any means to achieve his purpose. And it soon becomes clear that his aim is not to produce literary works for their own sake, like d'Arthez; from the beginning of the novel, Lucien's talent is a means of obtaining access to the aristocracy of Angoulême and the very first mention of his sonnets and his novel in *Illusions perdues* reveals that he is thinking of them as means of gaining 'enough money to pay his debt to his mother, sister and David' ['assez d'argent pour s'acquitter envers sa mère, sa sœur et David'] (CH V 233).

If Lucien is described as a woman, the pattern of his relations with his family, friends and mistresses sketches him as a *femme entretenue*. His brother-in-law, David, takes on the task of ensuring a 'carefree life' ['vie insouciante'] (CH V 147) for his friend: 'in this long-established friendship, one of them loved the other to the point of idolatry: it was David. And so,

Lucien assumed control like a woman conscious of being loved' ['[d]ans cette amitié déjà vieille, l'un des deux aimait avec idolâtrie, et c'était David. Aussi Lucien commandait-il en femme qui se sait aimée'] (CH V 146). This relation enables Lucien not only to accept money from his brother-in-law, but also to borrow money by forging his signature. Mme de Bargeton, whose 'mâle éducation' (CH V 154) is emphasised, also offers to support the aspiring poet as if he were a mistress:

> Yes, dear angel, I will put an oasis around you and in it you will live your poet's life – active, languid, indolent, industrious, pensive by turn. But never forget that you will owe your laurels to me, and that will be the splendid reward I shall reap for the pains I shall have to endure.
>
> [Oui, cher ange, je te ferais une oasis où tu vivras toute ta vie de poète, active, molle, indolente, laborieuse, pensive tour à tour: mais n'oubliez jamais que vos lauriers me sont dus, que ce sera pour moi la noble indemnité des souffrances qui m'adviendront.] (CH V 229)

In Paris, Lucien is not dependent only on Coralie but, indirectly, also on Camusot, her former lover, who has paid for her apartment and her expenses. D'Arthez, in his letter to Ève, concludes that Lucien 'is, forgive me for saying so, an effeminate little person who loves to show off' ['est, permettez-moi de le dire, une femmelette qui aime à paraître'] (CH V 578) – a judgement echoed by Ève who claims that 'in every poet, it seems to me, there's a pretty woman of the worst sort' ['dans un poète, il y a, je crois, une jolie femme de la pire espèce'] (CH V 653).

Lucien is not only guilty of what one of the first reviewers of the novel called 'this twin prostitution of love and art' ['cette double prostitution de l'amour et de l'art'][6] but also becomes a commodity himself: 'a fashionable commodity: discovered, put on the market, triumphant, out of style, thrown away'.[7] Significantly, he is often referred to as a work of art rather than a producer: for Mme de Bargeton, 'the poet was already poetry incarnate' ['[l]e poète était déjà la poésie'] (CH V 166); as mentioned above, according to d'Arthez, Lucien is not a poet but 'un homme de poésie', while Petit-Claud points out that he is 'un roman continuel' (CH V 717). In this context, his final act in the novel is only too well announced: when he is about to commit suicide, he meets a mysterious Machiavellian Spanish priest, Carlos Herrera (who will be revealed to be Vautrin from *Le Père Goriot* in disguise), agrees to become his secretary and signs a pact by which he sells himself, body and soul: 'I have bartered my life. I belong to myself no longer. I am more than the secretary of a Spanish diplomat, I am his creature' ['j'ai vendu ma vie. Je ne m'appartiens plus, je suis plus que le secrétaire d'un diplomate espagnol, je suis sa créature'] (CH V 724).[8]

The title of *Illusions perdues* seems to create the expectation that, after Lucien's illusions are dispelled, he will gain a better understanding of the world around him or, like the protagonist of a Goethean *Bildungsroman*, will advance towards a realisation of his genuine self in harmony with his *milieu*. But *Illusions perdues* is not a *Bildungsroman* or, at least, not a traditional one: on the one hand, Lucien, instead of finding his own self, loses all control over it and becomes an empty shell, a body animated by Vautrin's will. On the other, he does not seem to learn much, and his illusions are constantly renewed to the point that he sets out to conquer Paris again, even as Vautrin's 'créature'.[9]

However, the title does not refer exclusively to Lucien but also to other characters who lose their own illusions or, like David and Ève, lose their illusions about Lucien. Most importantly, it refers to the readers who will also lose all their illusions about the noble profession of authorship and of literary criticism.

At the same time, another kind of illusion the reader might be losing is fictional illusion: like Lucien who is introduced to the 'backstage area' of the book trade and the theatre industry, the reader is reading a novel about the making of novels. *Illusions perdues* is, quite explicitly, a reflexive novel and it is such in a specifically realist fashion. Unlike eighteenth-century, playfully reflexive fiction such as Diderot's novel *Jacques le fataliste*, it does not possess a self-conscious narrator who deliberately and explicitly flaunts the fictionality of the text; unlike modernist fiction, it does not primarily aim to foreground the opacity of language and the subjective character of any attempt at a representation of reality. What *Illusions perdues* stresses is not so much that a novel is made of words but that it is made of paper, composed by 'vendors of phrases' ['marchands de phrases'] (CH V 458), bought, sold and negotiated like any other product before it reaches the reader. In revealing the material and social conditions of its production, *Illusions perdues* shows that 'la prostitution de la pensée' is everywhere, and that *Illusions perdues* itself is an instance of it.

If *Illusions perdues* reflects (on) its own conditions of production, it also mirrors *La Comédie humaine*: in a letter to Mme Hanska, Balzac called the novel 'the main work within the work' ['l'œuvre capitale dans l'œuvre'] (LH I 650). Indeed, in many ways, *Illusions perdues* is a scale model of *La Comédie humaine*: it is one of the novels which contain the highest concentration of reappearing characters; it is a novel that moves from the provinces to Paris, depicts the life of provincial aristocracy, government officials, the professions of the printer, the publisher, the author, the journalist, the actress, the provincial lawyer and the worlds of the book trade and of boulevard theatre; at the same time, it is a study of the phenomenon that brings all of these together, the commodification of literature, culture and social life, expressed through the overarching metaphor of prostitution. In representing society as a spectacle, the 'coulisses' of the book trade and the life of authors, the novel approximates the very structure of *La Comédie humaine*, as Balzac had described it already in 1834 through a theatrical metaphor: 'the *manners* [*Études de mœurs*] are the *spectacle*, the *causes* [*Études philosophiques*] are the *backstage area and the stage machinery.* The *principles* [*Études analytiques*] are the *author*' ['[l]es *mœurs* sont le *spectacle*, les *causes* sont les *coulisses et les machines.* Les *principes*, c'est *l'auteur*'] (LH I 204; italics in the original).

In a similar spirit, a series of characters from *Illusions perdues* have been or can be read as either authorial or autobiographical *personae* of Balzac: David Séchard recalls his brief career as a printer; Étienne Lousteau and Émile Blondet his career as a journalist; Lucien his struggles as an emerging author, while d'Arthez can be seen as an idealised version of his authorial self and Vautrin as an incarnation of his idea of the author as a Promethean or Mephistophelean creator. However, independently of any potential correspondences with Balzac's own life or career, the authorial positions of d'Arthez, Lucien and Lousteau are typical positions occupied by the writing subject in the first half of the nineteenth century.

While the novel idealises d'Arthez's abstention from the literary market and demonises Lousteau's immersion in it, this opposition is undermined if one looks at *Illusions perdues* as a commodity. The mode of publication of the novel is quite representative both of Balzac's publishing strategies and of the main contradiction they (and Balzac's career in general) illustrate: his willingness to engage fully with the literary market while at the same time trying to redeem his work from the commodification this entailed.

While the twentieth- or twenty-first-century reader approaches *Illusions perdues* as a single novel, Balzac's contemporaries could not have done so. The first part of the novel, whose final title would be *Les Deux Poètes*, was published simply as *Illusions perdues* in 1837 in the eighth volume of Balzac's *Études de mœurs au XIXe siècle*. The only indication that this was not a separate work was Balzac's preface, which explained that what followed was only the 'introduction' of *Illusions perdues* (CH V 110). The second edition of the first part, still entitled *Illusions perdues* but without the preface, was published by Charpentier at the end of the first volume of a two-volume edition of *Scènes de la vie de province* in 1839. The second part, entitled *Un grand homme de province à Paris*, appeared also in 1839, in a two-volume edition, whose cover page or front matter did not announce it as the second part of a larger whole; the reader would have to read the preface to discover that the volume in his hands was the continuation of

Illusions perdues, to be followed by a final part. The third part was published three times in 1843: it was serialised in *L'État* as *David Séchard ou les Souffrances d'un inventeur*; it appeared in a two-volume edition, entitled *David Séchard* and accompanied by a preface which specified that it was the third part of *Illusions perdues*; finally, it was included, under the title *Ève et David*, in the eighth volume of *La Comédie humaine*, which brought, for the first time, all parts of the novel together.

But Lucien's adventures were not over at the end of the third part of the novel and would be continued in *Splendeurs et misères des courtisanes*, a novel with an equally complicated publication history, consisting of four parts, each of which was also published individually. While this novel can be seen as a 'sequel' of *Illusions perdues* in the modern sense of the term, its publication had started long before *Illusions perdues* had been completed. The first part of this novel, initially entitled *La Torpille* (and which would become *Esther heureuse* and finally *Comment aiment les filles*), opens at the Opera ball where Lucien announces to Mme de Bargeton and her new husband that he is authorised, by royal decree, to bear the name de Rubempré. Given that *La Torpille* was published in 1838, before even the second part of *Illusions perdues*, the reader who had left Lucien's story at the point where he had just been abandoned by Mme de Bargeton after their arrival in Paris, could easily mistake this for the second part of *Illusions perdues*; in fact, readers would have to wait five years in order to discover how Lucien reaches this point.

This fragmentary publishing practice was counteracted by a series of strategies which aimed to integrate not only the three parts of *Illusions perdues* (or the four parts of *Splendeurs et misères des courtisanes*) but also the entirety of Balzac's œuvre (a great part of which was published in serial form) into a 'vaste édifice' (CH V 110): all his works were eventually included in *La Comédie humaine*, they were classified in various series of *Études* and *Scènes*, and they contained reappearing characters which transformed Balzac's œuvre into an interconnected network of texts. By designating Vautrin, in *Splendeurs et misères des courtisanes*, as a 'kind of spinal column who connects, as it were, through his horrible influence, *Le Père Goriot* to *Illusions perdues*, and *Illusions perdues* to this Study' ['espèce de colonne vertébrale qui, par son horrible influence, relie pour ainsi dire *Le Père Goriot* à *Illusions perdues*, et *Illusions perdues* à cette Étude'] (CH VI 851), Balzac illustrated the way in which fragmentation could act as a unifying principle: not only Vautrin's role varies in each novel but their titles are often deceptive and do not reflect their changing focus and the fact that different characters assume and relinquish the role of the protagonist, in a process that resembles a relay race. *Le Père Goriot*, despite its title, is primarily a novel about

Illusions perdues: Writers, Artists and the Reflexive Novel

Rastignac who oscillates between the moral positions represented by Goriot and Vautrin. *Illusions perdues*, whose first pages give the mistaken impression that the protagonist is David Séchard, soon focuses on Lucien, while Vautrin appears only in its last pages, under an assumed identity. The title of *Splendeurs et misères des courtisanes* implies that it is a novel about the courtesan Esther who dies at the end of the second part; it is also the sequel of Lucien's adventures, who also dies at the end of the third part, leaving the role of the protagonist of the fourth part to Vautrin.

This disorderly publishing practice (which was not specific to *Illusions perdues*)[10] can be attributed, to a great extent, to the incompatibility between the exigencies of the increasingly industrialised book trade in Balzac's time and Balzac's totalising ambition in creating a work such as *La Comédie humaine*: Balzac indeed had agreements with various publishers and newspaper editors whose deadlines expired before he could complete a long novel with more than one part, such as *Illusions perdues*. However, reviewers would habitually impute commercial motives to Balzac, whether they commented on the fragmented publication of *La Comédie humaine* or on the unifying strategies Balzac employed.

In this sense, *Illusions perdues*, bound with the disreputable commercial practices of the book trade which it both illustrates and denounces, is a highly reflexive work not only as a novel and as a *mise en abîme* of *La Comédie humaine*, but also – and this is where the novelty of *Illusions perdues* lies – as a commodity. Balzac was not the first to depict the miseries and splendours of authorship:[11] in fact, his description of the book trade does not correspond to the time of the publication of the novel: Lucien's encounter with it is placed in the early 1820s before the emergence of the *roman-feuilleton* which would revolutionise and industrialise the literary market and the genre of the novel. However, the novelty of *Illusions perdues*, as Georg Lukács noticed, lies not simply in emphasising or deploring the commodification of literature and culture but in showing it in process:

> The fact that the spirit has become a commodity to be bought and sold is not yet accepted as a matter of course and the spirit is not yet reduced to the dreary greyness of a machine-made article. The spirit turns into a commodity here before our very eyes; it is something just happening, a new event loaded with dramatic tension.[12]

The 'dramatic tension' in question is not only a quality of Lucien's story but also of the publication history of *Illusions perdues* – a novel which is not only about performance but which also performed, as it were, the role of a commodity in order to redeem itself from its own commodification and emerge as a unified work.

NOTES

1. J. Janin, '*Un grand homme de province à Paris*, par M. de Balzac', *Revue de Paris*, 3ᵉ série, VIII (1839), 145–178 (p. 178).
2. J. Cherbuliez, '*Un grand homme de province à Paris*', *Revue critique des livres nouveaux*, VII (1839), 237–238 (p. 238).
3. A. de Vigny, *Œuvres complètes*, ed. F. Germain, A. Jarry and A. Bouvet, 2 vols (Paris: Gallimard, 1986–93), I, pp. 771, 792.
4. On the centrality of the metaphor of the theatre in *Illusions perdues*, see also P. Brooks, *The Melodramatic Imagination: Balzac, Henry James, Melodrama, and the Mode of Excess* (New Haven and London: Yale University Press, 1995; first published 1976), pp. 122–124.
5. On the characters' aesthetic views as echoing Balzac's own, see F. van Rossum-Guyon, *Balzac: la littérature réfléchie. Discours et autoreprésentations* (Montreal: Département d'Études Françaises, 'Paragraphes', 2002), pp. 179–199.
6. A. Dumartin, '*Un grand homme de province à Paris* par M. de Balzac', *L'Artiste*, 2ᵉ série, III (1839), 201–204 (p. 202).
7. F. Moretti, *The Way of the World: The 'Bildungsroman' in European Culture*, trans. A. J. Sbragia (London: Verso, 1987), p. 134.
8. On Lucien's relationship to Vautrin and the ways in which it was read in the nineteenth century and beyond, see M. Lucey, *The Misfit of the Family: Balzac and the Social Forms of Sexuality* (Durham, NC: Duke University Press, 2003), pp. 171–223.
9. On Lucien's inexhaustible illusions, see J.-D. Ebguy, 'L'Illusion retrouvée: *Illusions perdues*, un roman métaphysique' in J.-L. Diaz and A. Guyaux (eds), '*Illusions perdues*': *colloque de la Sorbonne* (Paris: Presses de l'Université de Paris-Sorbonne, 2004), pp. 119–136.
10. See S. Vachon, *Les Travaux et les jours d'Honoré de Balzac* (Paris: Presses du CNRS, 1992).
11. On the depiction of the drama of the (provincial) aspiring author and his relations to the publishers before Balzac, see P. Berthier, 'Le Thème du "grand homme de province à Paris" dans la presse parisienne au lendemain de 1830' in Diaz and Guyaux (eds), '*Illusions perdues*', pp. 25–50 and C. Haynes, 'An "Evil Genius": The Construction of the Publisher in the Postrevolutionary Social Imaginary', *French Historical Studies*, 30.4 (2007), 559–595 (esp. pp. 571–586).
12. Georg Lukács, *Studies in European Realism* (New York: Grosset and Dunlap, 1964), p. 60.

8

DOROTHY KELLY

Balzac, Gender and Sexuality: *La Cousine Bette*

Balzac's late novel of 1846, *La Cousine Bette*, places gender, family, sexuality and money at the heart of its conflict. Its textual system is firmly centred in the character, Lisbeth 'Bette' Fischer, the spinster 'spider' in the middle of its narrative web, who ensnares her family members in her plots. As an ugly, masculine, unmarried woman who works for a living, and who first has an intense friendship with a man, Wenceslas Steinbock, and then with a woman, Valérie Marneffe, she does not by any means occupy a 'normal' position in her society.

Throughout *La Comédie humaine* Balzac often places such marginal characters at the centre of his plots, marginal in the sense that they do not abide by the normative standards of the society of his time. As Michael Lucey has shown,[1] Balzac's texts reveal a deep interest in characters who, like Bette, have odd gender identities and non-normative sexualities. Balzac's novella, *Sarrasine*, features as one of its central characters a castrato singer who plays a woman's part in a production, which generates love and tragedy for the male character, Sarrasine. This text shows the destruction of Sarrasine's normative notions of gender, sexuality and love, and inspired one of the best known pieces of structuralist and post-structuralist literary criticism, Roland Barthes's *S/Z*.[2] The character Vautrin, an extremely powerful and dangerous criminal who becomes the head of the Sûreté police, loves men, and his main goal is to help several of them succeed in the upper echelons of society. Mariquita de San-Réal in *La Fille aux yeux d'or* keeps her female lover imprisoned in her Paris home, and murders her when she is unfaithful with Mariquita's own half-brother. Balzac's novels and short stories are peopled with 'feminine' men and 'masculine' women, and in one of his more fantastic novels, *Séraphîta*, the main character, an androgynous celestial being, is a man when seen by a woman, and a woman when seen by a man. The emergent realism of Balzac measures what we consider natural and real against what we consider unnatural and unreal. However, in so doing, it often puts their dividing line into question without fixing it in place.

Bette is one of these fascinating, non-normative characters, whose supposed main transgression is her non-married state, like her counterpart bachelor in *Le Cousin Pons*. Although Balzac writes in the Preface to *Pierrette* that celibacy is 'a state contrary to society' ['un état contraire à la société' (CH IV 21)] and that he harbours a deep hatred for 'celibates, old maids, and bachelors' ['les célibataires, les vieilles filles et les vieux garçons'(*ibid.*)], and although he constructs Bette as a frightening and dangerous character, he nevertheless represents in this novel how society itself creates Bette and how the alternative to spinsterhood, marriage, is perhaps worse. Thus, through *La Cousine Bette*, Balzac traces a vision of the lateness, decay and malfunctioning of the social order of his time through the malfunctioning of the institution of marriage. And as he shows the dissolution of that order, he lays bare its mechanisms to reveal that the violence of Bette's marginalisation is one of the causes of the novel's multiple tragedies.

Balzac divides his text into two large sections. The first, called the introduction by Balzac (CH VII 186), takes up about one-third of the book and gives us the background of Bette and her family. The end of this introduction marks a radical change in Bette and in the text, which then proceeds through the main plot of the story. In the introduction, Balzac describes the social forces and milieu that help create Bette's personality. As a woman in the society of her time, her main liability is her ugliness. Because she lacks beauty, which could be considered in Bourdieu's terms to be 'cultural capital' (a non-monetary quality that has worth in society), she has little value and is relegated to the margins of life by her family. Balzac explains that, as the ugly child living in an extended clan, she was sacrificed for her beautiful cousin, Adeline, and forced to work in the fields, whereas Adeline was coddled. Thus, early in the novel Balzac reveals the mechanism of social violence inflicted on Bette by her family, which Christopher Prendergast has analysed as the result of 'class attitudes and values' that mistreat poor cousins, a violence that understandably results in her resentment and revolt.[3] The jealous child Bette retaliates for this unfairness by attacking the very things that privilege Adeline: her beauty (she tries to pull off Adeline's lovely Grecian nose, much admired by old women) and her fine clothes (which Bette tries to rip and ruin).

As Pierre Bourdieu has well explained, the family must use certain strategies, in this case the privileging of one family member, to ensure the biological and social reproduction of the family group and the general family system itself.[4] Michael Lucey extends this idea when he describes how Bette's envy and hatred are in fact created as a by-product of the family system of alliance that metes out her cruel treatment.[5] Her family maximises its cultural and financial capital by pampering the daughter who, because she is the prettiest, has the best chance to cash in on her situation. This Adeline does by marrying the baron Hulot, thus giving her family (including Bette) access to substantial money and allowing the family (and the system) to produce children and reproduce itself.

In Balzac's description of Bette's personality, the jealousy that results from her mistreatment goes hand-in-hand with non-normal aspects of her behaviour: 'Jealousy was the fundamental feature of her character, full of *eccentricities*' (34) ['La jalousie formait la base de ce caractère plein d'*excentricités*' (CH VII 80)].[6] These oddities comprise her difference from others and make of her a difficult person to comprehend, as Hortense says: 'there is something about her I don't understand' (94) ['il y a quelque chose d'inexplicable en elle' (CH VII 133)]. In response to her strangeness, the family at times puts her in her place (which is a place of their devising) through a kind of quasi-affectionate name-calling that drives home her non-normative social status by identifying her abnormalities. This kind of labelling is one of the myriad ways in which this novel shows how abnormality is contained: Jann Matlock describes the representation of society's 'scrutinizing gazes',[7] and Lucey points out that Balzac's world is 'saturated in disciplines of enforced legibility and social control'.[8] Even one of the few ideal characters, the baron's brother, the maréchal Hulot, affectionately teases Bette, negatively targeting her spinsterhood by calling her a 'bad seed that refused to flower' (55) ['mauvaise graine qui n'a pas voulu fleurir' (CH VII 98).] Balzac's representation of these social interactions shows that human beings may be born with variously pretty or ugly bodies, but more importantly, they are then disciplined and categorised (in Foucault's sense[9]) by their physical and cultural environment (here the family in society). This formation by the milieu is a 'scientific' force that drives much of *La Comédie humaine*. Indeed, in this text, Balzac specifically states his case: 'Men always take on something of the surroundings in which they live' (235) ['L'homme prend toujours quelque chose des milieux où il vit' (CH VII 255)].

When Bette is brought to Paris and benefits from Adeline's marriage, she represses her resentment, accepts her fate as a subaltern, educates herself and learns a trade as an embroiderer. Although she leads an independent existence, she still needs her family for the clothing and meals they provide and, understanding these facts of life, she ingratiates herself with her family group, servants and all. Everyone says of her, 'She is a good, decent girl' (38) ['C'est une bonne et brave fille' (CH VII 84)], and she becomes the family confidante, calling herself 'the family confessional' (39) ['le confessional de la famille' (*ibid.*)] and learning everyone's secrets, which she does not betray in the introductory part of the text. This role of confidante is important later in the novel, when she rejects her role as the safe sounding board of the family and uses her knowledge to wreak havoc.

Balzac describes Bette's independence as a masculine trait, comparing her somewhat oddly (given that Bette is a spinster) yet still appropriately, to the independent seventeenth-century courtesan Ninon de l'Enclos: 'like Ninon, she had some masculine qualities' (38) ['elle possédait, comme Ninon, des qualités d'homme' (*ibid.*)]. In fact, like Ninon, Bette treasures her independence and fears 'any kind of tie' (37) ['toute espèce de joug' (CH VII 83)], particularly the constraint of marriage. She chooses to remain a spinster and refuses six suitors. Able to live in her own apartment, to earn a fair living with her embroidery and with the supplements provided by her family, she finds that she is happy (*ibid.*). But this contented life is described in terms that point out its difference from the norm when Bette is once again labelled with various kinds of outsider adjectives: she possesses 'the unusual quality seen ... in savages' ['cette singularité qu'on remarque ... chez les Sauvages'], and her character 'was very much like the Corsicans' (37) ['ressemblait prodigieusement à celui des Corses' (*ibid.*)]. Elsewhere she resembles various animals, such as 'monkeys, dressed up as women' (41) ['singes habillés en femmes' (CH VII 86)] and Hulot nicknames her 'Nanny-Goat' (40) ['Chèvre' (CH VII 85)]. The text specifically sets her up as a non-normative character, the 'misfit' of the family, to use Lucey's apt term, and as a social misfit more generally.

Her masculinity also appears in her physical body, particularly her thick uni-brow and her oversized arms and feet. This constructs for her a gender that is odd in the sense that is does not correspond to the ideal of normal femininity, and it also helps to highlight Adeline's feminine beauty. As Bette is a dark-haired 'peasant woman from the Vosges in the full meaning of those words, thin, dark, with shiny black hair' (34) ['Paysanne des Vosges, dans toute l'extension du mot, maigre, brune, les cheveux d'un noir luisant' (CH VII 80)], she neatly contrasts with the feminine and blond Adeline, who is also a peasant, but who belongs to the 'tribe' of women famous for their beauty, such as Madame du Barry and Diane de Poitiers: Adeline, 'one of the most beautiful of that divine race, had the sublime characteristics, the willowy figure, the seductive fabric of those women born to be queens' (27) ['une des plus belles de cette tribu divine, possédait les caractères sublimes, les lignes serpentines, le tissu vénéneux de ces femmes nées reines' (CH VII 75)]. Bette's ugly, peasant masculinity is the perfect foil for Adeline's 'noble', feminine attractiveness and constructs the ideal type of feminine beauty by detailing Bette's lack of it. Lucey goes so far as to describe a kind of pleasure taken in the description of Bette's (and her counterpart Pons's) strangeness when they are described 'in all their lack of normativity by a gaze whose goal is to assert the privilege of normativity by savoring its absence'.[10]

If Bette does not marry, she does engage in that seemingly odd relationship with Steinbock, a poor Polish count and artist whose life she saves when he attempts to asphyxiate himself and with whom she falls in love. She also later nearly marries another odd partner, the maréchal Hulot, a bachelor and thus an outsider like Bette, as neither one had complied with the bourgeois code of marriage: 'they had some things in common' (55) ['il se trouvait entre eux des ressemblances' (CH VII 98)]. Balzac underlines the bizarre nature of the alliance of Bette and Steinbock by emphasising their gender ambiguity, noting that, upon seeing them together, one would think that 'nature had made a mistake in allocating their sexes' in 'the alliance of this energetic woman and that weak man' (66, 69) ['la nature s'était trompée en leur donnant leurs sexes' in 'le mariage de cette énergie femelle et de cette faiblesse masculine' (CH VII 107, 110)]. Finally, if these two partners have non-normative gender identities, the power positions in their relationship also reverse what at the time would be normal male domination and female obedience. Having endured her position as subaltern, Bette develops '[t]he love of domination' (76) ['[l']amour de la domination' (CH VII 116)]. Steinbock is a possession, called a thing and a slave, and Bette is happy to have 'a man quite to herself' (78) ['un homme à elle' (CH VII 119)]. Here the man is the possession, and the woman provides him with money.

Bette, fifteen years older than Steinbock, also assumes the role of his mother, disciplining him to work on his sculptures and keeping him from succumbing to the temptations of Paris. 'I adopt you as my child' (71) ['je vous prends pour mon enfant' (CH VII 112)] she says, and here we see that mix of familial and sexual relationships that Balzac at times creates for his characters, such as for Goriot who is father and 'lover' to his daughters and to Rastignac, as Janet Beizer has so thoroughly traced.[11] This mixture presents a quandary for Bette because she cannot find any single, pre-determined sexual or familial role to play: 'She loved Steinbock enough not to marry him and too much to give him up to another woman. She couldn't resign herself to being only his mother but realised the folly of thinking of the other role' (78) ['Elle aimait assez Steinbock pour ne pas l'épouser, et l'aimait trop pour le céder à une autre femme; elle ne savait pas se résigner à n'en être que la mère, et se regardait comme une folle quand elle pensait à l'autre rôle' (CH VII 118–119)]. Even though their pairing cannot be contained within typical social definitions (and Prendergast has shown how the baron Hulot also cannot be named[12]), Bette wants to continue in this unnamable relationship. Her mixed identity as lover and mother symbolically transgresses familial rules by placing sexuality both inside and outside traditional systems of the family and its finances.[13]

Steinbock is himself a marginalised social being, a Polish immigrant with no friends and little means of survival in Paris. His alliance with Bette benefits both of them for a time and represents the first of a series of alliances between outcast characters. More importantly, this alliance takes place in a particular milieu that plays a crucial symbolic role in the text. The building that lodges Bette, Steinbock and Valérie is in the Doyenné quarter, a bizarre, dilapidated and marginalised neighbourhood near the Louvre. A kind of residue of the past that escaped demolition when Napoleon began but never finished the completion of the Louvre, Balzac writes that its inhabitants are probably ghosts (57) [CH VII 100]. This ghostly aspect also appears in the description of houses that are 'crypts, living tombs' (57) ['des espèces de cryptes, des tombeaux vivants' (CH VII 100)].

This dead, lifeless section of Paris is said by Balzac to symbolise 'the intimate alliance of poverty and luxury characteristic of the queen of capitals' (57–58), ['l'alliance intime de la misère et de la splendeur qui caractérise la reine des capitales' (CH VII 100)], the necessary presence of a pocket of the poor in the midst of the wealthy, that Balzac places in other works, such as *La Fille aux yeux d'or* and *Splendeurs et misères des courtisanes*. The spectral Doyenné quarter thus harbours and represents the marginalised, pushed-aside residues of Parisian society, the miserable ones who disappear into ghostliness and live anonymous existences, like Bette who resigns herself 'to being a nobody' (38) ['à ne rien être' (CH VII 84)].

This nothingness of marginalised identity gains significance when viewed through Terry Castle's observations on the representations of lesbians in literature.[14] Using Monique Wittig's discussion of women like Bette who refuse the 'economic, ideological, and political power of a man', Castle goes on to show how these women menace and haunt Western civilisation, which seeks to make them disappear and 'ghost' them. Most particularly, Castle demonstrates the ghosting of the literary lesbian, who disappears into spectral form in literature. Given that the intense friendship that develops between Bette and Valérie has been described by a number of critics as suggestively but not explicitly lesbian, the ambiguous nature of this relationship is itself a kind of 'ghosting' that maintains the indistinctness of its nature. How apt, then, that some of the spectres who haunt Bette's ghostly neighbourhood are Henri III and his favourites, a King and a court associated with homosexuality (57) [CH VII 100]. Homosexuality haunts this neighbourhood and this text without ever becoming completely visible. Before delving further into Bette's 'queer' relationship with Valérie (an illegitimate child who does not inherit from her father, who is therefore also an outsider), the relation of this half-dead neighbourhood to the particular historical moment of lateness that Balzac describes in the text, and the symbolic role of belatedness in the plot, need explanation.

The Doyenné ruins and dilapidated buildings aptly symbolise Balzac's views about the disappearance of certain buildings, which represent cultural elements of old Paris and French morality of the past. In a contemporaneous work, 'Ce qui disparaît de Paris' ('What Is Disappearing from Paris'), Balzac discusses the razing of marvellous buildings at the time, as well as the extinction of picturesque métiers, such as mending women, who appear to be statues in the niche of their makeshift shops.[15] Balzac remains ambivalent about this disappearance. If he seems to regret the demise of quaint street vendors, he praises the beginning of the modernisation of Paris in *La Cousine Bette* when he describes how *la Petite-Pologne* section of Paris is being bought up by speculation, with the positive result that the dangerous poor who live there are being driven out (444–445) [CH VII 436–437], a trend that accelerated later with Haussmann.

Bette, like her dated and declining Doyenné neighbourhood, belongs to the time before this modernisation and her belatedness is part of her strangeness. Balzac chooses her bizarre fashion sense to represent her outmoded being: when she gets new clothes, she immediately reworks them into the old-fashioned Empire style or that of her peasant garb (39) [CH VII 85]. She has long yearned for Adeline's yellow cashmere shawl, given to Adeline as a gift in 1808 (during the Empire) and which, in 1838, the date that marks the beginning of the novel, is quite worn and shabby and has been passed on to Adeline's daughter.[16] Bette's desire for a worn-out, dated fashion item symbolises her belatedness.

Adeline and her husband, the baron Hulot, are also residues of Napoleon's time, evidenced by the threadbare furniture in their salon, 'a corpse of the festivities of the Empire' (25) ['un cadavre des fêtes impériales' (CH VII 73)]. Hulot is immediately recognisable as one of the Empire's soldiers because of his clothing and demeanour; he has become 'one of those fine human ruins' (164) ['une de ces belles ruines humaines' (CH VII 193)]. When the Empire fell, Hulot's military service ended and he placed himself instead 'on active service with women' (29) ['en service actif auprès des femmes' (CH VII 77)]. Adeline specifically dates his infidelities to the end of the Empire, thus Balzac links the problems of the Hulot family (Hulot's bankrupting by his mistresses) to the end of Napoleonic heroism, which lives on in half-dead, degraded form in the baron's family and the dilapidated Doyenné neighbourhood.

It is in fact Bette's desire for the old-fashioned cashmere shawl that sets the machine of the plot in motion; it stands for the senseless and at times dangerous continuance of this leftover Empire society in a changed world. Hortense does not believe that Bette's lover, Steinbock, exists, and so she promises a trade with Bette: the shawl for proof of Bette's 'lover'. The evidence Bette brings is a silver seal made by Steinbock, which seals everyone's fate as Hortense becomes enamoured of its maker, as yet unseen. Steinbock, made real by this seal when before he was but 'a shadowy creature' (49) ['ce fantôme' (CH VII 93)], is aggressively pursued by Hortense, who proceeds to steal him from Bette.

Hortense does this by making her father, the baron Hulot, go with her to one of the shops in Bette's ghostly neighbourhood, where Steinbock has displayed a small bronze sculpture. Up until this time, we usually see Hortense in her own home, so her trek to the seamy side of town to pursue an unknown man whom she 'loves' certainly seems strange; with her father, she leaves her 'place', her proper milieu as a proper young woman. There, in the Doyenné neighbourhood, she meets and lures Steinbock, and, at the same time, her father exchanges his first conversation with Valérie while waiting on the street near the store (he had exchanged flirtatious glances with her before). Father and daughter thus make an odd trip together out of their own world and meet prospective lovers in Bette's ghostly, outcast neighbourhood. After meeting Steinbock, Hortense tells her father she has found an inexpensive husband in the store, which understandably surprises him, as it seems as if she had found the husband for sale there: 'A husband, my girl, in that shop?' (91) ['Un mari, ma fille, dans cette boutique?' (CH VII 130)]. After this shopping trip, Hulot begins to buy Valérie's favours. The journey of father and daughter to this degraded neighbourhood and their 'commerce' with and in lovers (Hortense buys Steinbock's statue) will set up the accelerated pace of the downward spiral of the Hulots.

When Bette learns that her entire family has been plotting behind her back to take her lover, Balzac describes the revolution that occurs within her as a kind of volcanic eruption, curiously aligning Bette with Vautrin in the famous scene of his arrest and the containment of his own volcanic eruption in *Le Père Goriot* (this similarity between Bette and Vautrin can be carried much further: marginality, rescues of future loved ones from suicide, intense same-sex relationships, unmarried status, magnetic gaze, vicarious living through an attractive other, and more). After the eruption cools, she accepts Valérie's invitation to join together in battle, and Bette promises that she will be everything to Valérie as she was to Steinbock. Indeed, the two relationships bear certain similarities because of their multiple and complicated natures: 'Besides, she [Bette] adored Valérie; she had made her her daughter, her friend, her beloved' (172) ['Elle adorait d'ailleurs Valérie, elle en avait fait sa fille, son amie, son amour' (CH VII 200)]. The word 'amour' hints at the homosexual nature of their relationship mentioned above. However, when Balzac more explicitly suggests a lesbian relationship, he also denies it: 'Lisbeth and Valérie offered the touching sight of one of those friendships between women which are so close and so unlikely that Parisians, always too quick to jump to conclusions, immediately dismiss them as scandalous. The contrast between the cold, masculine temperament of the Lorraine peasant and Valérie's warm creole nature gave substance to the calumny' (166) ['Lisbeth et Valérie offraient le touchant spectacle d'une de ces amitiés si vives et si peu probables entre femmes, que les Parisiens, toujours trop spirituels, les calomnient aussitôt. Le contraste de la mâle et sèche nature de la Lorraine avec la jolie nature créole de Valérie servit la calomnie' (CH VII 195)]. Balzac, as mentioned above, thus leaves the nature of their relationship vague, as he does with Bette's relation to Steinbock: family (daughter), friendship (friend), and love (amour) combine to make an indefinable liaison, a situation brilliantly analysed by Lucey.[17]

This nebulous love is homologous to the ghostly lesbian and to the living-dead Doyenné neighbourhood in which Bette, Steinbock and Valérie were confined at the beginning of the novel, but from which they now emerge, significantly after Hulot and Hortense make their incursion into the Doyenné. Balzac specifically couches this invasion of the space of the normalised by the marginalised in a social and spatial metaphor, underlining the physical infiltration of one milieu by another: 'This sketch will enable the innocent to appreciate the different kinds of havoc that women like Madame Marneffe wreak in families, and the way in which they attack poor, virtuous women, apparently so *beyond their reach*' (280 [emphasis mine]) ['Cette esquisse permet aux âmes innocentes de deviner les différents ravages que les Mme Marneffe exercent dans les familles, et par quels moyens elles atteignent de pauvres femmes vertueuses, en apparence *si loin d'elles*' (CH VII 294 [emphasis mine])].

This invasion is also associated with a kind of lethal contagion that is unleashed in Bette's revenge for the cruelty inflicted on her, a cruelty that the reader hears from her point of view when, after she learns that Hortense has stolen Steinbock, she tells her story to Valérie. She says that she had reconciled herself to her subaltern fate, but now her family has gone too far and taken the one thing that made her happy, her love for Steinbock. Balzac again displays the brutality of family politics, as everyone in Bette's inner circle – Hulot, Adeline, Steinbock and Hortense – have hidden their plans from her in an especially despicable exclusion. The family now privileges Hortense, just as they had privileged Adeline, and ironically now the family will itself create its own problems because of this final mistreatment of Bette. It is here where Balzac's significant and powerful metaphor of contagion describes what Bette had repressed when she had accepted her lowly status, and what this final blow will arouse in her: 'envy remained hidden in the depths of her heart, like the germ of a disease which can break out and ravage a town if one opens the fatal bale of wool in which it is enclosed' (36) ['l'envie resta cachée dans le fond du cœur, comme un germe de peste qui peut éclore et ravager une ville, si l'on ouvre le fatal ballot de laine où il est comprimé' (CH VII 82)]. Bette's family unwraps the wool that releases the plague.

Bette attacks Adeline by targeting the same things she attacked as a child: she aims to ruin Adeline's beauty: 'Oh, Adeline, you shall pay for this. I'll make you uglier than I am!' (110) ['Oh! Adeline, tu me le payeras, je te rendrai plus laide que moi!' (CH VII 146)]. And she aims to ruin Adeline financially and to acquire for herself all these things she missed by marrying the maréchal Hulot, the Count of Forzheim: 'She'll be in the gutter, but *I* shall be Comtesse de Forzheim!' (173) ['Elle sera dans la boue, et moi! je serai comtesse de Forzheim!' (CH VII 201)]. Bette becomes a 'power behind the scenes' (173) ['puissance occulte' (*ibid.*)], like an invisible social plague, as she moves among the various households, spreading her poison by wreaking havoc while her victims believe she is helping them. Significantly, it is another outsider, Valérie's Brazilian lover, who deliberately brings to Paris a different kind of 'plague' (an obscure tropical disease) that kills Valérie and Crevel. Bette will finally be killed by another disease, which was beginning to be associated at the time in part with the marginalised milieus of poverty and 'vitiated air' ['l'air vicié'] in Paris: tuberculosis.[18]

Valérie and Bette make a formidable couple, and their frightening power and success represent a kind of fear of the alliance of subalterns (women and the lower classes) in what Nicole Mozet calls the 'collective power' of women,[19] and in what Diana Knight describes as 'the near undoing of patriarchy by a spinster and a prostitute'.[20] Their dominance, once they cannily join forces, depends on working their plots together: 'As can be seen, these two women were as one. Everything Valérie did, even her most heedless actions, her pleasures, her fits of the sulks, were decided upon only after careful deliberation between them' (171) ['Comme on le voit, ces deux femmes n'en faisaient qu'une; toutes les actions de Valérie, même les plus étourdies, ses plaisirs, ses bouderies se décidaient après de mûres délibérations entre elles' (CH VII 200)]. And working their plots is, in fact, work, what Mozet views as the new political power of the people that threatens to establish itself:[21] whether embroidery, household management or prostitution, the work done by the company kept by Bette and Valérie becomes a productive, metaphoric financial 'company' when they merge their different talents. Through these two powerful women, the text portrays in frightening terms what might otherwise be positive 'desires for freedom, self-possession, and sexual liberty'.[22]

The targets of the pair are first and foremost men and their money: Valérie seduces and controls men to become rich, while Bette increases Valérie's and her own earnings with her superb management of Valérie's finances. Balzac turns them into Delilahs, the Biblical inspiration for the statue that Valérie commissions from Steinbock and for which she poses. The two women revel in their success while mocking the weaklings they make of men: 'they could laugh over the mischief they were jointly planning, over the folly of men, and count up together the accumulating interest of their respective piles of treasure' (172) ['elles pouvaient rire de leurs communes malices, de la sottise des hommes, et recompter ensemble les intérêts grossissants de leurs trésors respectifs' (CH VII 200)]. Bette takes her revenge on Adeline and Hortense by facilitating their husbands' infidelities and watching their suffering with pleasure: 'Tears rose in Hortense's eyes and Bette lapped them up with a look as a cat drinks milk' (218) ['Quelques larmes vinrent dans les yeux d'Hortense, et Bette les lapa du regard comme une chatte boit du lait' (CH VII 241)]. Bette also takes her revenge on Victorin, when his father-in-law, Crevel, transfers his affections and his wealth from his daughter (Victorin's wife, Célestine) to his new wife, Valérie (even though Valérie dies soon after). Meanwhile, Bette aims directly at the power positions of the family: 'She was looking forward to the joy of reigning over the family which had despised her for so long' (302) ['Elle jouissait par avance du bonheur de régner sur la famille qui l'avait si longtemps méprisée' (CH VII 313)].

In this extremely nefarious representation of the alliance of these two women, we see a kind of panic in the face of potential collective female power, what Mozet deems a diabolical alliance,[23] but one that at the same time exposes the malfunctioning of a family system that ties sexuality and gender to inheritance. Balzac clearly represents the breakdown of the family: marriages malfunction, inheritance is depleted or redirected to inappropriate family members, and those marginalised by the family take their revenge on it. Paradoxically, in order to save his family, Hulot must leave it, thus essentially breaking it up; he sees that, in his disgrace due to his fraudulent financial dealings, if he remained with his children and his wife, he would destroy them. He recognises something dreadful in his situation that 'degrades paternal authority and destroys the family' (351) ['ravale le pouvoir paternel et ... dissout la famille' (CH VII 355)]. The family seems to be at an impasse.

The most problematic participant in the ruin of the family is Adeline. She would, on the surface, appear to be the ideal wife at this time, subservient to her husband and selfless caregiver of the family. However, Balzac represents her as a hyperbolic self-sacrificer who has a blind fanaticism for her husband: 'she turned herself, in her inmost heart, into the humble, blind, devoted servant of the man who had made her life' (29) ['elle se fit, dans son for intérieur, la servante humble, dévouée et aveugle de son créateur' (CH VII 76)]. The narrator of *La Cousine Bette* directly criticises this obsessive submission of Adeline: 'The look with which the Baron rewarded his wife's fanatical devotion confirmed her opinion that gentleness and submission were a woman's most powerful weapons. In this she was mistaken. Noble feelings carried to extremes produce results similar to those of the greatest vices' (84) ['Le regard par lequel le baron récompensa le fanatisme de sa femme la confirma dans l'opinion que la douceur et la soumission étaient les plus puissantes armes de la femme. Elle se trompait en ceci. Les sentiments nobles poussés à l'absolu produisent des résultats semblables à ceux des plus grands vices' (CH VII 124)]. It is as if the code that grounded marriage in the submission of women carried within it the seeds of its own failure.

The malfunctioning of the institution of marriage can be seen as well when the narrator of the *Physiologie du mariage* asks if fidelity is impossible for men (CH XI 914). *La Cousine Bette* certainly provides evidence of this through Hulot, who is a kind of sexual addict who cannot stop his infidelities even after his philandering forces Adeline to debase herself by transgressing the codes of the good wife several times: she offers to sell herself to Crevel for the money that would save her uncle; she leaves the bourgeois household and goes out into the public sphere to earn a living by doing charitable work; she goes into league with her husband's former mistress, Joséphi, to try to locate him.

Most significantly, Adeline turns into the infamous hysterical woman when she is struck with constant trembling, 'the kind of out-of-control body nineteenth-century doctors associated with hysteria'.[24] Beizer shows convincingly how novelistic hysteria, in the case of *Madame Bovary* and in texts written later in the nineteenth century, serves as a means of constructing an image of woman's inherently flawed identity: 'Hysteria turns out to be just a way of labelling or highlighting the pathological feminine'.[25] Balzac in this novel indeed shows Adeline's flawed nature. Beyond this, however, he indicts the ailing social system of marriage and family that creates that flawed identity and causes her trembling malady. For most of her married life, she has been able to bear her husband's sexual mania, but when he steals from the state to make money to support his adulterous habit and taints the reputation of her family, particularly that of her uncle (who later, as she predicts, kills himself because of it), she succumbs to 'one of those violent nervous upsets that leave their mark forever on the body. Some days later she became affected by a constant nervous tremor' (304) ['l'une de ces révolutions nerveuses si violentes que le corps en garde éternellement la trace. Elle devint, quelques jours après, sujette à un tressaillement continuel' (CH VII 315)].

Shortly after this first attack, when she offers to prostitute herself to Crevel, she says that her heart is being ripped apart, 'drawn and quartered' (313) ['tiré à quatre chevaux' (CH VII 323)] (a ripping that Bette significantly wanted to do to Adeline's clothes), as competing family obligations confront her with irreconcilable contradictions. Matlock aptly notes a similarity between Balzac and Jean-Louis Brachet (a nineteenth-century doctor who wrote on hysteria), as both represent how women must hide their real feelings and keep up appearances, when the very act of hiding their real feelings can lead to illness: 'Doomed by her very attempts to model herself on social norms, to protect her husband's name, her family's tranquillity, and "appearances," a woman like Adeline winds up, in both Brachet and Balzac, tormented into convulsions.'[26] Her trembling resumes at two moments in her conversation with Crevel, first when he tells her that no one is seeking her favours the way they seek Valérie's, and second when she admits to herself that she is now like a prostitute: 'I offered myself to you like a prostitute' (321) ['je me suis offerte à vous, comme une prostituée' (CH VII 329)]. This second onset of trembling never stops, as if it were the marker of her split identity: 'She was trembling with the nervous tremor which, from that moment on, never left her' (321) ['Elle tremblait de ce tremblement qui, depuis ce moment, ne la quitta plus' (CH VII 330)].

Hortense, too, suffers nervous attacks when she finds out that Steinbock has gone to Valérie's, and later when she thinks Steinbock is the father of Valérie's unborn child. However, Hortense refuses to be the passive victim by accepting the situation: in making this decision, she specifically thinks of her mother's deplorable state as she decides not to be like her mother and instead leaves her husband: 'Her mother's image ['phantom' in the original French] appeared before her and wrought a complete change. She became calm and cold; she recovered her reason' (261) ['Le fantôme de sa mère lui apparut et lui fit une révolution; elle devint calme et froide, elle recouvra sa raison' (CH VII 277)]. Her brother, Victorin, also refuses to sit back passively and suffer. Instead, he arranges for the deaths of Valérie and Crevel. The Hulot children differ from their mother, as Hortense and Victorin move away from their parents' belated and half-dead social structure – the phantom Adeline that appears to Hortense – into the modern world. As Balzac says of Victorin, even though he is one of those people who are 'walking coffins containing a Frenchman of former times' (54) ['des cercueils ambulants qui contiennent un Français d'autrefois' (CH VII 97)], he is also part of the new world, 'the young men produced by the 1830 Revolution' (54) ['le jeune homme tel que l'a fabriqué la Révolution de 1830' *ibid.*]. Barbéris notes that Victorin's economic activity is also modern: he bases his fortune on real estate speculation rather than on a creative or productive activity.[27]

Money in Balzac's world is, of course, the basis of this new society, and one of the most important effects of this text is to show not only how money is connected to love and sexuality, but also how marriage, even though it has traditionally been linked to money, is essentially traffic in women, like prostitution, and in this text it is sometimes entwined with prostitution. Crevel will provide a dowry for Hortense's marriage if Adeline will sleep with him. The marriage between Victorin and Célestine, Crevel's daughter, was proposed by their fathers' prostitute mistresses (32) [CH VII 79]. And we recall that Hortense finds her husband in a store and, in a certain sense, buys his attention when she purchases his statue (just as a young woman's family would 'buy' a husband with a dowry).

Although the replacement of morality by money is a frequent theme in Balzac's works, in *La Cousine Bette* it has made the family and marriage unstable institutions. In this text, Balzac explores the stress placed on the family as money and individual satisfaction reign. When men are unfaithful and pursue their own desires heedless of their families, sex disconnects from marriage and becomes a commodity that undermines the family's well being. In order to survive, the family commits immoral and criminal acts. Hulot betrays and steals from the state to make money for his mistresses and his family. Hortense, who does not have enough money for an acceptable dowry, betrays her cousin, Bette, by 'stealing' her lover. Valérie's husband is a passive pimp who helps her manipulate her lovers to get favours and funds. Adeline attempts to sell herself for her family. And Victorin knowingly sets a murder in motion to help his family. Ironically, Josépha, Hulot's former mistress, seems to be one of the most moral of characters in the novel, when she saves Adeline and helps her try to restore her family. Josépha is also linked to great art and drama and is the mistress of one of the few real aristocrats in the novel, the duc d'Hérouville, although his diminutive size, as several critics have noted, reflects the diminished power and stature of the aristocracy.

Balzac places conclusions about this new society in the mouth of Bianchon, the upright doctor of *La Comédie humaine*: 'In the old days, money was not everything; it was recognised that superior values took precedence over it. There was nobility, talent, and service to the state. But today the law makes money a general yardstick' (434) ['L'argent autrefois n'était pas tout, on admettait des supériorités qui le primaient. Il y avait la noblesse, le talent, les services rendus à l'État; mais aujourd'hui la loi fait de l'argent un étalon général' (CH VII 428)]. In Balzac's view, the disappearance of honour leads

Balzac, Gender and Sexuality: *La Cousine Bette*

to the decay of French society in this novel: the heroism of the Napoleonic period is a ghost, and what takes its place is a society based entirely on money and self-interest, a society in which sexuality has been commodified and women's power seems threatening. Bette, the non-normative, marginal subject produced by this social and familial system, sees its flaws and uses them to undermine the very thing that made her. Her ultimate demise suggests that she is both the creation and the victim of the patriarchal society that Balzac evokes.

NOTES

1. M. Lucey, *The Misfit of the Family: Balzac and the Social Forms of Sexuality* (Durham NC: Duke University Press, 2003), p. 27.
2. R. Barthes, *S/Z* (Paris: Seuil, 1972).
3. C. Prendergast, *Balzac: Fiction and Melodrama* (London: Arnold, 1978), p. 108.
4. P. Bourdieu, *The Logic of Practice*, trans. R. Nice (Palo Alto: Stanford University Press), p. 189.
5. Lucey, *Misfit*, pp. 163–164.
6. Translations for *Bette* are from H. de Balzac, *Cousin Bette*, trans. S. Raphael, intr. D. Bellos (Oxford University Press, 1992). Page numbers are given after the translation.
7. J. Matlock, *Scenes of Seduction: Prostitution, Hysteria and Reading Difference in Nineteenth-Century France* (New York: Columbia University Press, 1994), p. 172.
8. Lucey, *Misfit*, p. 127.
9. M. Foucault, *Discipline and Punish: The Birth of the Prison*, trans. A. Sheridan (New York: Vintage, 1977).
10. Lucey, *Misfit*, p. 125.
11. J. Beizer, *Family Plots: Balzac's Narrative Generations* (New Haven: Yale University Press, 1986), pp. 132–135.
12. Prendergast, *Fiction and Melodrama*, pp. 166–167.
13. Lucey, *Misfit*, p. 161.
14. T. Castle, *The Apparitional Lesbian: Female Homosexuality and Modern Culture* (New York: Columbia University Press, 1993).
15. H. de Balzac, 'Ce qui disparaît de Paris' in *Le Diable à Paris: Paris et les Parisiens* (Paris: Michel Lévy, 1857), pp. 170–179.
16. Her cashmere shawl has been analysed by several critics, in particular by S. Hiner, 'Lust for Luxe: "Cashmere Fever" in Nineteenth-Century France', *The Journal for Early Modern Cultural Studies*, 5.1 (2005), 76–98.
17. Lucey, *Misfit*, pp. 154–156.
18. D. S. Barnes, *The Making of a Social Disease: Tuberculosis in Nineteenth-Century France* (Berkeley: University of California Press, 1995), pp. 32, 36–37.
19. N. Mozet, '*La Cousine Bette*, roman du pouvoir féminin?' in F. van Rossum-Guyon and M. van Brederode (eds), *Balzac et les parents pauvres* (SEDES/CDU, 1981), pp. 33–45.
20. D. Knight, 'Reading as an Old Maid: *La Cousine Bette* and Compulsory Heterosexuality', *Quinquereme* (1989), 67–79 (p. 71).

21. N. Mozet, 'Création et/ou paternité dans *La Cousine Bette*' in R. Le Huenen and P. Perron (eds), *Le Roman de Balzac: recherches critiques, méthodes, lectures* (Montreal: Didier, 1980), pp. 173–184 (p. 177).
22. Matlock, *Scenes*, p. 185.
23. Mozet, '*La Cousine Bette*', p. 35.
24. Matlock, *Scenes*, p. 174.
25. J. Beizer, *Ventriloquized Bodies: Narratives of Hysteria in Nineteenth-Century France* (Ithaca: Cornell University Press, 1994), p. 139.
26. Matlock, *Scenes*, p. 183.
27. P. Barbéris, Notes to Honoré de Balzac, *La Cousine Bette* (Paris: Gallimard, 1972), p. 368, note 1.

9

OWEN HEATHCOTE

Space, Religion and Politics in the *Scènes de la vie de campagne*

Introduction

Though famed for his descriptions of Paris, Balzac invested much of his creative energy in representing the French countryside. Since 'country and peasant life is awaiting its historian' ['la vie campagnarde et paysanne attend un historien'],[1] one of Balzac's ambitions was to engage with 'the major question of landscape in literature' ['la grande question du paysage en littérature'] (CH IX 922). This chapter accordingly examines Balzac's interest in small-town and rural spaces as illustrated by the four novels that make up the series of the *Scènes de la vie de campagne: Le Médecin de campagne, Le Lys dans la vallée, Le Curé de village* and *Les Paysans*. Except in *Les Paysans*, this emphasis on rural settings enables Balzac to foreground characters savouring a certain calm after a turbulent, even traumatic, life: 'Here then is rest after the agitation..., the gentle, uniform occupations of life in the fields after the stress of Paris, the scars after the wounding' ['Là donc le repos après le mouvement..., les douces et uniformes occupations de la vie des champs après le tracas de Paris, les cicatrices après les blessures'] (CH I 1148). Although past traumas may be perpetuated or even exacerbated by 'l'ombre et le silence' of the country, characters' attempts to work through these traumas often acquire a deep spiritual, even religious, dimension, especially when aided by the presence of high-minded friends and perceptive, devoted clergy. When suffering or traumatised characters actively embrace a certain beneficent mission in their country retreats, their endeavours also acquire a strong social as well as spiritual dimension. Such characters are consciously and actively repairing not just spiritual but cultural, social and economic disadvantage. Their mission is therefore not just – or even primarily – spiritual but, in the broadest sense, political – not least when, as in *Les Paysans*, any sense of true mission is absent or thwarted. It can be seen, then, that space, religion and politics are inseparable in the *Scènes de la vie de campagne*, making it one of the tightest but also one of the richest of Balzac's narrative groupings.

Although now seen as one of the most coherent sub-groups of the *Études de mœurs*, the *Scènes de la vie de campagne* were not always thus. After being classed as a *Scène de la vie de province, Le Lys dans la vallée*, for example, only became a *Scène de la vie de campagne* in the 'Furne corrigé' edition of *La Comédie humaine*. This migration affects not only any distinction between 'country' and 'provinces' but also the narrative environment in which *Le Lys* is found and interpreted. While the *Scènes de la vie de campagne* now usually open with *Les Paysans*, this text was an even later addition to the *Scènes de la vie de campagne*, being both incomplete and only published in 1855, after Balzac's death. It is, therefore, important to note that for some time the *Scènes de la vie de campagne* contained only two texts – *Le Curé de village* and *Le Médecin de campagne* – and that it is only belatedly that the *Scènes* now appear as the climax and end-point of the *Études de mœurs*. Balzac's creation of the rural spaces of the *Scènes de la vie de campagne* is therefore unpredictable and shifting – as fluid as the characters' own view of their own histories and their own trajectories. Given this fluidity, it is unsurprising that one of the features of space in the *Scènes de la vie de campagne* is that it can be moulded and remoulded. Like the composition and character of the *Scènes* themselves, space in the novels can be transformed in accordance with the changing needs of individuals and society.

Given that the rural spaces of the *Scènes de la vie de campagne* lend themselves to transformation, particularly when taken over by characters who are themselves engaged in similar processes of transformation, it is appropriate that both the spaces and the characters of the *Scènes de la vie de campagne* illustrate a transition towards some of Balzac's 'core values', such as those foregrounded in the 'Avant-propos' to *La Comédie humaine*. If the characters of the *Scènes* are reworking their priorities in settings that are themselves ready to be reworked, what better place for the rediscovery and the reintroduction of the political and religious values that Balzac feels were neglected or discarded by post-Revolutionary individualism and materialism, particularly under the July 1830 monarchy of the Orleanist Louis-Philippe? As Balzac writes in the 'Avant-propos': 'I am writing in the light of two eternal Truths: Religion and Monarchy' ['J'écris à la lueur de deux Vérités éternelles: la Religion, la Monarchie'] (CH I 13). To what extent, then, do the *Scènes de la vie de campagne* embody a successful return to these seemingly debased or neglected principles? To what extent do the four substantial novels of country life, in particular, *Le Médecin de campagne*, embody a religious and a political revival not only for at least some of their characters but for contemporary readers of *La Comédie humaine*?

Les Paysans (1844–55)

Written in part in 1844 but not published (unfinished) until 1855, *Les Paysans* is, despite its incompleteness, generally given pride of place at the beginning of the *Scènes de la vie de campagne*. Taken up by the early Marxist critic, Georg Lukács and by his Marxist/socialist successors, Pierre Barbéris, Pierre Macherey and André Wurmser, it remains one of Balzac's most important and influential novels. Most critics start from *Les Paysans* as the account of the tragic class struggle around a large country estate, Les Aigues, in the Burgundy of the 1820s. Les Aigues has been recently acquired by the former Napoleonic general, the Comte de Montcornet, who has moved there largely to please his wife, the aristocratic Virginie de Troisville. Unfortunately for the future of the estate, Mme de Montcornet is more interested in receiving her admirer, the Parisian journalist, Émile Blondet, than in cultivating her estate manager, Gaubertin, who had also hoped to buy the property. Once Montcornet dismisses Gaubertin for theft, the knives are out: an unholy alliance between Gaubertin, the local peasants (led by the Tonsard family at the local hostelry, the Grand-I-Vert) and a usurer from the nearby town of Blangy, the former Benedictine monk, Rigou, leads to the gradual but ruthless despoliation of Les Aigues, the murder of the faithful keeper, Michaud, and to Montcornet's eventual secession of the estate to the peasants, Gaubertin and Rigou. The opening adage of the novel – 'Who has land, has war' ['Qui terre a, guerre a'] – has been fulfilled: the Moncornets have been evicted and the estate has been torn apart and destroyed. Indeed, Montcornet himself later dies and the Countess and Blondet marry, passing what used to be Les Aigues on the way to their honeymoon destination.[2]

It can be seen from this summary that *Les Paysans* seems to offer relatively little evidence that Balzac was writing 'à la lueur de deux Vérités éternelles: la Religion, la Monarchie' – either the eternal truth of Catholicism or that embodied by the recently restored monarch, Louis XVIII (1814–24). In terms of religious or moral principles, the local characters are, as the local priest, the abbé Brossette, forlornly observes, 'people without religion' ['des gens sans religion'] (CH IX 110) with, for example, the apostate monk, Rigou, only interested in extending his property and his seraglio of nubile young women and with the peasants themselves consumed by 'peasant and proletarian hatred of the overlords and the affluent' ['la haine du prolétaire et du paysan contre le maître et le riche'] (CH IX 91).

Although the abbé Brossette is resignedly aware that 'only religion can repair so many ills' ['[l]a religion peut seule réparer tant de maux'] (CH IX 204), he also realises that the aristocratic Countess is more absorbed by her own pleasures than with the pillaging of Les Aigues (CH IX 220). Since Bonaldian social Catholicism can never be implemented without the estate owners' support, religion is as ineffectual as the law in inhibiting or in punishing the rapacity of the peasants and of the local, self-aggrandising bourgeoisie (CH IX 204).[3]

Why is the law as impotent as religion and why does the new monarchy not give more support to Les Aigues's new owners? One reason is that Montcornet is precisely the wrong person to take over the estate and does so at the worst possible moment in history. First, Montcornet is a former Napoleonic general whose strength and skills flourished in the battlefield rather than in the idyllic, indolent, feminised 'décor d'opéra' of the country estate. The general is an imperialist of the past rather than a monarchist of the present. Second, his wife may be an aristocrat but she has none of the legitimising history enjoyed by other local landowners such as the Ronquerolles and the Soulanges whose nearby estates go relatively unmolested. The Montcornets are thus caught between the outdated glamour of the past and any new-found prestige in the present. Third, after taking over the estate from the actress-singer Mlle Laguerre, the Montcornets fail to imitate the latter's different kind of aristocracy – her casual but much appreciated generosity towards local inhabitants. Fourth, it appears that the new regime is either too monarchic to bother itself with a Burgundy estate or insufficiently monarchic to risk inflaming a potentially violent province (CH IX 187–189). As in relation to religion, then, it appears that *Les Paysans* evinces a highly ambivalent, not to say negative, view of the Restoration monarchy. Both monarch and religion have to be appreciated, if at all, *in absentia* rather than, as might have been expected, as forces for regeneration in post-Revolution, post-Napoleonic France.

As a final note on the relations between space, religion and politics in *Les Paysans*, mention should be made of the role of gender and sexuality. As noted above, Les Aigues are feminised as a 'décor d'opéra', as a rural sanctuary for Mlle Laguerre and then for the Comtesse de Montcornet. It is also women who either directly or indirectly dominate the peasants – either through the violence of the female members of the Tonsard family or through Catherine Tonsard aiding her brother's attempted rape of La Péchina. Even Mlle Laguerre herself is manipulated by her chamber-maid, Mlle Cochet (Mme Soudry) and the upcoming bourgeois, Rigou, is, like Montcornet, manœuvred by a younger woman (CH IX 245). Throughout *Les Paysans* it is, then, the female characters who generally exacerbate the three-way class conflict (landowners, peasants, bourgeois) and who thus undermine the possible impact of social catholicism and the new monarchy. Whereas other novels in the *Scènes de la vie de campagne* have women as the incarnation of Catholic or royalist principles, the women in *Les Paysans* tend to subvert stability or obstruct restorative change.

Le Lys dans la vallée (1836)

The events and characters of *Le Lys dans la vallée* (1836) are even more embedded than *Les Paysans* in the early Bourbon Restoration. As Alain famously notes of *Le Lys*: 'It is the history of the Hundred Days, seen from a château in the Loire' ['C'est l'histoire des Cent-Jours vue d'un château de la Loire'].[4] Being the younger son of a well-connected aristocratic family, the narrator-hero of *Le Lys*, Félix de Vandenesse, is much better placed than the former Napoleonic general, Montcornet, to take advantage of the change in regime. As a teenager, Félix is propelled into representing his family at the Tours ball in honour of the King's nephew, the duc d'Angoulême, where he meets and falls for Henriette de Mortsauf, the 'lily' of the title, whose later recommendations and connections enable him to establish himself at court in Paris and become a private secretary to the King. While at court, Félix does not forget his strong, platonic relationship with Henriette but he also conducts a passionate sexual affair with the strong-willed English aristocrat, Lady Dudley. Once news of the affair reaches Henriette, her already delicate health deteriorates and she dies, in agony but subdued by opium, in her Clochegourde estate in the Indre Valley. At the request of his would-be new love, Natalie de Manerville, Félix confesses his past but she sharply dismisses him as a faithless, cold-hearted suitor: 'When one has crimes like this on one's conscience, one should at least keep them to oneself' ['Quand on a sur la conscience de pareils crimes, au moins ne faut-il pas les dire'] (CH IX 1228).

While the title of *Le Lys* seems to announce a paean to rural loveliness and serenity, it can be seen from this summary that the novel is no eclogue. Although Félix describes his return to the Indre Valley with a sensibility not unworthy of the Romantic poets, and although he and Henriette frequently savour the natural, and particularly the floral, abundance of Clochegourde, the countryside remains a setting for illness and pain, from Mortsauf's extreme irascibility as a returned *émigré* to his son's incipient consumption – and, finally, to Henriette's own suffering and death: 'Look at this valley, she said, showing me the Indre, it gives me pain but I still love it' ['Voyez-vous cette vallée, dit-elle en me montrant l'Indre, elle me fait mal, je l'aime toujours'] (CH IX 1157). Although, unlike Montcornet in *Les Paysans*, but like Véronique in *Le Curé de village* and Benassis in *Le Médecin de campagne*, Henriette succeeds in revitalising her neglected country estate, she still feels Clochegourde is a burden rather than a pleasure, a prison rather than a release (CH IX 1032–1033). It is, moreover, not Henriette but Félix who identifies her with the 'lily' and if she becomes a lily it is to please him more than herself (CH IX 1170). There is a sense, then, in which the countryside in/of *Le Lys dans la vallée* is an artificial rather than a spontaneous creation – the work of an (urban) outsider like Félix with his constant shuttlings between Clochegourde and Paris and with his carefully crafted bouquets. As Natalie de Manerville is quick to notice, Félix's love of Henriette and Clochegourde owes more to his own self-serving memory and the self-aggrandising 'labour necessary for the expression of ideas' ['travail que nécessitent les idées pour être exprimées'] (CH IX 970) than to the 'real' past and 'real' nature. As mediated through the eyes of the ultimately urban visitor, the countryside in *Le Lys* is, therefore, not so far removed from the 'décor d'opéra' of Les Aigues as seen through the eyes of the Parisian journalist, Blondet. Despite *Le Lys*'s title and its end-point position in the *Scènes de la vie de campagne*, there is, therefore, much to justify Balzac's uncertainty as to its classification and even to turn the countryside of *Le Lys* into Alain's (mere) angle, (mere) perspective on a more politically and socially important reality happening in the city and thus elsewhere. After being created through the poetics of Félix's memory, the pathetic fallacy of the correspondences between the characters and the Touraine countryside is therefore easily dismissed by Natalie de Manerville.

So what can be said about the role of politics and religion in *Le Lys dans la vallée*? As might be expected from the above remarks, the impact of the regime change represented by the advent of Louis XVIII is felt in Clochegourde – Mortsauf receives a new title and a pension and Henriette becomes 'one of the wealthiest heiresses of the Maine' ['l'une des plus riches héritières du Maine'] (CH IX 1039). However, since Henriette is unable to leave the Indre, the only immediate advantage she can obtain from her new status is to launch Félix's career in Paris. Once this is effected, any cross-fertilisation between the new regime and Clochegourde is of a purely personal nature, since, for example, Félix only returns to Clochegourde when on leave (CH IX 1110) rather than to aid the Mortsaufs in the regeneration of their estate or to give his hosts new insights into politics. Even if Félix's affair with Lady Dudley can be seen as the new regime contaminating the relative innocence of the countryside, that, too, is limited to its effect on one individual, Henriette, while the future of Clochegourde after her death is never explained. It follows that the politics of *Le Lys* are absorbed by the personal and it is only later in Félix's career – when Henriette is dead and after his travels to the countryside cease – that the impact of politics (and finance) on his marriage can be portrayed in *Une fille d'Ève* (1839). Indeed, as far as *Le Lys* is concerned, the whole point of 'la campagne' is that it should be largely out of politics and indeed out of time. Despite 'the magical transformation of the Restoration' ['[l]e coup de baguette de la Restauration'], in the countryside Félix reverts to being simply 'the serf of Clochegourde' ['le serf de Clochegourde'] (CH IX 1045). As time shows, moreover, Félix's political career is relatively short-lived, since he loses favour after the death of Louis XVIII.

In terms of religion, the votes are, perhaps more surprisingly, similarly out. On the one hand, Henriette rejects any sexual relationship with Félix, partly for the sake of her children but also because of her faith. She thus remains the incarnation of purity: 'She was ... THE LILY OF THIS VALLEY where she grew for Heaven by filling it with the perfume of her virtues' ['Elle était ... LE LYS DE CETTE VALLÉE où elle croissait pour le ciel, en la remplissant du parfum de ses vertus'] (CH IX 987). However, the role of God and religion for the Martinist[5] Henriette is less central and less crucial than one might expect: did Henriette die a fully Christian death or did she, as it might seem from her testamentary letter, regret her non-misspent life? Her remorse seems to be awakened by regret at non-commission rather than by sins of commission.[6] Relatedly, it has to be said that, although the priests of *Le Lys* are marginally more important than Brossette in *Les Paysans*, they remain silent witnesses to the action rather than its agents: 'the abbé de Dominis ... had decided to solve a number of problems and took cover in feigned absent-mindedness' ['l'abbé de Dominis ... avait pris le parti de chercher la résolution de quelques problèmes, et se retranchait dans une distraction affectée'] (CH IX 1118). As for the abbé Birotteau, he lacks his predecessor's apostolic strength, being merely 'an angel of sweetness who consoles instead of chastising' ['un ange de douceur qui s'attendrit au lieu de réprimander'] (CH IX 1121). With little moral or spiritual guidance from the professionals, Henriette's salvation or non-salvation seems to be a disconcertingly aleatory and individual affair from a writer claiming to be inspired by religion as one of the two eternal verities. Given that the priests of *Le Lys* offer no spiritual guidance and given that Louis XVIII is noted for epigrams rather than leadership (CH IX 1110), it has to be said that neither religion nor monarchy in *Le Lys* seems to offer either much-needed resolution to the traumas of the past or direction for the future. If there is optimism and vigour in *Le Lys*, it seems to belong, finally, only to the Touraine landscape – unless the latter is as arid as the 'landes de Charlemagne' or in mourning at the death of Henriette (CH IX 1197).

Le Curé de village (1841)

With *Le Curé de village* the reader engages with one of the 'core' texts of the *Scènes de la vie de campagne* since it and *Le Médecin de campagne* were the only two novels to be found in this category in volume 13 of the 1845 Furne edition of *La Comédie humaine*. In the same way, however, as *Le Lys dans la vallée* can be linked either with the countryside through its depictions of the Indre Valley or with a provincial town, Tours, *Le Curé de village* is, at least in the opening sections, linked to the town of Limoges more than to the village of Montégnac of later sections. Set in Limoges, the opening chapters of the novel evoke the early years of Véronique, only daughter of the rapacious, parsimonious scrap metal merchant, Sauviat, who eventually marries a man over twenty years her senior, the well-to-do banker, Pierre Graslin. Although highly respected and even admired in Limoges, it later emerges that Véronique must have been the woman for whom a local porcelain worker, Jean-François Tascheron, committed theft and murder in order to finance their joint elopement. After the capture and execution of Tascheron, who never reveals the identity of his accomplice, and after the death of her husband Graslin, Véronique withdraws to the undeveloped village of Montégnac where her money, her enrolment of a young, under-employed engineer, Gérard, and the help of the local population bring irrigation and new prosperity to the whole locality. The attentive local priest, the abbé Bonnet, sees that Véronique is thereby expiating her remorse for the past – embodied in her and Tascheron's son, Francis – and facilitates her public confession of her involvement in Tascheron's crime. Véronique dies penitent. As a sign of a new reconciliation and a new future, Gérard marries Tascheron's devoted sister, Denise, who becomes a second mother to the young Francis.

A number of conclusions can be drawn from the above, first about *Le Curé de village* as a *Scène de la vie de campagne* and, second, about the role of religion, politics and indeed royalty in the text. Notwithstanding the title and the categorisation of *Le Curé de village*, the novel is in many ways a town as much as a country text. It is in Limoges where Véronique passes her formative years, where she marries a banker and where she has her affair with Tascheron – who is an ex-peasant and now a porcelain worker. This past conditions all Véronique's subsequent actions: it is money inherited from her Auvergnat parents and husband in Limoges that finances her Montégnac initiatives and her seemingly indestructible, widowed mother accompanies her throughout. It is, moreover, the Paris engineer, Gérard, who makes the rural improvements possible and when he marries Tascheron's sister, Denise, he espouses a woman recently returned from New York who speaks of founding a Tascheron*ville*. In addition, Véronique's own emigration to Montégnac does not enable her to put down new (or old) country roots, but confirms her as a kind of *châtelaine* or *grande dame*: 'Mme Graslin was seen as the most distinguished person in the town and the most famous of its female inhabitants' ['Mme Graslin fut regardée comme la première personne de la ville et la plus célèbre du monde féminin'] (CH IX 679). Although seemingly unassuming, Véronique becomes, even in the country, a kind of instinctive cultural and social aristocrat. Much more than Henriette de Mortsauf, who commands the heart-felt admiration of her estate workers and who dies accompanied by 'a huge gathering' ['une foule immense'] (CH IX 1212), Véronique dies in her valley while never being totally of her valley. Véronique is on the earth (in all senses of the word earth), but only of the earth in as much as she, like the barren plain of Montégnac, can be almost miraculously brought to life. *Le Curé de village* is, therefore, only a country novel in as much as the country also incorporates and encrypts the town and in as much as its earth is symbolic and transformable. As we read in *Séraphîta*: 'the earth is ... the seedbed of Heaven' ['[l]a terre est ... la pépinière du ciel'] (CH XI 777).

Given that memories of the town underlie representations of the country in *Le Curé de village* it is interesting that representations of the clergy are similarly complex and multi-layered. For although the abbé Bonnet, the 'curé de village' of the title, is in principle the church's main representative in the novel, his role is one of witness and catalyst rather than Balzac's planned key protagonist. Self-effacing and reticent, Bonnet is overshadowed by more prestigious priests such as the new Bishop, Mgr Gabriel de Rastignac (CH IX 853) and his Archbishop, Mgr Dutheil, who officiates over Véronique's confession. By being administered by a 'prince de l'Église' in a ceremony normally reserved for Royalty (CH IX 860, 864), the increasingly aristocratic Véronique is removed still further from both countryside and rural religious practices. Her personal itinerary is thus consciously co-opted by a theatrical ritual designed not just to acknowledge her own Calvary but designed, like Tascheron's pre-execution repentance, to impress and improve the local population. Hence, in a period of heightened individualism, materialism and scepticism, 'religion appears once again as the great facilitator'.[7] The period of Louis-Philippe is, therefore, not only failing to give outlets to its young talent such as the *polytechnicien* Gérard but also allowing values such as morality, community and spirituality to fall into disrepair – like the desert of Montégnac. However, echoing aspects of Lamennais, Saint-Simon and Ballanche, and combining space, politics and religion, *Le Curé de village* offers a compensatory object lesson in material and spiritual regeneration.

Le Médecin de campagne (1833)

Although the earliest of the four texts of the *Scènes de la vie de campagne*, *Le Médecin de campagne* can be seen as their most complete expression – no doubt partly because 'campagne' actually figures in the title. Seen, at least initially, through the eyes of the retired Napoleonic soldier, Pierre-Joseph Genestas, the 'campagne' in question is a village in the hilly region of the Vercors, near Grenoble, where he is secretly searching for the well-known doctor Benassis, in the hope that the latter can improve the health of his adoptive son, Adrien. Thinking he is a casual visitor, Benassis offers Genestas hospitality and takes him to visit some of his many local patients who all laud both the doctor's unremitting medical interventions and his success in bringing economic progress to a backward region: small industries such as basket- and shoe-making prosper through new local initiatives and a newly built road to Grenoble that facilitates the import of fresh labour and the export of local productions. Particularly after listening in on another former soldier, Goguelat, recounting the celebrated 'histoire de Napoléon dans une grange', Genestas sees Benassis himself as 'le Napoléon de la vallée': although Benassis has unhesitatingly expelled a group of local cretins, he protects and encourages other marginals such as the sensitive creature of nature, La Fosseuse, and the former poacher, Butifer. However, as Benassis finally confesses to Genestas, his activities are personally motivated in that they are designed to re-channel and repair past guilt (an abandoned mistress) and past loss (a dead son) – a process inspired by the words '*Fuge, late, tace*' ['Flee, hide and be silent'] seen at the nearby Grande-Chartreuse and his own adopted motto '*aux cœurs blessés, l'ombre et le silence*' (CH IX 573, 574). Since one confession prompts another, Genestas reveals his own motives for visiting Benassis, leaves his son to recuperate, but returns after Adrien writes to him of the deeply mourned death of Benassis, the 'father' of the canton.

It can be seen that of all the texts in the *Scènes de la vie de campagne*, *Le Médecin* is perhaps the most successful in promoting the countryside as the ideal site for 'les cicatrices après les blessures'. With a doctor as its key protagonist, physical, mental and emotional therapy mirrors the social and economic recovery of a village and thereby of a whole region. The multiple narrators in the text – not only Benassis but Genestas, Goguelat, La Fosseuse and even, at the end, Adrien – bear multiple witness to the success of the 'nature cure', at least when driven and developed by a strong, central 'patriarch', the doctor Benassis. Single-minded and self-sacrificing, the doctor achieves for the region what the broader French regime (whether Grenoble or Paris) seems neither to have implemented nor even imagined. With its plural voices combining into a single message, *Le Médecin* indeed seems to offer 'perfect poetic, thematic and ideological unity' ['une parfaite unité poétique, thématique et idéologique'].[8]

This representation of rural revival in *Le Médecin* is, however, less clear-cut and utopian than it might seem. First of all, the nature of its village – whose identification 'in reality' has consumed considerable critical energies – is by no means isolated, with the success of Benassis's new measures depending on the proximity of Grenoble and the new link road to the town. Supported by the financial and administrative expertise of Benassis's friend Gravier, and benefiting from new buildings (whether homes or small factories) and the import of fresh labour with new, town skills, the village is, perhaps inevitably, becoming more bourgeois and urban.[9] *Le Médecin* can, therefore, even be seen as a text for city readers. As with all the other estates and villages in the *Scènes de la vie de campagne* – Les Aigues, Clochegourde, Montégnac – the town and its bourgeoisie are never so far away that their influence is not felt by both 'natives' and visitors alike – who, like Benassis himself, by definition come from outside. Indeed, these estates and villages are constantly being visited and appraised by outsiders – Blondet in *Les Paysans*, Félix in *Le Lys*, Gérard in *Le Curé de village* and Genestas in *Le Médecin*. As a result, the description of these villages may seem utopian but they are not, actually, remote, let alone utopian or 'nowhere'.

On the subject of religion, it is well known that Balzac described *Le Médecin de campagne* to Zulma Carraud as 'the Gospel in action' ['l'Évangile en action'] (Corr. I 838). Critics have, however, also noted that Benassis is a doctor, not a priest, and that although he takes over the former priest's house when he comes to the village, the new priest he appoints, the abbé Janvier, has an altogether minor role in the novel. While Benassis appreciates the cohesive potential of the Church as 'a complete system opposing man's depraved tendencies' ['un système complet d'opposition aux tendances dépravées de l'homme'] (CH IX 503) and, therefore, offering elevating *and subduing* ceremonies such as funerals, he himself is no church-goer. For him, ritual is more important than faith and economic (pre-socialist? Saint-Simonian?) initiatives have priority over the spiritual. Even his 'confession' to his new friend, Genestas, has little of the penitential, sacramental dimension of the confessions of Véronique or Henriette. Neither does his own death. It is, therefore, perhaps unsurprising that, contrary to Balzac's hopes, *Le Médecin de campagne* was not awarded the Prix Montyon as a work of witness and piety. Benassis may be a new Napoleon but he is no new Christ.

If *Le Médecin* is no more than programmatically Catholic, it is even less Royalist or Legitimist – despite Balzac's electoral ambitions at the time. While insistently advocating the importance of centralised power and, notoriously, the damaging effect of elections (CH IX 508), the text never suggests that any such centralised authority be established or re-established beyond Benassis's immediate canton. Evocations of Napoleon are pervasive, but often, as with the famous 'story in the stable', romanticised and even undercut via an unreliable narrator. There is, therefore, no advocacy of a return to an imperial regime (Napoleon III is still in the future) or of a revolution in favour of a new King or a different branch of the Monarchy. As Patrick Berthier observes, 'Benassis advocates strong power *whatever that power may be*' ['Benassis fait l'apologie du pouvoir fort *quel que soit ce pouvoir*'][10] and, despite the fact that, for R. Fortassier, 'paternal sentiment is present in all its grandeur' ['le sentiment paternel est là dans toute sa grandeur'],[11] for Barbéris 'no patriarchal perspective ends the book' ['[n]ulle vue patriarcale ne clôt le livre'].[12] Even more, then, than at the end of *Le Lys* and *Le Curé de village*, the future of the revitalised canton remains uncertain. Adrien has recovered but will join the army of his adopted father, Genestas, rather than continue the mission of Benassis as doctor-mayor. It would seem, then, that, having lost his own son, Benassis leaves an unspecified legacy beyond what is retained in the memory of those who knew him – and beyond the text we are now reading by the Napoleon of Letters that is Balzac.

Conclusion

It is evident from the above that, while illustrating Balzac's strengths as a 'paysagiste en littérature', the *Scènes de la vie de campagne* are very different from narrowly regional novels, whether set in Burgundy, the Vercors, the Limousin or even Touraine. It is evident, too, that they depart markedly from Balzac's claim to be writing 'à la lueur de deux Vérités éternelles: la Religion, la Monarchie'. While, in *Les Paysans*, the ex-Napoleonic general Montcornet and his aristocratic wife may occupy the moral high ground in relation to the rapacious peasants, they are too obtuse and too opinionated to cope with either peasants or the more sinister rising bourgeoisie of Blangy. In *Le Lys*, Henriette's motto of 'noblesse oblige' becomes with Félix a form of opportunism that sits neatly with the calculating politics of Louis XVIII and augurs well for Félix's future career, but provides no basis for generalised political or moral renewal. In *Le Curé de village* and *Le Médecin de campagne*, it is not the new regime but exceptional individuals who, for personal rather than political reasons, give impetus to backward regions. If the new Monarchies seem, therefore, to be unenterprising, unenlightened or simply off the novels' radar, then Religion, too, is often ill-served by morally admirable but counterproductively self-effacing clerics such as Brossette (*Les Paysans*), Birotteau (*Le Lys*), Janvier (*Le Médecin*) and, even, Bonnet in *Le Curé de village*. These priests may set an example but they are examples too easily ignored or avoided except by exceptional, motivated individuals. While the absence of any generalised political or religious revival thus leaves space for bourgeois opportunism and peasant depredations, it also, fortunately, leaves space for the individual moral and existential questionings that form the bedrock of the *Scènes de la vie de campagne*. The *Scènes* are, therefore, distinguished less by their much-analysed political or religious grandstanding than by the ways in which individuals like Henriette, Véronique and Benassis tackle the moral, social, spiritual and sexual implications of their passions, whether spent (Benassis), misspent (Véronique), unspent (Henriette) or overspent (*Les Paysans*). Since the relatively undeveloped spaces of the *Scènes* often lead, despite renewal, to decay and death, they also offer privileged sites for engaging with what it means to be human in *La Comédie humaine*. But given that being human entails dealing with both internal and external demons – such as Mortsauf's '*blue devils*' (CH IX 1151) – there is as much suffering as solace in the *Scènes de la vie de campagne*.

NOTES

1. *Contes bruns*, par une tête à l'envers. Balzac, Chasles, Rabou (Paris: Éditions des autres, 1979), p. 42. Unless otherwise stated, all the translations are my own.
2. Blondet and the Countess drive past the virtually derelict Les Aigues in the same way as Derville drives past the cadaverous Chabert at the end of *Le Colonel Chabert* and as Jules Desmarets drives away from Ferragus at the end of *Ferragus*.
3. As A. Watts points out, the bourgeois replacement of the nobility in the rural estates was typical of the early Restoration period (*Preserving the Provinces: Small Town and Countryside in the Work of Honoré de Balzac* (Bern: Peter Lang, 2007), pp. 163–165). It is, therefore, the bourgeoisie, who, as the main beneficiaries of the Revolution, initiate and control change.
4. Alain, *Avec Balzac* (Paris: Gallimard, 1937), p. 24.
5. From L.-C. de Saint-Martin (1743–1803), mystic and philosopher/theosopher, known also as 'le Philosophe inconnu' and cited in a number of Balzac novels, notably *Le Lys*.
6. Balzac famously attenuated Henriette's regrets under the influence of Mme de Berny: LH I 362.
7. Watts, *Preserving the Provinces*, p. 268.
8. P. Laforgue, *La Fabrique de 'La Comédie humaine'* (Besançon: Presses universitaires de Franche-Comté, 2013), p. 195.
9. R. Fortassier, Introduction to *Le Médecin de campagne*, CH IX 351–384 (364).
10. P. Berthier, 'Notice', *Le Médecin de campagne* (Paris: Gallimard, 'Folio', 1974), pp. 350–364 (p. 354). Italics in the original.
11. R. Fortassier, Introduction 378.
12. P. Barbéris, *Balzac et le mal du siècle: contribution à une physiologie du monde moderne*, 2 vols, II: *1830–1833: Une expérience de l'absurde: de la prise de conscience à l'expression* (Paris: Gallimard, 1970), p. 1899.

10

TIM FARRANT

Balzac's Shorter Fiction

Stories, Length and Relativity

One thing most people know about Balzac is that his work is long. Yet although *La Comédie humaine* is massive, and some of its fictions enormous, nearly all his novels, as well as the briefer narratives which make up more than half its works, were initially conceived as short fictions. These briefer works,[1] our main focus, we designate as Balzac's 'short' or 'shorter' fictions or stories[2] or tales. 'Short', because concentrated in subject, characters and scope; 'shorter', because necessarily more circumscribed than many of Balzac's other narratives, as well as, of course, the larger *Comédie humaine*. Balzac's 'novels' also combine the 'stories' (plotlines, careers, narrative trajectories) of their protagonists, as well as of lesser characters, and even *Splendeurs et misères des courtisanes*, the very longest, is made up of four shorter novels, which are themselves essentially stories. Stories, as gripping yarns and brief accounts, discursive mode and literary genre, are at the heart of Balzac's output: as its starting point (he began writing narrative as illustrations, philosophical examples; and short stories are the beginnings of even his longest, latest novels: *Splendeurs et misères, Le Cousin Pons, La Cousine Bette*); as themselves (the shorter fictions which make up over half *La Comédie humaine*); and as the microcosm(s) in tension with his macrocosm.

Such tensions, between microcosm and macrocosm, principle and practice, are highlighted by three examples: from Balzac's very first stab at narrative, in a teenage philosophical treatise; from the 1832 story *Le Curé de Tours*; and from a comment on the 1836 novel *Le Lys dans la vallée*. In the first, an axiomatic remark that all human affairs have as many sides as people who consider them is illustrated by an anecdote relating how two riders seeing a statue as respectively white and black discover that it is white on one side and black on the other: 'That's opinion' ['Voilà l'opinion'] (OD I 555). In *Le Curé de Tours*, the seemingly trivial conflict of clerics in the cloister of the cathedral at Tours is related to the apparent selfishness of men who carry

140

a science, a nation or laws in their bosom, which is, Balzac suggests, 'the noblest of passions, and in some way, the maternity of the masses' ['la plus noble des passions, et en quelque sorte, la maternité des masses'] (CH IV 244). And Mme de Mortsauf's unknown battle with passion in a valley of the Indre is perhaps as great as 'the most illustrious of battles ever known' ['la plus illustre des batailles connues'] (CH I 17). Balzac's two teenage riders imply the subjectivity (and undecidability) of perception and, like the two later examples, the dichotomy of microcosm and macrocosm, exiguity and extension. Short fiction is central to the conception and effect of *La Comédie humaine*, as the fundamental narrative manifestation of the example which demonstrates the larger truth or whole.

Balzac generally avoids traditional generic labels (*conte, nouvelle, histoire*), in his time largely devalued by overproduction during the *folie du conte*, the 1829–32 craze for tales, preferring those which were generically neutral, or polyvalent, evoking media outside or beyond literature. The *Scènes de la vie privée* (1830), his first volume of stories, carry a title which would eventually encompass some twenty-seven stories and novels, as well as being diversified, from *Eugénie Grandet* (1833), as *Scènes de la vie de province*, and subsequently *Scènes de la vie parisienne, politique, militaire* and *de campagne* under the general heading *Études de mœurs*. Likewise the *Romans et contes philosophiques* became, from 1834, the *Études philosophiques*, followed twelve years later by the seriously undernourished *Études analytiques*.

These labels, *scène* and *étude*, stress the visual, dramatic and objective, dignifying fiction with aesthetic and intellectual respectability and seeming generic invisibility, in line with Balzac's essentially mimetic desire to make genre transparent, to enable the reader to see through the text to the real. But this conflicts with the fact that this reality is recounted, is a vision, a perception, shaped by a narrator. This is apparent more in the earlier shorter fictions of *La Comédie humaine* (including *La Peau de chagrin*, first envisaged as a *conte fantastique*), where the narrator can, even in signal exceptions like *Sarrasine*, usually be identified with Balzac himself. This tension between objectivity and storytelling becomes acute with the systematic use of recurring characters after *Le Père Goriot* (1835), when a number, such as Bianchon or Bixiou, will become narrators, telling their own or their peers' stories in, say, *La Messe de l'athée* or *La Maison Nucingen*.

Genre then, is both central yet also almost does not matter, because it is content which defines, and helps subjects find, their form. One-line jottings were as likely to become novels as to remain as stories: *Les Souffrances de l'inventeur*, for example, eventually grew into *Illusions perdues*. Other ideas developed as both stories and novels – the text-nexus around celibacy pivoting on projects called *La Fleur des pois*, which stimulate works of differing lengths and composition: *Le Curé de Tours, Le Contrat de mariage*, the novel *La Vieille fille*, and which resonate into the next decade, in both a shorter fiction (*Pierrette*) and its companion novels in *Les Parents pauvres: Le Cousin Pons* and *La Cousine Bette*. Balzac's narratives struggle into being, long or short, large or small, like Rodin's sculptures of the author, surging upwards and onwards from their raw materials. Yet the big issues in Balzac's work, philosophy, history, sex and money, are most compelling when presented in the condensed quintessence of his stories.

From *La Comédie humaine*'s Beginnings to *Le Père Goriot*, 1829–35

These energies come together in a Big Bang at the inception of *La Comédie humaine*. The 1830 *Scènes de la vie privée* were born by downsizing the Scottian historical novel essayed in *Le Dernier Chouan* with anecdote-writing pioneered in his immensely successful 'How-to' guide for husbands hoping to stop their wives being unfaithful, the *Physiologie du mariage* (both 1829). Its grotesque recommendations undercut an overtly often reactionary viewpoint with one more compelling and subversive. The 1830 *Scènes* develop this, assuming a supposedly *conte-moral* mode in order to tell stories revealing the deficiencies of conventional marriage and its appalling inflictions upon women. Their brief narratives were driven by a collapse in traditional book (including multi-volume novel) publishing, and the rise of new forms of print media. Two kinds are especially relevant: the brief, pamphlet-like, often satirical *petit journal*, and the more intellectual literary review. Both pushed short fiction to the fore, giving it unwonted currency, appearing every few days or weekly, alongside other kinds of narrative (news, gossip, *faits divers*) surviving as best they could. The *petits journaux* where Balzac first published his stories, *La Mode, La Silhouette, La Caricature*, were mostly driven by pictures, as their very titles aver. Along with the other significant presence, after Scott, in Balzac's early writing, the German fantastic storyteller Hoffmann, these papers feed into the whimsical, imaginative, often phantasmagoric vision of the real developed at greater length especially in Balzac's early stories for the other kind of journal, the literary reviews: *L'Élixir de longue vie, Sarrasine* and *L'Auberge rouge*; a fantastic vision expanded in *La Peau de chagrin*, and which runs throughout, and arguably founds, *La Comédie humaine*.

The journals *Revue de Paris* and *Revue des Deux Mondes*, more book-like, appearing more leisurely, destined for the select library shelf, would feature Balzac's stories (along with others by high-end authors, notably Gautier, Mérimée, Stendhal) alongside portentous articles on history, geopolitics, the arts and economics. A third journal *L'Artiste*, of larger format and accordingly ambitious pretensions, would launch the following year, in 1831, and take notably Balzac's story *Le Colonel Chabert*. Balzac's storytelling in these organs peaked in the years of the *folie du conte* (1829–32) prior to an economic recovery and a turn towards the novel from 1833. The thirty or so stories Balzac wrote during the three years from 1829 form about two-thirds of those in *La Comédie humaine*, and nearly a third of its total number of fictions.

If most of Balzac's early tales were pre-published in newspapers, their decisive début was made in the book form of the 1830 *Scènes de la vie privée*. The manuscript of the first, now *La Maison du chat-qui-pelote*, *La Comédie humaine*'s initial fiction, reveals Balzac's strenuous efforts to shrink a discursive historical introduction and transfigure it as a scene; another reuses the pen-portrait of the miser Gobseck published earlier in *La Mode*. Such examples reveal something less manifest elsewhere, but fundamental – Balzac's blending of different genres, art-forms and modes of discourse in his new practice of brief narrative: an authoritative, ostensibly omniscient authorial account, inspired by the Scottian historical novel, mixed with presentation both visual and dramatic, concentrating action in dialogued set-piece scenes confronting opposing characters, but also making pictures in the mind. *La Maison* opens like an opera, its hero almost serenading his future lover at her window; Gobseck's portrait is a Dutch miniature, presenting the *Physiologie*'s theories and practices in action. Making a virtue of commercial necessity, Balzac turns what had hitherto been pigeonholed as the *conte*, a vehicle for intimacy, for depicting the kind of genre-scene that the large canvas of the historical novel would not allow. The *Scènes* were a game-changing gambit, reinventing the *conte* (disparaged as, variously, fairy-tale, moral tale, children's tale), and instituting the *scène* as a new, powerful, polyvalent and flexible genre in its own right – the major appellation of Balzac's creation, soon to include novels as well as stories, and in successive editions and eventually the *Comédie*, a form of newspaper or at least serial publication in instalments by other means.

The dominant note of Balzac's 1830 tales was personal and emotional, and fantastic during 1831; and the personal–emotional would characterise the stories of 1832, about marriage and relationships – *Madame Firmiani, Le Colonel Chabert, La Femme abandonnée*, and the works of 1833 and beyond, beginning with his biggest vignette of provincial constriction of natural affection, *Eugénie Grandet*. From the late 1820s, in *Les Deux rêves, Le Dernier Chouan* (of these four, the only novel), *Un épisode sous la Terreur* and *Adieu*, tales of history and revolution converge with the personal, the grand narrative with the secret history, love stories with philosophy and the fantastic, the absolute with the real. In *L'Élixir de longue vie*, the fantastic, Renaissance story of Don Bartholoméo's attempt to thwart mortality, and thereby the transmission of his biological and material inheritance, by getting his son to administer a long-life elixir at the moment of death, is married to reflections on present-day conditions of inheritance which interrupt its first edition and now form its preface. In *Sarrasine*, the phantasmagoric old man who appears at the opening turns out to be the incredible vestige of its once beautiful hero/ine, La Zambinella, a castrato opera-singer the artist Sarrasine fell in love with, believing her to be a woman. S/he, bridges, yet cruelly illuminates, the gulf between what might seem ideal and what seems real, between the spiritual and the material, as well as suggesting some very contemporary interrogations of gender.[3]

Sarrasine and *L'Élixir* are about the tipping point, the moment at which returns, family, amorous, aesthetic and/or financial, diminish or disappear. Not by accident were they written in the slipstream of the July Revolution, which instituted a bourgeois constitutional monarchy founded on imperatives of self-interest and Guizot's get-rich-quick watchword, 'Enrichissez-vous!' The three key tales of the next year, 1831, recount desires which go too far: *Le Chef-d'œuvre inconnu*, where the painter Frenhofer, who falls in love with the 'woman', 'la belle noiseuse' supposedly depicted in his artwork (a painting in which all others can see only a mess of disordered strokes, apart from a perfectly painted foot); *L'Auberge rouge*, which recounts (or rather, leaves us to infer, via incomplete information like *Sarrasine*'s) that the banker Taillefer has murdered the merchant Walhenfer for his wealth; and *La Peau de chagrin*, where an incredible premise, a wild-ass's skin which can satisfy every desire in return for a claim on its holder's life, is exploited, like the long-life elixir, as an utterly credible metaphor of what can happen when cupidity becomes too omniscient: self-negation, destruction, death. They are early warnings of capitalism's ultimate logic, at the moment of its birth.

Perhaps the main social manifestation of capitalism is individualism, the pursuit of subjective imperatives above all else. This hegemonic subjectivity is the driver both in these fantastic tales and in subsequent 1832 stories where the personal dominates, and the subjective is the common factor, the pivotal viewpoint from which all else is seen. *La Grande Bretèche*, *La Grenadière*, *Madame Firmiani*, *Le Colonel Chabert*, *Le Curé de Tours*, *La Femme abandonnée*, all tell tales of protagonists who sacrifice others or are sacrificed themselves to overweening and unconquerable desires. But one of the things which distinguish these tales from their predecessors is their dependence, for their narrative spring, on an uncertainty, and on the search for a fuller account of the facts of their situation. *Madame Firmiani* begins with speculation on the nature of its protagonist, as well as of her mysterious absent husband, before performing an act of gradual revelation – a pattern followed also in *La Grenadière*, more brutally in *La Grande Bretèche*, *Le Colonel Chabert* and *Le Curé de Tours*, which relates how a naïve priest is stripped of his home and status: both teacup-storm and earth-shattering catastrophe. *La Femme abandonnée* recounts the cool cruelty of a man's desertion of his dear, but married, mistress for a more advantageous match. These stories use similar roles (abandoned woman, absent husband, trusting priest or lover) but seen from different viewpoints, to explore situations and relationships in the round. The personal, the emotional, they seem to suggest, can be just as astonishing and unknowable as can the fantastic; the gold-standards of integrity and authenticity can be as elusive and illusory as the magic skin or the philosopher's stone.

This shift from the imaginary and/or imaginative to the emotional, from the fantastic to the real, heralds a development from stories centred essentially on the experience of single protagonists towards longer works turning more on the experience and interrelations of characters as objective social types and roles. In the novel *La Recherche de l'absolu* (1834) the scarcely credible 'science' of *L'Élixir de longue vie* or *La Peau de chagrin* is transmuted into the alchemist Claës's marginally more plausible quest for gold, recounted in terms of its ultimately tragic impact on his family (who pay the price for his obsession which, needless to say, like his predecessors', turns out to be sterile). And where his stories begin with, or depict, a problem, his novels will set out a project, and pursue it in at length in a more developed social context than is possible in stories, beginning with the problem-novel *La Peau de chagrin: Histoire des Treize*, *Eugénie Grandet*, *La Recherche de l'absolu*, all demonstrate that projects, personal, philosophical or social, can be more protracted, more complete, and just as catastrophic as the problems of his stories.

But it is, of course, not just, or at all, as forerunners of his novels that Balzac's stories are important. They are, crucially, significant in their own right, representing centres of investigation, viewpoints on society, presenting the actors of Balzac's *Comédie* but seen, importantly, from the outside, from the collective perspective, as social types or figures on its stage. One of the striking things about Balzac's stories, certainly pre-*Goriot*, is how very few are first-person narratives,[4] and how, even in those which are, the narrator is a quasi-authorial observer, a spectator or even eavesdropper, avid for information, for knowledge about the world he is describing, an outsider, like the reader, dying to be in the know. Both first and third-person narrators treat people from the outside as enigmas which may or may not be solved: the old man who was apparently a female, La Zambinella *(Sarrasine)*, Mme de Dey

(*Le Réquisitionnaire*), Stéphanie, the deranged heroine of *Adieu*[5] who has lost her mind in Napoleon's retreat from Moscow, the mysterious storyteller Hermann (*L'Auberge rouge*), Madame Firmiani, Colonel Chabert, later Facino Cane or Diane de Cadignan in the stories which bear their names. The real is a mystery inviting speculation which may, or may not, pay off.

For all this general externality and supposed authority of perspective, Balzac's stories do not deliver complete *ex cathedra* truths or unproblematic facts about characters or situations, the 'real causes of events' promised by Herrera/Vautrin/Collin (*Illusions perdues*, CH V 695). Their perceptions are fragmentary, leaving the reader to piece together such coherence as he or she can. We reach the end of *Sarrasine* having linked the extravagant old (wo-) man of the opening and the beautiful castrato at its core, but we are less certain of whether Balzac might be identified with the narrator or even Sarrasine, any more than we could prove Taillefer's guilt in *L'Auberge rouge*.[6] We build some sort of picture of Madame Firmiani from the viewpoints of sixteen different social types (CH II 142–147), yet we never really discover what she has done with her absent, unseen husband, 'le problématique Firmiani' (CH II 151). After initial scepticism, we do find out about her male analogue, the destitute old soldier who turns up one day at the lawyer Derville's chambers, claiming to be the Napoleonic Colonel Chabert, come back from his presumed grave to reclaim his sometime wife and supposed widow, since advantageously remarried. But the truth revealed turns out to concern not his identity (which is authentic), but society's management and reconfiguration, thereof. It is throughout a matter of obliteration and rewriting, of telling, and retelling, the latest, politically correct (politically conformist) version of the story, in line with the shifting historical goalposts of the Bourbon Restoration, from the lawyer's clerks' initial drafting of Louis XVIII's edict restituting property to Royalist émigrés (and dispossessing Imperial beneficiaries like Chabert) to Chabert's final self-deletion in the madhouse, crossing out his name on the ground, crying 'Pas Chabert! pas Chabert!' [Not Chabert! not Chabert!'] (CH III 372).

This centrality and relativity of perspective highlights a crucial paradox in Balzac's creation, one fundamental to its genesis, suggestiveness and effect. It aspires, from its inception, to an absolute: philosophical, from Balzac's teens, and from his maturity a philosophically underpinned, yet totalising mimetic absolute, aspiring to a complete description of, and for, contemporary society. The 1830 *Scènes de la vie privée* are written 'in hatred of the silly books [moral tales] which mean spirits have presented to women to this day' ['en haine des sots livres que des esprits mesquins ont présentés aux femmes jusqu'à ce jour'] (CH I 1173), initiating the *scène* as the dominant taxonomic category of *La Comédie humaine*. The *Contes drolatiques* (1831, 1833, 1837) replicate Renaissance tales, attempting to reanimate a kind of Gallic 'merrie France'; yet Balzac completed only three of the ten cycles initially envisaged, just as he finished only two-thirds of the works planned for *La Comédie humaine*. From early on, Balzac's projects were marked out as and conceived as systems of stories. Balzac's enterprises – *scènes, dixains, Comédie* – have the merit of aspiring to some formal shape, logic and coherence in the otherwise often-chaotic cacophony of the *folie du conte*. In trying to show contemporaries as others saw them, to 'tell Roman life to the Romans' ['raconter la vie romaine aux Romains'] (*Une fille d'Ève*, preface, CH II 267), they sought a necessary estrangement and objectification of the familiar, and a resultant intensification of perception. Yet the pattern of comparison and contrast, of action and reaction which makes Balzac create Chabert as a mirror-image of Firmiani, Goriot as the angelic opposite of the deadly Grandet, or *César Birotteau* as the novel twin of the story *La Maison Nucingen*, if it describes and to some extent explains a process of conception and composition, never completes the longed-for whole. *Le Colonel Chabert* and *Madame Firmiani*, *Eugénie Grandet* and *Le Père Goriot*, *César Birotteau* and *La Maison Nucingen* do not, cannot give us the whole story, because the whole story could not, cannot, be given. The very suggestiveness of *La Comédie humaine* lies in its uncompleted vistas, its unintended poetry, in what we might speculate and imagine about the regions never written about and which we therefore cannot visit, as much as in the pleasures of discovering those we can.

Interweaving Characters and Narratives: *Le Père Goriot*, Convention and Watershed, 1835–39

Another way of understanding the issues of completeness, coherence and wholeness is via the relevant compositional processes, which involve narrating the tales of one or more main characters, either in single narratives or stories or incorporated into a novel. *La Peau de chagrin* has one protagonist, Raphaël; *Eugénie Grandet*, Balzac's first widely read and successful realist novel, interweaves the tales of two, Eugénie and her miser father (with her cousin Charles as the transient catalyst who seduces her and her fortune). *Le Père Goriot* combines three, Goriot, Rastignac and Vautrin. Yet, despite their relative self-containedness, these novels are not complete in themselves. *Eugénie Grandet* finishes with a shortfall, an incompletion rather like Chabert's, if differently configured: Eugénie ends up without Charles, living out the lonely existence pre-programmed by her father. *Le Père Goriot* closes with Rastignac's ambiguous challenge to the city he wants to conquer: 'It is down to the two of us now!' ['À nous deux maintenant!'] – Rastignac and

Paris? Or Delphine? (CH III 290) It is an end more like a beginning: Rastignac's story, and those of others (Vautrin, Bianchon, Mmes de Beauséant, Restaud and Nucingen, those of Nucingen himself) must be told elsewhere.

Le Père Goriot is a convention, a gathering of characters whose stories have already been told in previous tales of La Comédie humaine (Mme de Restaud's in Gobseck, Rastignac's in Étude de femme) or which have yet to be related. Creatively, Le Père Goriot is a watershed, initiating the systematic use of characters who will recur in other fictions. Some of them are retreads – the first, indeed, is Mme de Beauséant, who gains this name on folio 17 of the manuscript, replacing a hitherto anonymous marquise. Mme de Beauséant's reappearance here, following her star role in La Femme abandonnée, is thus a convenient post-rationalisation; more substantial characters, Bianchon, Nucingen, Vautrin, were still awaiting the telling of their tales in La Messe de l'athée; La Maison Nucingen, Illusions perdues and Splendeurs et misères.

The impact of Balzac's innovation was radical. From being largely centripetal, turned inward upon themselves in terms of character, subject and event, Balzac's fictions gradually became more, and also centrifugal, drawn outward by the gravitational forces of centres of interest in his other fictions. From 1835 and Le Père Goriot, Balzac's stories (and some novels: La Muse du département, for example) become as much a question of playing catch-up with figures who previously had only passing mentions or walk-on parts; a matter of filling the gaps, of telling the stories of hitherto bit-players, or having them tell the stories themselves. La Fille aux yeux d'or and Le Contrat de mariage (1834–35) do this symmetrically, in a way similar to Grandet and Goriot, as opposing instances of virtue and vice, naivety and knowingness: de Marsay appears, breathless after a torrid gender-bending adventure with Paquita, to counsel the respectable Manerville on marriage. But La Messe de l'athée with L'Interdiction (both 1836) will be the first Comédie humaine tales to use established characters and their narratives within the story to inflect the course of the action. In the first, Bianchon recounts seeing his medical mentor, Dupuytren, secretly attending Mass. Like other stories of 1836–39, it deals with dichotomy and paradox: the atheist in quest of transcendence; musical idealists, Gambara, Massimilla Doni, limited by the constraints of the material; a former potentate, Facino Cane, reduced to begging in a bar; a mediocre artist, Pierre Grassou, outstripping aesthetically superior peers. All these names are tales, and every tale is a question answered, at least in part. In L'Interdiction, Dr Bianchon and Rastignac (who already met as students in Goriot) take Bianchon's uncle Judge Popinot to hear the society lady Madame d'Espard's claims that her estranged husband is mad.[7] When the honest Popinot tells d'Espard of his wife's slander, he is replaced by another judge, Camusot. By the end of *L'Interdiction*, Mme d'Espard seems to have won, but we have to wait until part I of *Splendeurs et misères* (1843), where Camusot plays a major role, to learn the final outcome: that her husband has been acquitted.

It is no doubt *La Maison Nucingen* (1838) which most effectively reconciles the roles of answering questions and acknowledging the implications, role and importance of stories, and the tales it, and society, tells. But as well as recounting how Nucingen made his fortune, *La Maison Nucingen* reveals a more cynical Rastignac than the relatively innocent one of *Goriot*, and a whole network of speculation driven by communication, gossip and covert conversations. More fundamentally, it illustrates that all narrative is a matter of perspective, delivered and/or perceived from one viewpoint which, in relation to all others, is necessarily oblique – here, the private room in which Nucingen's (and other) stories are told by people including Finot, Blondet, the financier Couture and Balzac's fictional caricaturist, Bixiou. At the end, Finot realises that there were people overhearing next door. But, as Bixiou ripostes, there are always people next door – that is, with other angles from which stories can be heard or told.

Stories are indissociable from the trajectories of Balzac's characters; they take their tales and histories with them, but also leave narrative traces behind. These features, along with the inevitable partiality and incompletion of perspective, are recognised by Balzac's preface to the 1839 story *Une fille d'Ève*. Balzac warns us that we will encounter some characters in mid-life, others at their beginnings, that we will have the middle of a life before its beginning, or the death before the birth. This is because, he says, it is thus in real society, where we may meet someone we have not seen for a decade who will recount the vivid history of the intervening years. Sometimes the history will come in bits, the next day or even a month later. 'Nothing is of a single piece in this world, everything is a mosaic. You can only recount chronologically the history of the past, a system inapplicable to a present which is on the move' ['Il n'y a rien qui soit d'un seul bloc en ce monde, tout y est mosaïque. Vous ne pouvez raconter chronologiquement que l'histoire du temps passé, système inapplicable à un présent qui marche'] (CH II 265). This is why Balzac's fictions do not give us potted biographies like Rastignac's, uniquely (if ironically) vouchsafed us in this preface (CH II 265–266): life is not lived or experienced, and therefore cannot necessarily best be recounted, diachronically.

Serialisation and Storytelling, 1836–45

There are also, however, other, more practical publishing (commercial and compositional) reasons why Balzac's later stories assume the forms and content they do.[8] In 1836, Balzac's *La Vieille fille* had pioneered newspaper novel-serialisation in Émile de Girardin's broadsheet *La Presse*. Girardin introduced fiction as a way of selling papers across political boundaries, enlarging markets by transcending readers' ideological allegiances. With its graphic account of its protagonist's sexual frustrations, Balzac's novel was a *succès de scandale*; *La Maison Nucingen* was supposedly a milder successor, and between 1836 and 1841 Balzac produced a number of longer stories or short novels recounting near-miss love affairs which tease and test the boundaries of conventional morality, if not beyond repair. In *Une fille d'Ève*, Marie de Vandenesse is taken to the edge of adultery with the disreputable journalist Nathan, but is saved by a combination of her husband's generosity (monetary and moral) and the jealousy of Nathan's mistress Florine. In *La Fausse maîtresse* (1841), Laginski's factotum Paz conceals his passionate love for Laginski's wife Clémentine by a feigned affair with a horsewoman, Malaga, even allowing Clémentine to assume that Laginski's debts are his own, run up with this false mistress, in order to protect his master, enduring Clémentine's opprobrium when she discovers and dismisses him. Paz obeys, but not before sending her a letter revealing his passion and his motives, and he remains secretly to watch over her and save her from a later crisis which leaves her longing for the man, Paz, who has shown complete integrity and never broken any moral law.

In presenting partial, unrealised or transcended love affairs, these novellas correspond to the logic of Balzac's post-*Goriot* stories, in which there can never really be an ending, and there are always other stories. Events and individuals are often subject to a degree of remote or invisible control, paying lip service to an ostensible morality covering the latent passion beneath. But they also answer the needs of a significantly female readership seeking the novelistic *frisson*, the fantasy absent from their lives which Flaubert's Emma Bovary would try to realise. The six- to eight-instalment fictions prevalent in newspapers between *La Vieille fille* and the advent of the full-blown serialised novel with Sue's *Les Mystères de Paris* (1842–43) attempt to swell the quintessentially Romantic, feminine novella into novel forms of reality: witness Balzac's short novel *Albert Savarus* and his long story *Honorine* (1842, 1843), whose protagonists spin various yarns in ultimately futile quests to seduce and secure those whom they love, but cannot have.

The convergence of publishing imperative and creation, almost heedless of readership and largely centred on Balzac's world, is best exemplified by his

1843 story *Autre étude de femme*. Assembled mainly from tales and pen-portraits earlier published as framed narratives or articles in other serialised enterprises, like the panoramic collections of pictures of contemporary social types, *Les Français peints par eux-mêmes*, *Autre étude*, on one level, makes a virtue of necessity – filling volume II of *La Comédie humaine*, which had itself begun, from April 1842, to appear in instalments, rather like a newspaper or *Les Français* itself. Yet *Autre étude de femme* also confirms something more fundamental about narratives, especially Balzac's short narratives: that they are in fact cycles of stories, told by characters who, by this point in Balzac's creation, by dint of their many reappearances, have assumed substance and standing in a world which, in its own time, paralleled the real one, and for posterity, has largely replaced it. By *Autre étude de femme*, Balzac's world has become so 'centrifugal' that only its characters and character-narrators can hold it together; the authorial narrator is like an unseen camera, filming others who have now completely achieved the ability to act and speak in their own right.

This centrifugalism reaches a climax with the late tales *Un homme d'affaires* (1844) and *Les Comédiens sans le savoir* (1845). The first is a fiction of almost impenetrable complexity, indissociable from its subject, the arcana of commerce. But instead of merely recounting that complexity (as does, for example, *La Maison Nucingen*), *Un homme d'affaires* leads us to experience it – to run our heads against the brick wall of incomprehension which we may also meet when presented with the misbehaviour of opaque insider traders. *Les Comédiens sans le savoir* is less interstitial than its predecessor: a place of encounter, like the Pension Vauquer, the floor of the Bourse or the Bal de l'Opéra (depicted by Balzac in the closely contemporary *Splendeurs et misères*), but better adapted, like *Splendeurs* itself, to the linear organisation of the organ in which it appeared, the *feuilleton*. The premise, an exploration of Paris by a provincial, Gazonal, as he encounters a series of Parisian types, replicates the process of wandering. The 'plot' is simply a matter of chance encounter, thereby expressing a reality of urban life. *Les Comédiens sans le savoir* also realises, perhaps more than any of Balzac's previous narratives, the dramatic potential present in embryo in his first *Scènes*. It is a script more than a story, its personnel more or less free agents, apparently unbound by any detectable authorial agenda other than to let them speak and be. As its title implies, *Les Comédiens sans le savoir* is about the spectacle, instruction and amusement we may unconsciously provide for others, its dialogue reminding us that *La Comédie humaine* is a conversation as much as a drama, its players also free agents who act and react on reality's great stage.

Short(er) Fiction and *La Comédie humaine*

Balzac's shorter fictions are the most dialogic element in his output, or perhaps rather, the element which is most central to the dialogic, to the multiplicity of perspectives which makes up and characterises *La Comédie humaine*. His *Comédie* both is and is more than the sum of its narratives, whether shorter fiction or novels; it could be read mechanically, starting at the beginning, with a story (an emblematic, artist/aristocrat-versus-bourgeois drama), *La Maison du chat-qui-pelote*, and ending with *La Comédie humaine*'s final work, which is in many ways a string of anecdotes, *Petites misères de la vie conjugale*, whose elongation shows the limits beyond which short fiction cannot satisfactorily be stretched in newspaper-serialised publication.

The *Petites misères* illustrate why *La Comédie humaine* was not and could never have been seamless or continuous, unproblematically diachronic, a single narrative, or simple story; the early project for an *Histoire de France pittoresque* on this model, with a novel for each century, was soon abandoned, doubtless for this amongst other reasons. It is true that the 'Avant-propos' falls back towards its end, on a rationale which is vestigially diachronic (each of the series of *Scènes* 'formulating an era of human life' ['formule une époque de la vie humaine'], beginning with childhood and adolescence in the *Scènes de la vie privée*: CH I 18) before moving to a more thematic organisation. But the 'Avant-propos' actually gives no indication of the order in which *La Comédie* should be read, beyond that in which it is presented, and the real key to reading it is doubtless provided by that preface to *Une fille d'Ève*: 'il n'y a rien qui soit d'un seul bloc en ce monde, tout y est mosaïque'. Short(er) narrative is the fundamental organising principle of *La Comédie humaine*, which depends centrally for its effect on relativity of perspective and perception, and on each narrative's being relatively shorter than the others, and smaller or more exiguous than the whole. That whole, the 'tout', makes a picture; but the picture is a mosaic, with all that implies in terms of fragmentations, divisions, and boundaries, parts and wholes and (in)completion, and Balzac's model is the nineteenth century, a model which is extremely mobile and difficult to keep in place (CH II 265).

Balzac revisits this image of mobility in three dimensions in the 'Avant-propos'. The sentence which begins 'In reading attentively the table of society' ['En lisant attentivement le tableau de la Société'] presents a two-dimensional table (or, implicitly, picture: the French is suggestive, if not ambiguous) of Society (Balzac's capital letter indicating, like his creation, very much High Society) which is 'cast from life' ['moulée sur le vif'] (CH I 12), and where passion is both the binding social element and the agent of destruction. What this means for *La Comédie humaine* overall is that its fundamental organising principle is not diachronic or thematic, but narrative; and this principle is most original, intense and quintessential in brief narrative. Balzac's shorter fictions are characterised, more than the novels, by the ways in which the loop between passion as creation and passion as destruction is short-circuited, and their habit of returning, revisiting and reconfiguring the present in the light of the past before propelling their victims into a future often hobbled by the dead weight of previous deeds. *Sarrasine* and *Le Colonel Chabert* would be key examples, but there are others,[9] including *La Peau de chagrin*, where a flashback structure creates a compression akin to brief narrative. There is no Balzac protagonist who is not as much in thrall to past misdeeds and mishaps as potentially freed by chance.

Balzac's shorter fiction is, then, the fundamental organising principle of his creation. His stories are concentrates of tensions unleashed and expanded in his longer narratives. They can be anthologised as quintessences of a larger world, as in Paul Bourget's headily distilled 1907 selection, which stresses the standing of Balzac's stories as the equal of his novels, his mastery at compressing terror into a second, or Alan Raitt's soberer 1964 anthology, both worth consulting, like the more recent translation collections of Peter Collier and Peter Brooks.[10] They can be gathered in compendious collections,[11] or, as single pieces, dismembered, most microscopically by Roland Barthes,[12] but never put to death. Pierre Laforgue sees them as manifestations of Romantic eros; Scott Carpenter as traces of excess; Max Andréoli, *La Maison du chat-qui-pelote* as a rebus; Owen Heathcote as expressions of violence; Diana Knight the artist stories as critique of prostitution.[13] There is no end to their resonance.

Two J's – journalism and Henry James, one of the most percipient critics of French literature – perhaps best summarise the vital dichotomies and paradoxes of Balzac's work. James noted in Balzac something visceral and fundamental: 'Balzac affects us ... as personally overtaken by life, as fairly hunted and run to earth by it';[14] and this is most manifest in the stories, because they deal first-hand with raw passions, concentrating within limited confines, and more than longer fictions, on pointful, dramatic events. If scenes of conflict loom throughout Balzac's novels, themselves structured by lay-lines of hostility with the clash of opposing camps of characters writ large, these moments of confrontation are found in essence in the stories, not, in fact, reduced or distilled, but stated in the simplest form, from which the novels will be expanded. And it is the characteristic of Balzac's stories to allow wider perspectives and bigger questions to be intuited, even before the conception of the larger series – the *Études de mœurs*, the *Études philosophiques*, the never realised *Études de femmes* or *Études sociales* – of which they would be but part.

Balzac's stories have a way of punching above their weight which can be traced back to their origin in his youthful philosophical questing, less as exempla than as speculations on the key dilemmas at stake. So there is hardly a Balzac story which is not riven by such themes; however you sample them, the geno- (and pheno-) type appears. As Baudelaire observed, 'everyone in Balzac, even the concierges, is touched with genius' ['chacun, chez Balzac, même les portières, a du génie'];[15] but his remark could be extended to cover almost everything in his work. In *Le Réquisitionnaire*, a Royalist aristocrat, Mme de Dey, dies at the very moment her son is executed many leagues away; the microcosm always hints at a bigger picture, 'a whole world in a prodigiously exiguous summary of space and time' ['tout un monde dans un raccourci prodigieusement exigu d'espace et de matière'].[16] We are told all we need to know, and yet left wanting more. The isolated, but perfectly painted foot which ends *Le Chef-d'oeuvre inconnu* speaks volumes on unrequited ambition and desire. In *La Grande Bretèche* (1832), now part of *Autre étude de femme*, the husband's final reminder to his wife, whose lover he has had walled into a cupboard, 'You swore on the cross that there was nobody there' ['Vous avez juré sur la croix qu'il n'y avait là personne'] (CH III 729), is both factually accurate and morally abominable. The literalism of his utterance is juxtaposed to the infinity of her love, and to the paradoxically Christ-like selflessness of the woman who, to stay true to her own heart, bore false witness. Marsay's flippant closing verdict on Paquita, 'She died.... Of her breast' ['Elle est morte.... De la poitrine'] (CH V 1109) – supposedly of tuberculosis, but in fact by her lesbian lover Mariquita's dagger – shrinks the immensity of passion to a mammary, revealing its own horrific misogyny, the unspeakable inhumanity of reducing a human being to a thing. Balzac's stories embody, more intensely than any other part of his creation, the electric resonance of the real, and the fundamental perceptual link between short and long, small and large: the principle that for any one of us, like *Le Lys dans la vallée*'s Mme de Mortsauf, an unknown private battle can be 'peut-être aussi grande que la plus illustre des batailles connues' ('Avant-propos', CH I 17).

It is (*pace* James) a journalist, Nicholas Lezard, who hits the nail most firmly on the head. Commenting on Peter Brooks' selection of Balzac's stories, having sympathised with those daunted by the idea of reading *La Comédie humaine*, he proffers the tales as an elegant solution, providing 'a thorough feeling for the joys of Balzac ... without the massive digressions that can clog up longer works ... You get the sense that you are reading an undeceived, undeceivable adult – albeit one with a highly developed sense of the melodramatic, and of the potency of story itself ... never a dull moment, with ruin or scandal always but a step away ... And the great thing about work this entertaining is that it's still exciting nearly 200 years on. It isn't just a bridge, it's a fully functioning time machine. I strongly recommend you hop on'.[17]

It's hard to disagree with that (or with Lezard's designation of Brooks's selection of Balzac stories as an excellent way in). But one could add that the stories are not just an appetiser for the Gargantuan *plats* of the novels, fit for the gigantic appetites of Rabelais's hero, but the very quintessence of Balzac's opus: the surest, purest formulation of a creation which, if it is anything, is above all a Glory of Stories.

NOTES

1. Essentially, but not exclusively, in broadly chronological order: *Les Deux rêves, La Maison du chat-qui-pelote, La Paix du ménage, El Verdugo, Le Bal de Sceaux, La Vendetta, Gobseck, Étude de femme, Une double famille, Adieu, L'Élixir de longue vie, Sarrasine, Une passion dans le désert, Un épisode sous la Terreur, Le Réquisitionnaire, L'Auberge rouge, Les Proscrits, Maître Cornélius, Jésus-Christ en Flandre, Le Chef-d'œuvre inconnu, Le Message, Madame Firmiani, Le Colonel Chabert, Le Curé de Tours, La Bourse, La Grenadière, La Femme abandonnée, Les Marana, La Grande Bretèche, L'Illustre Gaudissart, Un drame au bord de la mer, Melmoth réconcilié, La Fille aux yeux d'or, La Messe de l'athée, L'Interdiction, Facino Cane, La Confidence des Ruggieri, Pierre Grassou, Gambara, La Maison Nucingen, Massimilla Doni, Les Secrets de la princesse de Cadignan, Un prince de la bohème, Z. Marcas, La Fausse maîtresse, Une fille d'Ève, Honorine, Autre étude de femme, Gaudissart II, Les Comédiens sans le savoir, Un homme d'affaires*.
2. For a fuller explanation of the rationale for this choice, see T. Farrant, *Balzac's Shorter Fictions: Genesis and Genre* (Oxford University Press, 2002).
3. See Dorothy Kelly's chapter in this volume.
4. The exceptions are: *Les Deux rêves* (now part III of *Sur Catherine de Médicis*), *Sarrasine, L'Auberge rouge, Le Message, Un drame au bord de la mer, La Maison Nucingen* (first-person plural – the narrator and his (unnamed) companion overhearing, and therefore framing, a conversation between Finot, Blondet, Couture and Bixiou), *Z. Marcas*, although a number contain framed first-person narratives (*Gobseck, Le Colonel Chabert, Honorine* and, most memorably, *Autre étude de femme*, which incorporates earlier first-person narratives (notably *La Grande Bretèche*)).
5. See S. Felman, *La Folie et la chose littéraire* (Paris: Seuil, 1978).
6. See P. Citron, 'Interprétation de *Sarrasine*', AB 1972, 81–95; D. Kelly, 'Balzac's *L'Auberge rouge*: on reading an ambiguous text', *Symposium*, 36 (1986), 32–44.
7. Cf. A. Mikhalevitch, *Balzac et Bianchon* (Paris: Champion, 2014).
8. Cf. M.-È. Thérenty, *Mosaïques: être écrivain entre presse et roman, 1829–1836* (Paris: Champion, 2003), pp. 587 et seq.

9. *Le Réquisitionnaire, Un drame au bord de la mer, La Messe de l'athée, Facino Cane.*
10. H. de Balzac, *Contes choisis*, intr. P. Bourget (London: J.M. Dent & Co.; New York: G.P. Putnam's Sons, 1907); H. de Balzac, *Short Stories*, ed. A. Raitt (Oxford University Press, 1964); *The Girl with the Golden Eyes and other stories*, intr. P. Coleman, trans. P. Collier (Oxford World's Classics, 2012); *The Human Comedy: Selected Stories of Honoré de Balzac*, intr. P. Brooks, trans. L. Asher, C. Cosman and J. Stump (New York: N.Y.R.B. Books, 2014).
11. I. Tournier (ed.), H. de Balzac, *Nouvelles et contes* I 1820–1832, II 1832–1850 (Paris: Gallimard, 'Quarto', 2005, 2006); F. Lacassin, *La Comédie des ténèbres* (Paris: Omnibus, 2006).
12. In *S/Z* (Paris: Seuil, 1970), an unremitting (if supremely insightful) dissection of the mechanisms of this (and purportedly) any narrative. Barthes's analysis, like Citron's 'Interprétation de *Sarrasine*', was inspired by J. Reboul's essay 'Sarrasine ou la castration personnifiée' (*Cahiers pour l'analyse*, 7.5 (March–April 1967), 91–96).
13. M. Andréoli, 'Une nouvelle de Balzac: *La Maison du chat-qui-pelote*', AB 1972, 41–80; P. Laforgue, *L'Éros romantique: représentations de l'amour en 1830* (Paris: Presses universitaires de France, 1998); O. Heathcote, *Balzac and Violence: Representing History, Space, Sexuality and Death in 'La Comédie humaine'* (Oxford: Peter Lang, 2009); D. Knight, *Balzac and the Model of Painting: Artist Stories in 'La Comédie humaine'* (London: Legenda, 2007).
14. H. James, 'Émile Zola', *The Atlantic Monthly*, August 1903, 193–210 (p. 208).
15. C. Baudelaire, 'Théophile Gautier [I]' in C. Pichois and J. Ziegler (eds), *Œuvres complètes*, 2 vols (Paris: Gallimard, 'Pléiade', 1975–76), vol. II, p. 120.
16. Bourget (intr.), Balzac, *Contes choisis*, p. xv; Raitt (ed.), Balzac, *Short Stories*, p. 61.
17. 'The Human Comedy: Selected Stories by Honoré de Balzac', *The Guardian*, 25 March 2014. [accessible on line via: www.theguardian.com/books/2014/mar/25/human-comedy-balzac-review-nicholas-lezard; consulted 5 October 2015].

11

ANDREW WATTS

Adapting Balzac

Adaptations of Balzac's work have a long history. During the author's lifetime, many of his novels and short stories were adapted for the Parisian stage, and often enjoyed considerable popularity. In January 1835, the Théâtre du Gymnase presented a highly successful version of *Eugénie Grandet* under the title *La Fille de l'avare*, which ran for more than 300 performances. In April 1835, the Théâtre des Variétés and the Théâtre du Vaudeville both staged versions of *Le Père Goriot*, barely a month after the first complete edition of the novel had gone on sale. For Balzac, adaptations such as these proved both a blessing and a curse. On the one hand, they served as valuable promotional vehicles for his work. On the other hand, the inadequacy of early nineteenth-century copyright law meant that these plays were usually staged without his permission, and he earned no money from them. Given his own ambitions to succeed as a playwright, and the financial debts against which he struggled for most of his adult life, it is not surprising that Balzac was largely contemptuous of the practice of theatrical adaptation, which he denounced as a blatant violation of an author's intellectual property.[1]

Adaptations of Balzac nevertheless extend well beyond the confines of the stage. Since the nineteenth century, recreations and 're-imaginings' of his texts have proliferated in different media, most notably film, television and radio. Drawing on case studies from each of these three media, this chapter examines the key artistic and commercial imperatives that have driven this ongoing fascination with *La Comédie humaine*. In addition to explaining why Balzac continues to inspire new adaptive projects, one of the aims here is to challenge some of the negative critical stereotypes surrounding re-inventions of his work. Often derided for their supposed mediocrity, or labelled inferior to their prestigious source material, adaptations of Balzac can appear as richly complex works of art which engage both with the possibilities and constraints of their own media, and with the ideological concerns of their time. Equally, they can help us to explore aspects of *La Comédie humaine* that critics have frequently overlooked or neglected. This is particularly true in the case of radio, a medium that proves well equipped to emphasise the importance of sound to Balzac's depiction of French society. While standing as artistic achievements in their own right, many of these adaptations invite us to think about Balzac in new ways, and in so doing deepen our understanding of his work. Moreover, the vibrancy of adaptation studies as an academic discipline renders a fresh appraisal of adaptive interest in Balzac both necessary and timely. Over the past ten years, a growing number of scholars – among them Deborah Cartmell, Linda Hutcheon, Thomas Leitch, Julie Sanders and Imelda Whelehan – have argued compellingly that adaptation warrants greater study as a unique form of creative expression. Moving away from an earlier tradition of fidelity criticism, which judged adaptations according to how closely they resembled their source texts, research in this area has focused increasingly on why certain authors prove so adaptable, and what recreations of their work can tell us about the richness of adaptation as an artistic process.

Balzac and Cinema

From the short films of the silent era to the lavish Hollywood productions of more recent times, cinema's love affair with Balzac is an enduring one. Many of the novelist's most celebrated works – and others that are not so well known – have been adapted for the big screen, often on more than one occasion. To date, there have been at least thirteen different versions of *La Peau de chagrin*, eleven of which have been produced outside of France, and no fewer than seven films based on *La Duchesse de Langeais*. The reasons for which filmmakers have shown such enthusiasm for adapting Balzac are varied. Some, of course, have been motivated primarily by commercial gain. As a classic nineteenth-century novelist, Balzac has a name capable of attracting audiences and generating box office revenues. Others have identified his work as a hallmark of artistic excellence and cultural prestige, and adapted him in the hope that these associations might rub off on their own creative output – a concern that was especially prominent among early cinematographers as they struggled to establish their new medium. Perhaps most importantly, however, successive generations of filmmakers have considered Balzac's work tailor-made for the big screen. His fiction abounds in captivating stories, dramatic situations and memorable characters. Moreover, as Anne-Marie Baron has shown, his realism is infused with an acute visual sensibility – a probing attentiveness to the way people and places look – that lends itself readily to cinema.[2] Not only does Balzac tell great stories, he tells them in a way that invites us to see them unfolding in our mind's eye. It is by no means surprising, then, that his work has continued to resonate so strongly with filmmakers. As director Max de Rieux summarised in 1928 while completing his version of *La Cousine Bette*, *La Comédie humaine* appears as 'a long screenplay filled with riches' ['un long scénario plein de richesses'],[3] a corpus of material with inbuilt cinematic potential.

Silent filmmakers were quick to recognise the artistic and commercial possibilities of adapting Balzac. Between 1906 and the onset of sound film in 1927, at least eighty-two such adaptations were either produced or planned in Europe and North America. Studios in France, Germany and Italy were responsible for the majority of these films. However, as cinema hungered for new scripts and narrative material, the vogue for adapting Balzac also spread to Hollywood. In 1921, Metro Pictures (subsequently Metro-Goldwyn-Mayer) released *The Conquering Power*, a reworking of *Eugénie Grandet* directed by Rex Ingram, starring Rudolph Valentino. With a screenplay by June Mathis, who had worked previously with Ingram on *The Four Horsemen of the Apocalypse* (1921), *The Conquering Power* presented itself as a modernisation of Balzac's novel. Accordingly, Valentino's Charles Grandet arrives in Saumur in a chauffeur-driven sedan and wearing an elegant travelling suit, elements which reflect the actor's own playboy reputation and growing star status at this time.

Mathis's screenplay also makes numerous changes to Balzac's plot. The most significant of these comes at the end of the film, where in deference to the Hollywood requirement of a happy ending, Charles returns from Martinique to ask for Eugénie's hand in marriage. It is also in its creative departures from the source text, however, that *The Conquering Power* reveals its innovativeness. Among the most memorable sequences in the film, and one which again has no equivalent in the novel, is the scene in which Grandet's coins take on the form of a living creature. As the old miser tries desperately to escape his strongroom, this monstrous personification of gold warns 'now you are mine!', before the walls of the room close in and Grandet is buried beneath his fortune. Though *The Conquering Power* takes considerable liberties with its literary source, ultimately the film delivers a warning about the destructive power of money that echoes Balzac's pessimistic vision in *Eugénie Grandet*.

In contrast to their North American counterparts, silent filmmakers in France were often cautious in adapting Balzac. Mindful of the author's cultural importance, they tended to adopt fidelity as their guiding principle. However, this desire to remain faithful to their source material was by no means incompatible with creative experiment, as Jean Epstein demonstrated in his 1923 adaptation of *L'Auberge rouge*. Epstein had never adapted a literary text before alighting on Balzac's short story, which he felt would enable him to reach a large audience and, more importantly, showcase the

Figure 2: Rudolph Valentino (Charles) with Alice Terry (Eugénie) in *The Conquering Power* (1921, dir. R. Ingram).

technical possibilities of his medium. The opening sequence of the film illustrates neatly the director's adaptive method. Introducing each of the guests at a Paris dinner party, Epstein manoeuvres his camera around the table in a circular motion before contemplating the scene from above. This technique represented a significant innovation compared to earlier silent films, which traditionally were shot with a camera facing the actors and fixed in one position.

Epstein's ambition, however, was not simply to cause spectators to marvel at his dexterity as a filmmaker. He also wished to demonstrate that Balzac's narrative could be expressed in uniquely cinematic language. This aim is reflected in the sequence in which the film's protagonist, Prosper Magnan (played by Léon Mathot), is tempted to murder the wealthy diamond merchant with whom he and his friend Taillefer are sharing a room. As Magnan wrestles with his conscience, a thunderstorm drenches the eponymous inn with rain. Created in the studio with thousands of gallons of water provided by the Paris fire brigade, this storm functions as the visual centrepiece of the film. However, the effect on screen proves as intricate as it is spectacular. Linking the thunderstorm outside with the storm that has erupted in Magnan's head, Epstein's final edit cuts in an image of diamonds falling like drops of rain. A further series of shots proceeds to emphasise the young man's murderous thoughts, as bolts of lightning slash across the screen.[4] As well as rivalling the special effects beloved of early North American filmmakers, with *L'Auberge rouge* Epstein showed that silent film was eminently capable of rendering the psychological complexities of the Balzacian text.

As silent cinema gave way to sound film after 1927, Balzac seemed to fall out of fashion with French filmmakers, who increasingly turned away from literary texts in favour of scripts that dealt with contemporary subject matter. The outbreak of the Second World War and the subsequent German Occupation nevertheless re-ignited cinematic interest in *La Comédie humaine*. Between 1940 and 1944, seven film versions of Balzac appeared in France, making him the most adapted author of the Occupation after Georges Simenon.[5] The majority of these productions, which included reworkings of *La Duchesse de Langeais* (1942), *Le Colonel Chabert* (1943) and *La Rabouilleuse* (1944), were period costume dramas. Only two – André Cayatte's *La Fausse maîtresse* (1942) and Pierre Blanchar's *Un seul amour* (1943), based on the short story *La Grande Bretèche* – re-situated Balzac in a contemporary setting. Most of these films also performed well at the French box office, especially Jacques de Baroncelli's *La Duchesse de Langeais*, which boasted a screenplay by the celebrated playwright Jean Giraudoux. Critics nevertheless remain divided as to why French filmmakers embraced *La Comédie humaine* so enthusiastically during this period. According to Jacques Siclier, adaptations of classic plays and novels were more likely to evade censorship because they appeared far removed from the concerns of the early 1940s, and therefore were not considered a threat by the German occupiers or the Vichy government.[6] Jean Tulard, on the other hand, claims that Balzac's popularity with both audiences and filmmakers was driven by a desire to escape the grim reality of everyday life under the Occupation. For many, Balzac offered a reassertion of French culture in the face of Nazi oppression.

This escapist impulse is evident in Robert Vernay's adaptation of *Le Père Goriot*. Made in 1944 but not released until 1945, Vernay's film seeks to dazzle audiences with lavish costumes and interiors emphasising the privileged lifestyle enjoyed by Balzac's fictional aristocrats. In his sequences depicting the homes of Madame de Beauséant and Madame de Restaud, the director employs a series of high- and wide-angle shots which invite us to contemplate the chandeliers, fine glassware and vast polished floors. Moreover, the film eschews some of the bleaker moments in the source text, most notably Goriot's burial at Père Lachaise. Unlike the novel, Vernay's adaptation ends with the glamorous spectacle of a high-society ball, where Rastignac waltzes with his mistress Delphine.

While Vernay's film strikes a determined contrast with the hardships of the Occupation, it also echoes the socio-political context surrounding its production. The portrayal of Vautrin's arrest presents an intriguing parallel with this contemporary context, since it reflects the practice of *délation* and the denunciation of suspicious persons or activities to the Nazi occupiers. In the film sequence, upon hearing the footsteps of the police outside, Vautrin (played with suitable menace by Pierre Renoir) asks which of the boarders has betrayed him. The camera pans around the dining room, eventually reaching Poiret and Mademoiselle Michonneau, who shuffle nervously in the corner. Recognising the traitors in his midst, Vautrin spits in Poiret's face before the boarders call for the two spies to be evicted from the house.

Figure 3: The police arrest Vautrin (Pierre Renoir) in *Le Père Goriot* (1944, dir. R. Vernay).

The boarders, meanwhile, quickly forget that Vautrin is a convicted criminal, and express their disgust at the underhanded way in which he has been ensnared. Even as he encourages spectators to leave behind the bitter experience of the war, Vernay underscores the preoccupations of his own era.

With the growing accessibility of television, cinematic interest in Balzac slowed noticeably in the second half of the twentieth century until the heritage cinema movement brought the adaptation of literary classics back into vogue. In the late 1980s and early 1990s, filmmakers returned to *La Comédie humaine* with fresh enthusiasm. In France, Yves Angelo directed a new version of *Le Colonel Chabert* (1994) starring Gérard Depardieu (whose own affection for Balzac would see him take on the role of the novelist himself in a 1998 television film for French broadcaster TF1). On 12 June 1998, two Balzac adaptations were released simultaneously in the United States: *Passion in the Desert*, directed by Lavinia Currier, and *Cousin Bette*, a very liberal retelling of Balzac's 1846 novel directed by Des McAnuff. The aftershocks of the heritage movement continued to be felt during the first decade of the new millennium in France. In 2007, Jacques Rivette directed a highly faithful retelling of *La Duchesse de Langeais* under the original title of Balzac's novella, *Ne touchez pas la hache*. The film is particularly notable for the way in which it captures Balzac's fascination with private life. By confining the action mostly to the interior spaces of the Faubourg Saint-Germain, Rivette focuses our attention on the intimate power struggle between the Napoleonic veteran Montriveau and the aristocratic Antoinette de Langeais. In his pursuit of fidelity, the director also rectifies some of the omissions made by Baroncelli in his 1942 film, which at the insistence of German censors cut the scene in which Montriveau threatens to brand the Duchess with a red-hot iron, as well as the subsequent depiction of her attempted kidnapping from a Spanish convent.

Rivette's concern with fidelity in *Ne touchez pas la hache* also highlights Balzac's artistic debt to the theatre. As Mary M. Wiles observes, the prologue to the film draws extensively on theatrical imagery, especially in its use of curtains as structuring devices.[7] In the opening sequence, Montriveau, played by Guillaume Depardieu, recognises the voice of Antoinette singing behind the curtains of the convent chapel, where she is living as a nun under the name Sœur Thérèse. Having secured a meeting with his former love, the General waits for another curtain to be opened to reveal Antoinette standing, as if centre stage, in the middle of a convent cell. However, this encounter comes to a sudden end when Antoinette reveals that Montriveau is in fact her lover, prompting the Mother Superior to pull the curtain angrily. Signalling the transition to the next scene, Rivette cuts to yet another set of curtains, which open to reveal the Paris drawing room of the Comtesse de Sérizy five years before. Such references to the theatre are an established feature of Rivette's films. In *Ne touchez pas la hache*, however, they also call attention to the theatricality of the source text, in which Balzac concludes the final meeting between Antoinette and Montriveau in explicitly dramatic terms: '"Mother," cried Sister Thérèse in Spanish, "I have lied to you, this man is my lover!" The curtain fell at once' ['"Ma Mère," cria la sœur Thérèse en espagnol, "je vous ai menti, cet homme est mon amant!" Aussitôt le rideau tomba'] (CH V 923). In emphasising the theatrical resonance of this key moment in *La Duchesse de Langeais*, Rivette demonstrates his fidelity to Balzac's plot, and his ability to express cinematically the influences that frame the novelist's own work.

Balzac and Television

Like cinema, television has continued to draw inspiration from *La Comédie humaine*. In France, more than forty films and mini-series based on Balzac texts have been produced for the small screen, including versions of *Le Colonel Chabert, Eugénie Grandet, Le Père Goriot* and *Illusions perdues*. The novelist's work has also featured prominently on television in other countries, especially during the 1960s and 1970s, when television sets became more affordable and the medium began to reach mass audiences worldwide. Between 1965 and 1971, three Balzac adaptations – *Eugénie Grandet, Père Goriot* and *Cousin Bette* – appeared on British television, as the BBC devoted a new Saturday evening slot to recreations of texts from outside the domestic canon. In 1971, Spanish television also produced a five-part adaptation of *Le Père Goriot, Papá Goriot*, followed by a twenty-part serial broadcast under the same title in 1976. In the twenty-first century, Balzac's fiction continues to prove attractive to television. His dramatic plots and larger-than-life characters are of course valuable resources for television just as they are for cinema, particularly in the case of serial adaptations which seek to retain viewers from one episode to the next. No less importantly, his works are out of copyright, and thus provide inexpensive source material for television producers, who typically operate with much smaller budgets than their counterparts in cinema.

However, television's fascination with *La Comédie humaine* cannot be attributed solely to commercial considerations. As many television production companies – and, more specifically, directors and screenwriters – have recognised, Balzac's fiction also proves inherently suited to this medium. Many of his stories deal with everyday domestic life, a feature particularly in keeping with television, which is often watched within the privacy of the home. Moreover, Balzac's realist aesthetic translates readily to the small screen. As Kate Griffiths points out, television has traditionally used narrow shots and close-ups to a much greater extent than cinema.[8] The medium thus represents a natural context in which to recreate Balzac's enthusiasm for describing physical details such as clothing and facial expressions. The intensely visual nature of his fiction has clearly inspired television practitioners to return repeatedly to *La Comédie humaine* in their pursuit of narrative material. In 2004, scriptwriter Jean-Claude Carrière speculated that television has adapted Balzac so often because 'we work in the same way' ['nous procédons de la même manière.'][9] Like Balzac, television drama revels in capturing that which can be seen and observed.

By the 1950s, television producers in France had awakened to the possibility of exploiting these connections between their medium and *La Comédie humaine*. Having operated with only a limited portfolio of entertainment programmes during the 1940s, over the next decade the French national broadcasting agency RTF (Radiodiffusion Télévision Française) increased its output of drama serials in an attempt to encourage more of the country's households to acquire a television set. Literary adaptations proved a key part of this strategy, as the 1957 mini-series *Vautrin*, written by Jean Vertex and directed by André Leroux, illustrates. Focusing on the adventures of Balzac's infamous master-criminal, the series reworked elements of *Le Père Goriot*, *Illusions perdues* and *Splendeurs et misères des courtisanes*. More importantly, it adopted a three-part format clearly designed to sustain the curiosity of viewers. Echoing the way in which Balzac sought to maintain public interest in his work by having Vautrin appear in different novels in *La Comédie humaine* – as well as in a stage play, also entitled *Vautrin*, in 1840 – RTF used this fictional character to build audience loyalty both to the series and to television as a medium.

As French television audiences continued to grow during the 1960s, RTF and its successor ORTF (Office de Radiodiffusion Télévision Française) began to consider how Balzac could be used to educate as well as entertain viewers. Accordingly, the agency adopted a scholarly approach to *La Comédie humaine*, recruiting directors and screenwriters to recreate Balzac's work faithfully on screen. Yves-André Hubert's 1964 version of *La Cousine Bette* reflects this emphasis on fidelity, as does ORTF's decision to engage Jean-Louis Bory to write the screenplay for the film. A novelist and academic, Bory was an enthusiastic reader of nineteenth-century French literature, and had previously published a study of the criminal underworld in *La Comédie humaine*, 'Balzac et les ténèbres'. However, he was by no means afraid to make changes to Balzac's plot in adaptation. The most notable of these comes at the end of the film, where it is Bette, rather than her sister Adeline, who witnesses Hulot's tryst with the kitchen maid.

In Bory's rewriting of this key scene, the eponymous spinster returns to bed and promptly dies, her hand resting limply on the bed covers as the final credits roll. This ending eschews the domestic tragedy envisioned by Balzac, who in the novel highlights the humiliation and powerlessness of the saintly Adeline in the face of her husband's serial infidelity. Bory's emphasis on Bette's failure makes the ending of the film more accessible – and potentially more satisfying – to a television audience.

It would nevertheless be wrong to assume that ORTF's version of *La Cousine Bette* merely dilutes the complexity of the source text. In directing this film, Hubert demonstrated his ability to overcome some of the technological difficulties associated with adapting Balzac for television. Before the 1970s studio cameras were heavy and slow to manoeuvre, making it difficult to create a sense of movement on screen. Consequently, as Sarah Cardwell explains, television dramas tended to rely heavily on dialogue, giving them the rather static feel of stage plays.[10] These problems are evident in Hubert's adaptation of *La Cousine Bette*, where many of the verbal exchanges between the characters are long and linguistically complex – features that can become tiresome for the viewer. The director offsets these shortcomings with his inventive use of camera angles and *mise-en-scène*, not least to convey the sensuality of Valérie Marneffe. In the first sequence in which actress Claudine Coster appears on screen, the camera captures Hulot's desiring gaze, but remains behind Valérie, playfully tantalising the viewer with the prospect of seeing her face. In a further sequence that emphasises her sexual allure, Valérie sits to the extreme left of frame while Hubert fills the rest of the shot with the men – among them Crevel, Hulot and Steinbock – who have fallen under her spell. As both sequences illustrate, the director exploited the restricted movement of the camera in order to communicate the mixture of curiosity and erotic desire that Valérie arouses at the level of the plot, and potentially in the viewer.

By the early 1970s, television versions of Balzac were firmly established as a staple of programming schedules in France. Over the following decade, this enthusiasm for adapting the novelist's work intensified, a development that can be attributed – at least in part – to the break-up of ORTF in 1974. The French government's re-organisation of the national television industry resulted in the creation of three separate state-owned channels – TF1, Antenne 2 and FR3 – which thereafter would compete for viewers and advertising revenue. Television producers identified Balzac as a name with probable appeal for audiences in this new competitive era. Between 1974 and the introduction of commercial television in France in 1982, each of the country's three channels commissioned films based on Balzac texts. Alongside its output of light entertainment programmes and popular

Figure 4: Alice Sapritch (Bette) and Jacques Castelot (Hulot) during filming of *La Cousine Bette* (1964, dir. Y.-A. Hubert).

drama series, TF1 produced an extensive catalogue of Balzac adaptations during this period, including Alain Boudet's *Une ténébreuse affaire* (1975), Guy Jorré's *Pierrette* (1979) and Pierre Badel's *Adieu* (1982). In an attempt to secure their own share of the national television audience, the remaining channels also turned to Balzac. In 1981, FR3 commissioned Marcel Cravenne to direct *Ursule Mirouët*, while Antenne 2 produced versions of *La Peau de chagrin* (1980) and *Le Lys dans la vallée* (1981), directed by Michel Favart and Fabrice Maze, respectively.

The 1970s and early 1980s also witnessed significant developments in the way in which the novelist's work was presented on screen. The introduction of lighter, more mobile cameras gave directors greater flexibility to combine studio production with on-location filming, enabling them in turn to capture more of the detail of Balzac's plots than had been possible before. In 1980,

Gabriel Axel harnessed these technological improvements to striking effect in his adaptation of *Le Curé de Tours* for Antenne 2. With a screenplay by Pierre Moustiers (who subsequently recreated both *L'Interdiction* and *Eugénie Grandet* for French television), the film appears as a faithful reworking of Balzac's novella. Like the source text, Axel's version begins with the priest François Birotteau (played by Jean Carmet) making his way through the streets of Tours in a torrential storm. The sequence follows Balzac's plot closely. Birotteau attempts to distract himself from the freezing rain with thoughts of warmth and good company. Like Balzac, Axel grants us access to the character's mind, cutting in two shorter sequences indicating where Birotteau would prefer to be at this moment. Bordered by a pink haze which emphasises their dream-like quality, one scene shows the priest enjoying a game of cards with his aristocratic friend Madame de Listomère, the other him bathing his feet in front of a roaring fire. By combining interior and exterior shots, Axel efficiently defines Birotteau's personality, underscoring that devotion to material comforts motivates the character more than religious calling.

The opening to the film demonstrates, however, that Axel does not simply transfer Balzac's work to the screen without imposing his own artistic concerns on the production. In adapting *Le Curé de Tours*, he also explores how to re-present his source material in a televisual way, as when Birotteau sits down to breakfast with his landlady Mademoiselle Gamard and her other lodger, abbé Troubert. The scene highlights Mademoiselle Gamard's persecution of Birotteau. In this sequence, the three protagonists sit facing camera, Troubert surrounded by butter, jam and a basket of bread at one end of the table, Birotteau with only a cup of coffee at the other. Axel omits much of the realist detail of the equivalent scene in the novella, in which Balzac describes the dining room with its scratched table cover and dog curled up next to the stove. The director's *mise-en-scène* nevertheless proves doubly effective here, reflecting both the silent tyranny to which Carmet's character falls victim, and Balzac's own belief in the wider significance of the apparently trivial details of everyday life. This understated film sequence captures the richness of meaning inherent in the source text precisely by exploiting the straightforwardness of the small-screen image. As John Ellis explains, television typically avoids complex, detailed images in favour of a 'stripped-down' aesthetic more in keeping with the financial constraints under which most broadcasters operate.[11] By mobilising this convention in his own film, Axel asserts his ability to retell *Le Curé de Tours* in a uniquely televisual manner.

By the late 1980s, French television's interest in *La Comédie humaine* dwindled as heritage cinema sparked a surge in big-screen adaptations of literary classics. However, Balzac by no means disappeared from the national television landscape. In the 1990s, television adaptations of his work acquired a new driving force in the form of director Jean-Daniel Verhaeghe. Inspired by his passion for nineteenth-century literature, Verhaeghe has directed five Balzac adaptations to date: *L'Interdiction* (1993), *Eugénie Grandet* (1994), *La Duchesse de Langeais* (1995), *Le Père Goriot* (2004) and *La Maison du chat-qui-pelote* (2009). The majority of these films reflect his commitment to high production values and fidelity to his source material. However, in an increasingly competitive and fragmented television industry, Verhaeghe has been forced to consider how to make Balzac's work appeal to the widest possible spectrum of viewers.

As Isabelle Mette has shown, the impact of these commercial pressures is reflected in Verhaeghe's version of *La Maison du chat-qui-pelote*.[12] Based on the opening novel of *La Comédie humaine*, the film depicts the contrasting marital fortunes of two sisters, Augustine and Virginie, who grow up in the eponymous shop owned by their father Monsieur Guillaume. With a running time of one hour, this short adaptation is designed to retain the attention of viewers who can now choose between multiple forms of film, television and online entertainment. To further maximise ratings, it also features popular stars such as comedian Régis Lapasle (Guillaume) and actress/singer Arielle Dombasle (Duchesse de Carigliano). It is perhaps not surprising, then, that the film disappointed some critics, who accused its director of eliding the complexities of Balzac's narrative.

Such negative appraisals nevertheless overlook the more original aspects of the film, such as its use of music and nursery rhymes. In a scene with no direct equivalent in the novel, Augustine tries to impress her artist husband Théodore de Sommervieux by learning to play the piano. The melody she practises originates in the traditional French nursery rhyme 'Ah! vous dirai-je maman', set to music by Mozart around 1781, and better known to Anglophones as 'Twinkle, Twinkle, Little Star' and 'The Alphabet Song'. In the film, the melody and its corresponding lyrics, in which a child complains to her parents of her unhappiness, function as a poignant metaphor for Augustine's marital disappointment. Her attempts to play the piano fall on the increasingly deaf ears of Sommervieux, who gradually loses interest in his beautiful but unsophisticated wife. The melody is also heard in the closing sequence of the film. These musical references do more than merely serve the needs of the plot. By evoking 'Ah! vous dirai-je maman', Verhaeghe throws into relief Balzac's own exploitation of fables and children's literature. While the source text does not cite the nursery rhyme, it does recall La Fontaine's fable 'Les Loups et les Brebis' (1668) by comparing Augustine's determination to win back her husband to the courage of sheep who remain brave only as long as the wolf is away. Far from providing only facile entertainment for a mass audience, Verhaeghe thus demonstrates – perhaps unintentionally – that he and Balzac are engaged in the same process of adaptation. Like the novel on which it is based, the television version of *La Maison du chat-qui-pelote* appropriates earlier literature and redeploys it in a new work of art.

Balzac and Radio

Balzac has been adapted extensively for the airwaves. In France, radio dramatists have produced more than fifty versions of his work. Many of these date from the 1950s and early 1960s, when television was still establishing itself as a popular medium. These adaptations draw mainly on a familiar cluster of texts from *La Comédie humaine*, including *Le Colonel Chabert*, *Le Père Goriot* and *La Fille aux yeux d'or*. French radio has also created some highly ambitious re-imaginings of Balzac's fiction. In 1963, for example, Marcel Sicard directed *Lucien de Rubempré*, a serial in 115 parts which recounted the adventures of the eponymous hero and situated them within the much broader narrative span of *La Comédie humaine*. More recently, in 2014, France Culture produced a ten-part version of *Petites misères de la vie conjugale* which updated the author's reflections on middle-class marriage for a twenty-first-century audience. Yet radio's enthusiasm for adapting Balzac is by no means confined to France. In the United States in 1953, Sir Laurence Olivier presented and starred in radio dramatisations of two Balzac short stories, *La Bourse* and *La Grande Bretèche*, for the NBC series 'Theatre Royal'. Adaptations of Balzac have also featured on British radio, most recently in 2014, when the BBC reworked *Eugénie Grandet*. This extensive corpus has been largely neglected by critics, many of whom consider radio an outdated medium unworthy of serious scholarly analysis.

Radio nevertheless offers valuable insights into Balzac's work, not least by drawing attention to his artistic interest in sound. While Balzac is well known for his visual sensibility, his fiction also contains numerous references to music, voices and the noises generated by the bustle of everyday life. In *La Comédie humaine*, the novelist encourages his readers to hear as well as picture the world he describes. In *Les Chouans*, for example, he evokes the sound of the owl call used as a signal by the Breton guerrillas. Sounds also indicate moments of high drama in Balzac, as with the loud knock at the door heralding the unexpected arrival of Charles Grandet in *Eugénie Grandet*. As an auditory medium, radio is especially well suited to capturing these sounds – an advantage that radio dramatists have long since recognised and exploited. By the 1950s in France, radio versions of Balzac had become particularly adept at using sound effects to articulate the 'sonorous' elements of their source material, as Pierre Billard demonstrated in his 1957 version of *Une ténébreuse affaire*. Like the novel, this radio dramatisation begins with the former bailiff Michu loading his gun, before his dog starts to bark furiously. The barking prepares the listener for the subsequent introduction of the policemen Corentin and Peyrade, and anticipates both the fear and hostility that their investigation will provoke among the fictional inhabitants of Nodesme.

Billard also moves beyond the simple reproduction of sounds described by Balzac, exploring how sound can be used to represent other non-visual elements of the novelist's work, such as the thoughts and feelings of specific characters. Billard demonstrates his awareness of these artistic possibilities in his reworking of *L'Auberge rouge*, which he adapted alongside *Une ténébreuse affaire* for the popular crime drama series 'Les Maîtres du mystère' in 1957. Just as Epstein had done in his silent film version of Balzac's short story, Billard mobilises the language of his own medium to convey the mental torment experienced by Prosper Magnan. As the young surgeon contemplates murder, we hear the sound of his laboured breaths as he struggles against his desire to steal Walhenfer's gold. The extradiegetic music accompanying this sequence illustrates the ebb and flow of his murderous thoughts by increasing in volume every time Magnan appears on the brink of striking the decisive blow. As Walhenfer snores loudly, a church bell tolls in the distance, further exacerbating Magnan's anxiety since he has only a few hours in which to carry out the murder and make good his escape. The blindness of radio heightens the potency of these sounds. The listener can only imagine what is happening on air so the dramatic tension in waiting to discover if Magnan commits the crime becomes all the more acute. Moreover, this blindness proves highly evocative of the source text, in which Balzac declines to show the moment at which Walhenfer is killed – a feature of the story readily appropriated by Billard, whose version of *L'Auberge rouge* drowns out the murder with a musical scene transition.

With the exponential growth of television audiences during the 1960s, radio's enthusiasm for adapting Balzac began to wane. However, despite this changing media landscape, radio broadcasters continued to commission new versions of the novelist's work, both in France and abroad. In the United Kingdom, the BBC retains interest in *La Comédie humaine*, particularly on Radio 4, a station with a long tradition of adapting canonical literature. After producing a three-part dramatisation of *La Cousine Bette* in 2000, the station returned to Balzac in 2011, re-imagining *La Peau de chagrin* as *The Wild Ass's Skin Reloaded*. Written by Adrian Penketh and directed by Toby Swift, this hour-long drama shifts the historical setting of Balzac's story from nineteenth-century Paris to contemporary London, and reinvents the fictional Raphaël de Valentin as an unemployed investment banker, Rupert Verdit. Fascinated by the enduring resonance of his source material, Penketh set out to produce a script that he describes as 'claustrophobic and dark'.[13] Accordingly, his version opens with the blaring music of a strip club, where Rupert spends £50 on a lap dance after the stripper refuses his request simply to talk.

Despite its pessimistic tone, *The Wild Ass's Skin Reloaded* gestures playfully towards its own status as an adaptation. Tongue-in-cheek references to the source text abound, most notably – and paradoxically – in the sequence in which Rupert contemplates suicide. When the former banker gives away his debit card to a homeless man on a bridge overlooking the Thames, the PIN code he tells the stranger to remember is 1831 – the year in which *La Peau de chagrin* was published. Having delayed his plunge into the river, Rupert then wanders into an antiques shop, where, in a nod to the name of Balzac's own protagonist, the assorted objects include an original painting by Raphaël. Penketh may not expect the listener to recognise these allusions, but he clearly revels in the adaptive pleasure of reinventing *La Peau de chagrin* in a new temporal and geographical context.

In contrast to *The Wild Ass's Skin Reloaded*, Radio 4's version of *Eugénie Grandet* strives to achieve a faithful representation of its source material. Directed by Gordon House and broadcast in 2014, this two-part adaptation makes minimal changes to Balzac's plot, notably removing Grandet's stutter in order to make the character more intelligible for a radio audience. With a cast of established actors that includes Sir Ian McKellen (Grandet) and Shirley Dixon (Nanon), this radio play also reflects the high production values typically associated with Radio 4 drama. However, like Penketh in *The Wild Ass's Skin Reloaded*, writer Rose Tremain brings fresh perspective to Balzac's work, here recasting Nanon as narrator. The switch from the third-person narration of the source text makes good sense for radio. As a servant, Nanon offers an inside account of life in the Grandet household. This perspective also lends itself readily to the intimacy of the medium, which requires the listener to visualise the narrative using his or her own imagination.

More importantly, Tremain's decision to have Nanon relate the story reshapes our response to the character and the drama as a whole. The impact of this change in narrative perspective is illustrated by the final sequence in the play, in which Nanon reflects on her marriage to Cornoiller. While in the novel Balzac observes discreetly that the servant 'passed from the state of girl to woman' ['passa de l'état de fille à celui de femme'] (CH 3 1176), Tremain's Nanon voices a much more explicit account of her sexual awakening. 'Cornoiller, well, he liked the hot and shameless side of marriage,' she reveals, 'and bless me, but I grew to like it too.' This admission provides a humorous ending to the plot, foregrounding the physical delights of marriage experienced by a character who at the start of episode one had described herself as 'big and ugly'. At the same time, however, Nanon's revelation strengthens the contrast between her happiness and Eugénie's barren widowhood. Unlike the novel, in which Eugénie finds at least some consolation in religion and charitable works, at the end of the radio play she sits alone in her father's strongroom while Nanon and Cornoiller sleep next door. By placing the servant at the heart of her narrative, Tremain invites us to see – or rather hear – Balzac differently.

Conclusion

That Balzac has inspired the adaptive imagination is beyond doubt. Since the earliest theatrical versions of his work in the nineteenth century, artists have recreated his texts in a variety of different media. Whether working in film, television or radio, many have sought to attract audiences, make money and garner cultural legitimacy from Balzac's name. Often, they have been drawn to the extraordinary richness and artistic flexibility of their source material. With its thrilling plots and vibrant characters, *La Comédie humaine* continues to prove uniquely adaptable. As I have shown in this chapter, not all adaptations of Balzac deserve the bad press they sometimes receive. In cinema, silent films such as Jean Epstein's *L'Auberge rouge* pushed their medium to its technical limits in order to represent the complexities of Balzac's fiction on screen. On television, directors, like Yves-André Hubert, who exploited the slowness and rigidity of the studio camera in his version of *La Cousine Bette*, have engaged with the constraints of their medium. Finally, radio dramatisations of Balzac emphasise the novelist's fascination with the artistic possibilities of sound. Above all, however, adaptations of Balzac challenge us to reconsider how we think and write about the process of adaptation itself. As Thomas Leitch observes, there is an established tendency among critics to condemn adaptations as parasites which feed off the lifeblood of artistically superior works. Yet as Leitch points out, continuing this parallel between adaptation and vampirism, it is often the source texts themselves which assume 'the status of undead spirits whose unnaturally prolonged life depends on the sustenance they derive from younger, fresher blood – through the process of adaptation'.[14] Far from draining the lifeblood from his work, adaptations have helped to sustain Balzac's artistic afterlife, and in so doing, reinforce his enduring appeal.

NOTES

1. For further discussion of Balzac's attitude towards stage adaptations of his work, see S. Paraschas, '"La Contrefaçon spirituelle": Balzac and the Unauthorized Stage Adaptations of Novels' in N. Archer and A. Weisl-Shaw (eds), *Adaptation* (Oxford: Peter Lang, 2012), pp. 67–78.
2. A.-M. Baron, *Balzac cinéaste* (Paris: Klincksieck, 1990) and *Romans français du dix-neuvième siècle à l'écran: problèmes de l'adaptation* (Clermont-Ferrand: Presses universitaires Blaise-Pascal, 2008).
3. M. P., 'Avant *La Cousine Bette*: Quelques minutes avec Max de Rieux', *Cinémagazine*, 27 (6 July 1928), 13.
4. For a detailed analysis of the shots used in this sequence, see R. Abel, *French Cinema: The First Wave, 1915–1929* (Princeton University Press, 1984), p. 354.
5. J. Tulard, 'Les Adaptations cinématographiques des romans de Balzac entre 1940 et 1944', AB 1996, 389–394 (p. 389).
6. J. Siclier, *La France de Pétain et son cinéma* (La Flèche: Henri Veyrier), p. 117.
7. M. M. Wiles, *Jacques Rivette* (Urbana, Chicago and Springfield: University of Illinois Press, 2012), p. 128.
8. K. Griffiths, '*Chez Maupassant*: The (In)Visible Space of Television Adaptation' in K. Griffiths and A. Watts, *Adapting Nineteenth-Century France: Literature in Film, Theatre, Television, Radio and Print* (Cardiff: University of Wales Press, 2013), pp. 143–171 (p. 149).
9. *Le Père Goriot* (2004, dir. J.-D. Verhaeghe) [on DVD].
10. S. Cardwell, 'Literature on the Small Screen: Television Adaptations' in D. Cartmell and I. Whelehan (eds), *The Cambridge Companion to Literature on Screen* (Cambridge University Press, 2007), pp. 181–195 (pp. 185–186).
11. J. Ellis, *Visible Fictions: Cinema, Television, Video* (London, Boston, Melbourne and Henley: Routledge & Kegan Paul, 1982), pp. 129–130.
12. I. Mette, 'Exploitation et valorisation du patrimoine audiovisuel français: l'exemple des adaptations télévisées de Balzac conservées par l'INA', www.enssib.fr/bibliotheque-numerique/documents/49091-exploitation-et-valorisation-du-patrimoine-audiovisuel-francais.pdf, pp. 72–73 [Accessed 31 July 2015].
13. A. Penketh, 'Adapting Balzac for the Friday play', www.bbc.co.uk/blogs/radio4/entries/831c58ce-4352-3894-a128-48b216e19776 [Accessed 5 August 2015].
14. T. Leitch, 'Vampire Adaptation', *Journal of Adaptation and Film Performance*, 4.1 (2011), 5–16 (p. 6).

12

SCOTT LEE

Balzac's Legacy

It would be difficult to overstate the influence Balzac has had on other writers since his death in 1850. Widely considered to be the initiator of the modern novel because of the realism he is seen to bring to this literary form, Balzac is an inescapable literary reference to the present day, first and foremost because of the sheer volume of his output and the immense range of genres and subjects he explored. Having produced close to a hundred works in the span of approximately twenty years, the author of *La Comédie humaine* stands as a sort of literary monument, a father figure for the generations of writers which succeeded him. The fictional universe he created, unparalleled in its imaginative scope, was to cast a long shadow over writers both in his native France and around the world. Balzac was himself influenced by writers as diverse as Rabelais, Scott, Hoffmann and Sterne; it is thus no surprise that his own writing, bearing the mark of these writers, is difficult to categorise.

What is it about this vast life-work that is sufficiently innovative to engender such a lasting legacy? The most salient feature of Balzac's reputation, immediately following his death, was that of a realist. In his famous Preface of 1842 to *La Comédie humaine*, Balzac sets out, as 'secretary of French society', to represent the whole of society in the first half of the nineteenth century. His plan is not only ambitious, it is highly structured, organised along the lines of an eighteenth-century scientific enterprise into a series of Studies: Manners, Philosophical, Analytic and 'Scenes': private, provincial, Parisian, political, military and country life. While his great œuvre remained incomplete at the time of his death, it can be rightly claimed that Balzac's work constitutes an invaluable historical document of life in early nineteenth-century France. Whether it be his depictions of the military battles of the Grande Armée in *Le Colonel Chabert* or *Adieu*, his portrayal of bourgeois domestic life in *Eugénie Grandet* or *La Femme de trente ans*, or his depiction of the printing business in *Illusions perdues*, Balzac shows himself to be a passionate, even obsessive chronicler of the world his characters inhabit. Unlike the Romantics for whom the self is the major preoccupation, Balzac takes as his main focus contemporary society in all its variety, as the headings of *La Comédie humaine*'s sections suggest. Perhaps the most remarkable feature of his realism are his elaborate descriptions of people and especially objects: the minute detailing of the lawyer's office at the beginning of *Le Colonel Chabert*, the threadbare furniture of la maison Vauquer in *Le Père Goriot*, or the house of Mme Camusot towards the end of *Le Cabinet des antiques*.

Another innovative feature of Balzac's realism is his technique of reappearing characters, inaugurated in 1834 during the composition of *Le Père Goriot*. Well-known characters such as Rastignac, Vautrin and Rubempré, instead of being limited to a single work, reappear in other novels and short stories, playing roles of varying degrees of importance. As Graham Robb points out, the advantages of this device were 'enormous: We get to know these characters in exactly the same way we become familiar with real people, little by little, by personal acquaintance or hearsay ... By treating his characters as people who change and grow old, Balzac launched the novel into a new dimension – passing time, where life and death are real.'[1] For Maurice Souriau, writing in 1888, the technique constituted 'one of the greatest advances ever made in novelistic technique'.[2] Not surprisingly, this innovation was to have a lasting legacy, most notably in the work of Zola, to which we will return later. Yet another dimension of Balzac's originality in the realm of realism is his depiction of urban life, the teeming pulse of the city, chiefly Paris under the Restoration and the July Monarchy. If Balzac sought above all to portray *l'homme social*, man in his social context, it makes sense that his novels, and not just those figuring in the *Scènes de la vie parisienne*, depict protagonists in an urban setting. In Balzac, modern realism manifests itself as urban realism, and Paris itself, in works such as *Le Père Goriot, La Fille aux yeux d'or* and *La Cousine Bette*, is presented as a complex, sordid, multifarious space of interaction. That the city should take centre stage in a novelist's work marks a notable shift in literary practice from the Romantic period, where the emphasis is frequently placed on pastoral scenes. 'Balzac's descent into the street is a great moment in literature'.[3]

Balzac's predilection for urban settings is not merely aesthetic, for it follows another reality of early nineteenth-century France, namely the rise of the bourgeoisie and capitalism. While Balzac's enormous personal debts and attempts to evade his creditors no doubt encourage critics to underline the prevalence of money in his work, they are also a reflection of the social reality under the July Monarchy. He was perhaps the first writer to grasp that the individual's destiny in the era of capitalism was inextricably linked to the laws of economics. His novels and stories – from *La Peau de chagrin* in 1831 through *Eugénie Grandet, Illusions perdues, Gobseck* and *La Cousine Bette* – vividly show the ravages of money's pernicious influence in human relations.[4] Balzac's portrayal, in *Les Paysans*, of the economic reality of peasants in the early nineteenth century so impressed Marx that he makes a number of references to this text and others in *Capital*, including *Gobseck* and *Le Curé de village*. Dostoevsky, whose first publication was a translation of *Eugénie Grandet*, shares a similar admiration for the transition we see in Balzac from the relative stability of Romantic values to their subordination, with the advent of industrial society, to the implacable laws of capital. *Crime and Punishment* bears the influence of Balzac's great novel in its portrayal of suffering, as does *The Brothers Karamazov* in its treatment of anti-clericalism and greed. Much more recently, Thomas Piketty, in his bestselling work *Capital in the Twenty-First Century* (2013), makes frequent reference to Balzac's profound understanding of the economic situation in France in the early nineteenth century. The central thesis of Piketty's book is the longevity of inherited wealth and the inability of the meritocracy to bridge the gap between those who inherit wealth and those who attempt to gain it through hard work. Both *Le Père Goriot* and *César Birotteau* (along with the novels of Jane Austen in the British context) are cited as illustrations of the 'hyper-concentration of capital', specifically of inherited wealth, and the futility of hard work or education in enabling social mobility. Piketty takes Vautrin's speech to Rastignac in *Le Père Goriot* as an accurate reflection of an economic reality in which social success can only be achieved by wealth, and in which wealth is only attainable though inheritance. When a twenty-first century treatise on capitalism contains the section headings 'Vautrin's Lesson' and 'Rastignac's Dilemma', and when a comparison is drawn between the career of César Birotteau and that of the founder of the cosmetics company L'Oréal, it may be said with confidence that Balzac's legacy continues to be strong.

Alongside works of realism, however, Balzac also produced, especially early in his career, works of a pronounced supernatural bent, influenced as he was by the tales of Hoffmann. Novels and stories such as *La Peau de chagrin, Louis Lambert, Melmoth réconcilié* and *Séraphîta* explore both the physical and metaphysical dimensions, the consequences of unbridled ambition, the prototype of which is embodied in the wild ass's skin which shrinks as Raphael de Valentin's wishes are made.[5] Baudelaire was among the first to see Balzac's legacy as being that of a visionary rather than a realist: 'I have often been astounded that Balzac's great legacy was to have been an observer; it always seemed to me that his principal virtue was to have been a visionary, a passionate visionary.'[6] *La Comédie humaine* is a hybrid artistic construction, the work of a 'voyant', as both Chasles and Gautier saw him, and a realist, intrepidly laying bare the often-dark truth of human relations.[7]

Balzac's willingness to plumb the depths and complexities of human nature is an enduring aspect of his legacy. The most frequently recurring charge levelled against him is that of immorality, of choosing to depict the duplicity at the heart of French society in the age of social upheaval during the great capitalist expansion of the Restoration. Beyond the criticisms regarding the scabrous content of his works, perhaps the most common negative evaluation concerns his 'mauvais style', or poor writing style. On the one hand, his descriptions are seen to be too minute and elaborate; on the other, pushed to write quickly and abundantly to pay his debts, Balzac is seen as an exceptionally poor writer. Brunetière sees him as 'one of the worst writers who ever tormented the poor French language';[8] as we shall see, this is a widely held view, even amongst writers who claim Balzac as a positive influence. His technique of reappearing characters also comes in for negative comment, seen as it was as a manifestation of his inability to satisfactorily conclude his works, and as a way for the author to publish unfinished novels. Ambivalence is a general and abiding characteristic of his legacy, one that perhaps goes hand in hand with his attraction to difficult, ambiguous, often tortured characters, and a reputation for exaggeration and stylistic excess. In the second half of the nineteenth century, while Balzac's reputation among his fellow writers remains to a certain extent equivocal, *La Comédie humaine* begins to emerge as a 'classic', as a work that will stand the test of time.

The publication of Flaubert's *Madame Bovary* (1856) coming just six years after Balzac's death meant that comparisons between the two authors were inevitable. These associations were all the more inescapable given that Flaubert's masterpiece bore the sub-title *Mœurs de province*, in apparent homage to Balzac's *Études de mœurs*. Yet an account of Balzac's influence on Flaubert, the nineteenth century's great master of realism, is certainly more complicated than this putative nod to a literary predecessor would suggest. Like many literary critics during Balzac's lifetime and after his death, Flaubert found it difficult to reconcile the greatness of Balzac's insights with his poor writing style. 'What a man Balzac would have been, had he known how to write. That was all he was missing.'[9] The other main flaw Flaubert sees in Balzac's style is his habit of intervening editorially, of inserting his own personal opinions in the course of his novels, an unsurprising criticism given Flaubert's strict credo of authorial impersonality. Despite these misgivings regarding Balzac's stylistic deficiencies, Flaubert cannot avoid the immense influence of his literary forbear. Upon the publication of *Madame Bovary*, much is made of the long shadow cast by Balzac on

Flaubert, specifically with regard to the novel's realism and perceived immorality. In his correspondence, Flaubert himself admits to a certain anxiety of influence: 'I fear writing like Paul de Kock or like Balzac in the style of Chateaubriand.'[10] Later, in his working notes for *L'Éducation sentimentale*, he warns himself against imitating Balzac: 'Be wary of *Le Lys dans la vallée*.'[11] Whether Flaubert perceived Balzac's legacy to be negative or positive, it looms large in his mind as he readies himself to put pen to paper.

Balzac's influence on Flaubert may well be intractably ambivalent, yet he did consider *La Cousine Bette* to be a masterpiece, and upon Balzac's death allowed that 'When a man one admires dies, one is always sad … Yes, he was an immense fellow who courageously understood his era'.[12] This nod to Balzac's ability to document the reality of life in early nineteenth-century France points to what may be Balzac's most lasting influence on the author of *Madame Bovary*. It has become a critical commonplace to assert that Flaubert is the more 'modern' writer: less digressive, less prone to making editorial comments on his characters and their context, a better stylist and most importantly, capable of constructing an impersonal narrative voice, where meaning is conveyed by the materiality of the fictional world constructed. *La Comédie humaine*'s depiction of bourgeois life opened up the possibility of the universe which Flaubert creates in works such as *L'Éducation sentimentale, Un cœur simple* and *Bouvard et Pécuchet*: in Balzac as in Flaubert, elaborate descriptions are not superfluous or self-indulgent, but heavily invested with meaning. Flaubert may have had less grandiose ambitions than his predecessor, yet Balzac's passion for detail and his ability to show that 'people and the objects around them are organically interrelated'[13] are among the most important aspects of his influence on Flaubert.

The case of Zola, whose sprawling series of novels, *Les Rougon-Macquart* (1870–93), tracing the destiny of a family under the Second Empire, largely inspired by *La Comédie humaine*, is at once a more straightforward and more complicated history of influence. As the leader of the Naturalist movement in France, Zola's appreciation of Balzac's work was both polemical and aesthetic. Balzac is a constant reference for Zola, his greatest influence and inspiration. Taking as his starting point Taine's laudatory article on Balzac in 1865, Zola sees in Balzac the preeminent author of his time, who 'crushes the whole century. Victor Hugo and the others, in my opinion, disappear before him.'[14] The structure of *Les Rougon-Macquart*, a series of inter-linking novels whose unifying element is the destiny of a single family and a realistic portrait of life under the Second Empire, is an obvious nod to Balzac's highly structured *Comédie humaine* and its intent to represent life under the Restoration and the July Monarchy. As a result of such direct inspiration, it is not surprising that Zola's 'anxiety of influence' is more acute than that admitted to by Flaubert. Indeed, Zola goes so far as to create a series of notes at the beginning of his career, just prior to the publication of *La Fortune des Rougon* (1871) entitled 'Differences between Balzac and myself', in which he addresses the question of Balzac's influence on the work he is setting out to create. As might be expected of the founder of French naturalism, Zola affirms therein that 'My work will be less social than scientific ... the setting will be more limited than that of *La Comédie humaine*. I do not wish to depict contemporary society, but a single family, by showing the dynamics of race modified by environment.'[15] While distinguishing his work – more scientific, less ambitious – from that of Balzac, Zola at the same time makes a sustained effort to appropriate him for the Naturalist movement. He reads Balzac's *Le Cabinet des antiques* as a political novel, sees Grandet as an illustration of the theory of the influence of *milieu* on man and considers *La Cousine Bette* to be an experimental novel in which Hulot is subject to a series of ordeals in order to show the functioning of the mechanism of passion. He explains Balzac's sympathies for the monarchy and the aristocracy as an unfortunate case of bad faith: 'don't listen to him, he is lying to himself, he worked for the future, he recounted the faltering murmurs of universal democracy'.[16]

While it is difficult to accept Zola's position that Balzac was an unwitting naturalist or 'scientist in literature', it is undeniable that, unlike Flaubert, Zola openly acknowledges Balzac as his greatest influence. We see hints of Balzac's *Pierrette* in *La Fortune des Rougon*, of *La Cousine Bette* in *Nana*, of *Le Curé de Tours* in *La Conquête de Plassans*. Zola is a veritable disciple of Balzac, as the famous caricature (1878) by André Gill succinctly illustrates: Zola, holding a copy of the *Rougon-Macquart*, is seen saluting the bust of Balzac, who returns the gesture. Indeed, Zola's admiration for the author of *La Comédie humaine* and his concern for the latter's legacy motivates him to push for a sculpture of Balzac, 'the greatest of our novelists', to be erected in Paris, albeit without success. While there is far from a perfect correspondence between the ideological content of Zola's œuvre and that of Balzac's *Comédie humaine*, it seems nonetheless reasonable to conclude that Zola's mimetic, documentary impulse to account for the reality of an era is most certainly the result of Balzac's influence.

The great Anglo-American writer Henry James (1843–1916) may arguably be Balzac's most enthusiastic disciple in the English-speaking world. Like Zola, James sees himself as 'an emulous fellow worker, who has learned from him more of the lessons of the engaging mystery of fiction than from any one else'.[17] Unlike Zola, James expresses his admiration and his indebtedness without the pronounced anxiety of influence we see in the French naturalist or even in Flaubert. In James's view, Balzac is 'the father of us all', 'our towering idol';[18] *La Comédie humaine*, for its part, 'hung before us in the space of twenty short years ... remains one of the most inscrutable, one of the most unfathomable, final facts in the history of art'.[19] James's astonishment at Balzac's artistic achievement can be traced to what he perceives to be the chief characteristic of his work, namely realism. Balzac's immersion in and understanding of the society in which he lived was, in his view, 'a superb foundation for the work of a realistic romancer';[20] 'his strength was to lie in representing the innumerable actual facts of the French civilisation of his day'.[21] In this line of thought, he considered *Le Père Goriot* to be a masterpiece: 'it easily ranks among the few greatest novels we possess',[22] given its portrayal of the excesses of paternal love and of the cut-throat nature of social aspiration during the Restoration.

Nevertheless, James was acutely aware of his predecessor's shortcomings. Like virtually all writers who cite him as an important influence, James's view of Balzac is frequently ambivalent. He notes that Balzac's works and characters give far too much play to the theme of money: 'the great general protagonist is the twenty-francs piece';[23] he also concurs with other detractors who judge Balzac to be lacking in moral sense, finding him 'morally and intellectually ... superficial'.[24] As for Balzac's tendency to expound philosophical views in his fictional work, James is unequivocal: 'from the moment he ceases to be a dramatist Balzac is an arrant charlatan ... It all rings false – it is all mere flatulent pretension'.[25] The unfiltered, unrefined nature of Balzac's writing is however not, in James's view, a sufficiently serious defect to condemn his art; quite the contrary, James sees the ungainly aspects of Balzac's prose as a reflection of their creator's immersion in the world he creates: 'with all his faults of pedantry, ponderosity, pretentiousness, bad taste and charmless form, his spirit has somehow paid for its knowledge. His subject is again and again the complicated human condition; and it is with these complications as if he knew them ... by the history of his soul and the direct exposure of his sensibility.'[26] We see evidence of Balzac's influence throughout James's fiction, though this inspiration is more pronounced at the beginning of his career. The novella 'The Lesson of the Master' (1888), a tale of the artist's life showing the dangers of the imagination, owes much to Balzac's *Le Chef-d'œuvre inconnu*; James's great 'novel of things', *The Spoils of Poynton* (1897), in which we see the struggle to hold on to beautiful objects, brings to mind *Le Curé de Tours*, as well as Balzac's novel of an obsessive art collector, *Le Cousin Pons*. And in *The Ambassadors* (1903), James's tale of Paris, we see echoes of Balzac's *Louis Lambert*, at least onomastically, in the character of Lewis Lambert Strether, as well as of his short story *Madame Firmiani*, whose plot closely resembles that of

James's novel, namely the civilising role of an aristocratic woman in the life of an ambitious young man.

Oscar Wilde, whose admiration for Balzac is legendary – '[La Comédie humaine] is really the greatest monument that literature has produced in our century'[27] – shares James's feeling that in Balzac, the real is overtaken by the fictional: 'after reading the Comédie humaine one begins to believe that the only real people are the people who have never existed ... A steady course of Balzac reduces our living friends to shadows, and our acquaintances to the shadows of shades.'[28] One is reminded in this regard of Wilde's statement that the death of Lucien de Rubempré was one of the greatest tragedies of his life. Wilde's assessment echoes that of other critics, who, given Balzac's immersion in the fictional universe he creates, question the realism of La Comédie humaine. One contemporary critic goes so far as to maintain that Balzac's ultimate ambition was not to 'copy the real, but rather to rewrite it, in sum, to reinvent it', and that we would do well to see him as having 'more in common with the Harry Potter series by J. K. Rowling, or with Tolkien's The Lord of the Rings cycle'.[29] By creating a self-contained fictional universe, Balzac's work can in a sense be categorised as fantastical.

Among French writers of the twentieth century, Marcel Proust's work – both his criticism and fiction – stands out as being profoundly influenced by Balzac's Comédie humaine. Proust's correspondence and notes attest to his marked interest in Balzac, whose novels and short stories he read voraciously, even as an adolescent. His sprawling multivolume novel, À la recherche du temps perdu, is littered with references to Balzac's works. And yet, despite his indebtedness to his predecessor, Proust's admiration for Balzac is not unalloyed. In the posthumous collection of critical essays entitled Contre Sainte-Beuve, Proust offers a decidedly ambivalent interpretation of Balzac's œuvre. Like Henry James's essays, Contre Sainte-Beuve constitutes a sustained effort to come to terms with Balzac's legacy at the turn of the twentieth century. And like James, Proust finds Balzac's aesthetic instincts to be wanting: 'The vulgarity of his sentiments is so great that life could not make up for it ... I dare not speak of the vulgarity of his language. It corrupts his very vocabulary.'[30] Proust, like Flaubert, considers Balzac's narrative technique to be unnecessarily overt, lacking in subtlety: 'in Balzac, there is strictly speaking no style. Balzac's style doesn't reflect, it explains.'[31] However, despite seeing Balzac's poor style as a significant shortcoming, Proust admires what he interprets as the truth of Balzac's characters, his ability to make them come to life: 'This same man who naively expounds his historical and artistic views, etc., conceals the most profound intentions.'[32] Proust is impressed by his predecessor's capacity to create characters whose realistic quality is a function of their psychological truth, rather than their conformity to an extra-fictional reality; this constitutes the core of his argument against Sainte-Beuve: 'Instead of speaking of Balzac's thirty-year-old woman, [Sainte-Beuve] speaks of the thirty-year-old woman outside of Balzac.'[33] Balzac's technique of reappearing characters, which Proust greatly admires and which allows the verisimilitude of the characters to develop and deepen, is one of the great legacies which Proust takes up and incorporates into *À la recherche du temps perdu,* where the reader comes to know in all their complexity characters such as Swann, Charlus, Albertine and Odette, precisely because they appear at different intervals, and in different contexts, in the various volumes of Proust's masterpiece. The great lesson of Balzac's realism, for Proust, resides in its capacity to accord a literary value, and therefore a meaning, to aspects of our lives that are otherwise 'too contingent. But it is precisely the law of these contingencies which is revealed in his work'.[34] Balzac's fiction gives meaning to our lives, it makes sense of the apparently accidental, meaningless aspects of our real-world experience. One can understand Proust being inspired by this 'law' of Balzac's fiction, given the power, in *À la recherche du temps perdu,* of seemingly random events (like the taste of the madeleine dipped in tea) to allow access to the submerged, 'other' dimension of memory.

The low point for Balzac's literary legacy came in the late 1950s and 1960s with the arrival of the New Novel [Nouveau Roman] in France, an avant-garde movement whose goal was to free the novel from what its proponents considered to be the bourgeois values of the nineteenth century. The putative leader of the group, which also included novelists such as Nathalie Sarraute, Claude Simon and Michel Butor, was Alain Robbe-Grillet, whose manifesto *For a New Novel* [*Pour un nouveau roman*] (1963), called for a renovation of the novel form, inherited from the nineteenth century, centred on character and plot. For Robbe-Grillet and the New Novelists, Balzac is the very model of such a 'bourgeois' literature that purports to naively represent reality in an unproblematic fashion: 'everything tended to impose the image of a stable, coherent, continuous, unequivocal, entirely decipherable universe. Since the intelligibility of the world was not even questioned, to tell a story did not raise a problem. The style of the novel could be innocent.'[35] Like virtually all critics of Balzac during and after the author's lifetime, Robbe-Grillet does not fail to find fault with Balzac's overly intrusive style, his tendency to tell instead of show and his overpowering narrative omniscience. While it takes little effort to show that the universe Balzac created is anything but homogeneous and unproblematic, but rather one of heterogeneity and discontinuity, it nevertheless remains that Balzac became the whipping boy of the New Novelists, whose exponents disdained plot, linearity and character study. One could rightly claim that the 'Balzacian novel' was indeed a sort of straw man invented by the New Novelists to identify novels from the nineteenth or twentieth centuries which continued to tell stories.

Roland Barthes's *S/Z* (1970) marked another milestone in Balzac criticism, and constitutes an intriguing attempt to show the Balzacian text as an example of the 'classic' or 'readerly' [*lisible*] text in which language is seen to be a transparent vehicle for communicating meaning, unlike the modern or 'writerly' [*scriptible*] text, which refers not to an extra-textual reality but to the play of its own internal discourse. Breaking Balzac's short story *Sarrasine* (1830) into 561 numbered fragments or 'lexias' [*lexies*], Barthes's study, in a demonstration of the extreme limits of structuralism, systematically reveals the assumptions underlying the text's enunciations and the ways in which the latter conform to a series of five codes. Like the New Novelists, Barthes views Balzac's story as adhering to a 'simple representative model', as being 'modestly plural', as assuming the 'naturalness' of the ideologies (social status, beauty, moral rectitude) it puts forth, unlike 'modern texts', which ironically announce the artificiality of their own discourse. Yet, perhaps despite himself, Barthes's reading of the short story ultimately reveals it to be highly resistant to the categories in which he seeks to arrange it. Barthes delivers a wonderfully subtle reading of the work which highlights its modernity, most notably its questioning of the boundaries of desire and sexual identity, all the while attempting to maintain the readerly/writerly distinction. In the final analysis, it is ironic that Barthes would choose *Sarrasine* as his analytical guinea pig, given that it is arguably one of the most modern texts of all *La Comédie humaine*, a text that Camille Paglia qualified as 'the century's first completely Decadent work'.[36] Indeed, the effect of *S/Z* was, perhaps paradoxically, to revitalise appreciation for Balzac's works with the renewed conviction that, far from being 'modestly plural', they reveal themselves, on the contrary, to be immensely polyvalent and complex, allowing for multiple interpretations and lending themselves to myriad critical approaches.

Many modern writers can also be seen as inheritors of Balzac's literary legacy. James Joyce, while not overtly claiming Balzac as an influence, shares the latter's fascination with the city as the site of the subject's questioning of his or her place in modern society. At least one critic has pointed out that *Dubliners* shares with *La Comédie humaine* a sort of synecdochical strategy whereby the dramas occurring in the capital city serve as a means to represent the modern dilemmas of the whole country.[37] Italo Calvino, for his part, elucidates more explicitly his admiration for Balzac and the prescient quality of the latter's depiction of the city. In his essay 'The City as Novel in Balzac', Calvino sees Balzac as being among the first writers to conceive of the city as 'language, as ideology'.[38] He considers the *Histoire des Treize* trilogy

(*Ferragus, La Duchesse de Langeais, La Fille aux yeux d'or*) a veritable 'topographical epic' of Paris, anticipating the popular and literary creations of the nineteenth and twentieth centuries in which the 'Superman takes his revenge on the society that has outlawed him': *The Count of Monte Cristo, The Phantom of the Opera, The Godfather*. Calvino's admiration for his predecessor extended to his attendance in 1968 at Barthes's seminar on *Sarrasine* and his decision to write prefaces for a number of Balzac's texts published in a collection he directed for the Italian publisher Einaudi. It is perhaps surprising to learn that the great American writer Jack Kerouac, a pioneer of the Beat generation and an avant-garde stylist, also cites Balzac as a seminal influence, claiming in 1965 that 'Balzac was the great giant who made me want to create a world too, which will never be anywhere near as huge as the *Comédie humaine*'.[39] Kerouac envisioned organising his works under the over-arching title of *The Duluoz Legend*, replete with recurring characters, whose purpose, enunciated in 1947, was 'Balzacian in scope – to conquer knowledge of the U.S.A. (the center of the world for me just as Paris was the center of the world for Balzac)'. Such was the influence of Balzac on his own work that he qualified his roman-fleuve in 1957 as 'a modern subjective *Comédie humaine*'.[40] Like Balzac, Kerouac's grand project remained unfinished at the time of his death; in its ambition to offer a faithful representation of American society in the twentieth century, his work testifies to the enduring influence of his French predecessor.

In the wake of the New Novel's period of formal experimentation and disdain for traditional narrative structure, contemporary French writers, in what has been termed a 'return to story', acknowledge more readily their debt to Balzac. In both his essays and fictional work, Pierre Michon (b. 1945) makes frequent reference to *La Comédie humaine*. The first chapter of his essay *Trois auteurs* is an impressionistic homage to Balzac's life, works and the characters he created. He imagines meetings between Balzac and Stendhal, Baudelaire and George Sand, and intertwines reflections of his own encounters with Balzac's work in an attempt to explain his fascination with his predecessor. In contradistinction to the New Novelists, what Michon appreciates most in Balzac is his 'unqualifiable pleasure of writing', the fact that Balzac, unlike Flaubert, does not disappear from his texts: 'I never forget Balzac when I read him ... I am told that it is a fault of Balzac's, this impossibility to disappear from his text: I don't agree.'[41] The novelist Richard Millet (b. 1953) can also be seen to participate in this renewed appreciation for Balzac's writing. In his own work, Balzac's works remain a sustained influence, whether it be *La Rabouilleuse* in his *Lauve le pur* (2000), *Béatrix* in *L'Écrivain Sirieix* (1992) or *Le Lys dans la vallée* as a source of inspiration in the short story 'Octavian' (*Cœur blanc*, 1994).

In Millet's fiction, Balzac becomes part of the narrative texture, both a source of literary inspiration and an integral plot component. The parodist and historical novelist Patrick Rambaud (b. 1946) pays an unusual tribute to Balzac in his novel *La Bataille* (1997), a depiction of the battle of Essling (1809) involving Napoléon's army, and the 'completion' of the novel of the same name which Balzac projected to write early in his career, but never finished. Far from the anxiety of influence felt by Flaubert and Zola, Rambaud and other contemporary writers overtly and proudly claim Balzac as a seminal influence and literary inspiration. By far the most explicit example of Balzac's enduring legacy among contemporary writers is the novel *Balzac and the Little Chinese Seamstress* [*Balzac et la Petite Tailleuse chinoise*] (2000) by the Chinese novelist and cinematographer Dai Sijie (b. 1954), in which Balzac's novels figure prominently, principally as a symbol of freedom of expression, forbidden during the Chinese Cultural Revolution. The novel, adapted as a film by the author himself in 2002, is a story of the power of narrative as a means of escape, seduction and identity in which several novels by Balzac – among them *Ursule Mirouët, Le Père Goriot* and *Le Cousin Pons* – serve as a symbol of Western culture and its promotion of individualism and the power of female beauty. While not inspired by the style or thematic content of Balzac's novels, Dai Sijie's widely read work stands as a testimony to what may be Balzac's most powerful legacy, namely his unmatched storytelling ability.

Balzac's legacy as creator of the modern novel and as a founder of literary realism is particularly astounding, given that it has been established to a certain extent *despite* him, notwithstanding an array of perceived deficiencies: a poor writing style, encyclopedic digressions, questionable philosophy, a tendency to tell rather than show. His most attentive readers, like the generations of writers whose work he influenced and continues to influence, rightly see these stylistic elements as forming an integral part of Balzac's innovation according to which *everything* in the literary text signifies; in so doing, they locate Balzac's genius in his ability to communicate something other, something timeless from the detailed observation of his own era: for Balzac depicted *l'homme social* in the grips of a particularly modern dilemma, namely the subject's place in a society where economics outstrips individuality. If identity is no longer a given (and one is reminded here of the character of Vautrin, by turns bourgeois, priest and criminal, a prototypical example of Balzac's notion of the fluidity of identity) but rather subordinated to an alienating structure, how does one go about making sense of one's place in the world, of giving meaning to one's existence? The categories taken to be 'natural' – family relationships, sexual identity, morality – are systematically shown in Balzac's work to be unnatural, relativised by the great upheaval wrought by the advent of market capitalism. In its relentless depiction of the individual's struggle with the forces that seek to define it, Balzac's *Comédie humaine* has lasting appeal ultimately because it takes as its subject what it means to be human in our modern, or postmodern, world.

NOTES

1. G. Robb, *Balzac* (London: Picador, 1994), pp. 254–255.
2. M. Souriau, 'Balzac et son œuvre', *La Revue de l'enseignement secondaire et de l'enseignement supérieur*, 1 September (1888). Quoted by D. Bellos, *Balzac Criticism in France 1850–1900* (Oxford University Press, 1976), p. 160.
3. Robb, *Balzac*, p. 70.
4. See Allan Pasco's chapter 'Balzac, Money and the Pursuit of Power' in this volume.
5. See David F. Bell's chapter 'Fantasy and Reality in *La Peau de chagrin*' in this volume.
6. C. Baudelaire, *Œuvres complètes*, 2 vols (Paris: Gallimard, 'Pléiade', 1976), vol. II, p. 120, my translation. Unless otherwise indicated, all translations are my own. Given the number and linguistic variety of sources referenced, I am including English translations only.
7. See the chapter '*Le Père Goriot: Arrivisme* and the Parisian Morality Tale' by Armine Kotin Mortimer in this volume.
8. F. Brunetière, *La Revue des deux mondes* (15 June 1880). Quoted by Bellos, *Balzac Criticism*, p. 139.
9. G. Flaubert, *Œuvres complètes*, 16 vols (Paris: Club de l'honnête homme, 1971–76), vol. 13, p. 268. Quoted by A. Raitt, 'Le Balzac de Flaubert', AB 1991, pp. 335–361 (p. 349).
10. *Ibid.*, p. 143. Quoted by Raitt, 'Le Balzac de Flaubert', p. 343.
11. G. Flaubert, *Carnets de travail*, ed. P.-M. de Biasi (Paris: Balland, 1988), p. 290. Quoted by Raitt, 'Le Balzac de Flaubert', p. 353.
12. G. Flaubert, *Œuvres complètes*, p. 96. Quoted by Raitt, 'Le Balzac de Flaubert', p. 341.
13. G. Robb, *Balzac*, p. 257.
14. É. Zola, letter of 29 May 1867 to Valabrègue. Quoted by C. Becker, 'Zola et Balzac', in AB 1996, 937–948 (p. 39).
15. Quoted by Bellos, *Balzac Criticism*, p. 108.
16. É. Zola, in *La Tribune* (31 October 1869). Quoted by Bellos, *Balzac Criticism*, p. 121.
17. H. James, *The Question of our Speech: The Lesson of Balzac; Two Lectures* (Boston and New York: Houghton Mifflin, 1905), p. 70.
18. *Ibid.*, pp. 67 and 116.
19. *Ibid.*, p. 75.
20. H. James, *French Poets and Novelists*, intr. L. Edel (New York: Grosset and Dunlap, 1964), p. 92.
21. *Ibid.*, p. 70.
22. *Ibid.*, p. 105.
23. H. James, *French Poets*, p. 72.

24. *Ibid.*, p. 88.
25. *Ibid.*, p. 88.
26. *Ibid.*, p. 94.
27. O. Wilde, 'Balzac in English' in R. Ellmann (ed.), *The Artist as Critic: Critical Writings of Oscar Wilde* (New York: Random House, 1968), pp. 29–32 (p. 29).
28. *Ibid.*, p. 30.
29. F. Schuerewegen, 'Le démiurge pris au piège', *Le Magazine littéraire*, 509 (June 2011), 84–85 (p. 85).
30. M. Proust, *Contre Sainte-Beuve* (Paris: Gallimard, 'Folio', 1954), pp. 187 and 189.
31. *Ibid.*, p. 200.
32. *Ibid.*, p. 210.
33. *Ibid.*, p. 219.
34. *Ibid.*, p. 217.
35. A. Robbe-Grillet, *For a New Novel: Essays on Fiction*, trans. R. Howard (New York: Grove Press, 1965), p. 32.
36. C. Paglia, *Sexual Personae: Art and Decadence from Nefertiti to Emily Dickinson* (London and New Haven: Yale University Press, 1990), p. 389.
37. B. Tadié, 'Balzacian Ghosts in "The Boarding House"', *European Joyce Studies*, 19 (2010), 31–41 (p. 35).
38. I. Calvino, *Why Read the Classics?* trans. M. McLaughlin (New York: Pantheon, 1999), p. 140.
39. J. T. Jones. *Jack Kerouac's Duluoz Legend* (Carbondale and Edwardsville: Southern Illinois University Press, 1999), p. 25.
40. A. Charters (ed.), *Jack Kerouac: Selected Letters*, 2 vols (New York: Penguin, 1999), vol. 2 (1957–1969), p. 55.
41. P. Michon, *Trois auteurs* (Paris: Verdier, 1997), p. 28.

Epilogues

Dual Balzac

CHANTAL CHAWAF

Balzac is an Überwriter. He endows writing with a supernatural vitality that enables the imaginary to overflow into the non-fictional. Is this because the essence of his death-defying language encompasses elements of the mother and elements of the father, the core conditions for human reproduction embraced by the art of the novel? Is the hypnotic gift of life in this visionary work so true that actual society seems to be merely its inner double?

Let us look at the mother factor: at the age of fifty, in a letter Balzac reminds his mother of 'the impact of her angry, steady looks with which you terrified your children when they were fifteen years old' ['l'effet des regards irrités et fixes avec lesquels tu terrifiais tes enfants quand ils avaient 15 ans' (Corr. V 510)]. Balzac did not get on with his mother. His letters to Evelyne Hanska prove it: 'My mother and I have no sense of mutual understanding' ['Ma mère et moi nous ne convenons point réciproquement' (LH I 471)]; 'I have had neither mother nor childhood' ['Je n'ai eu ni mère, ni enfance' (LH I 625)]; 'if you knew what my mother was like! ... She is a monster and a monstrosity! ... she is *killing my sister* having already killed my poor Laurence and my grandmother. ... I have almost broken off any contact with my mother. There would have been no alternative. ... We thought she was mad. W[e] consulted the doctor who had been her friend for 33 years, and he replied: "Alas! She is not mad, she is vicious!"' ['si vous saviez ce qu'est ma mère! ... C'est à la fois un monstre et une monstruosité! ... elle est en train *de tuer ma sœur*, après avoir tué ma pauvre Laurence et ma grand-mère. ... Moi j'ai failli rompre avec ma mère. Ce serait une nécessité. ... Nous l'avons cru folle. N[ous] avons consulté le médecin qui est son ami depuis 33 ans, et il nous a répondu: – "Hélas ! Elle n'est pas folle, elle est méchante!"' (LH I 607. Emphasis in the original)]; 'I am going to work on *La Cousine Bette*, a frightening novel, since the main character is in part my mother ... ' ['Je vais me mettre sur *La Cousine Bette*, roman terrible, car le caractère principal sera un composé de ma mère ... ' (LH II 232)]. Balzac is on the point of denying his mother's existence: 'I have never had a mother' ['Je n'ai jamais eu de mère' (LH II 146)].

However, Balzac is unable to erase his mother: the prodigious creator who gives birth to the whole of humanity, to an entire world, is in competition with his mother who produces only individuals. Balzac rises above the physical womb on whom the unloved son no longer depends. He invents his own metaphysical womb: 'chance has forced me to write my desires instead of fulfilling them' ['le hasard m'a constraint à écrire mes désirs au lieu de les satisfaire.' (LH I 301)] Rather than castrating him, Balzac's emotional void enriches him. His creativity replaces that of his mother: 'I love like a woman, and with the energy of a man' ['j'aime comme une femme, et avec l'énergie d'un homme.' (LH II 644)] He will draw on this energy at its source, in the body of the woman, in the women he will love. Stéfan Zweig is shocked by this and will judge Balzac to be deferential and devoid of masculine dignity in all his relationships with women: 'Inexplicably servile as he is, he does not counter the authoritarian demands of his sovereign lady with true male courage' ['Dans une inexplicable servilité il ne sait pas opposer aux exigences autoritaires de sa souveraine un vrai courage viril'[1]]. According to Zweig, Balzac adopts a position of total submission; he kneels before his lady and sacrifices his own personality. In actual fact, one could say that Balzac is grafting female passivity on to his own activity as a male, as he communicates erotically with (a) woman, his 'unique terrestrial religion' ['seule religion terrestre' (LH I 24)] as he, the passionate lover, declares!

Sexed identity does not confine him, it makes him multiple; he expands and becomes complete. As he writes in *Modeste Mignon*: 'do not hold it against me for having something of the woman about me, is that not the right of the poet?' ['ne m'en voulez pas d'avoir été quelque peu femme, n'est-ce pas le droit du poète?' (CH I 532)] Théophile Gautier admires his friend for his ability to inhabit different bodies for this is, as he explains, the source of 'those of his characters [who are] endowed with a profound and intimate existence' ['De là viennent ces personnages ... doués d'une existence intime et profonde'[2]]. It follows that two periods alternate throughout the genesis of Balzac's novelistic genius as it unfolds and develops until his death. Firstly, during the time of his liv*ed* writing when, nursing his childhood wounds, he is drawn into incestuous love (Berny, d'Abrantès, Hanska) and then the time of his liv*ing* writing when, reassured, he becomes the titanic mother who gives unceasing birth to the plots and the characters of *La Comédie humaine*, as he brilliantly transposes the matter of experience into verbal life. Théophile Gautier, in his book of memoirs written shortly after Balzac's death, records how Balzac recommended his friends find 'a strange literary hygiene', 'an absolutely total chastity' that 'would develop to perfection the powers of the mind' and 'faculties hitherto unknown' ['une étrange hygiène littéraire', 'la chasteté la plus absolue', 'développait au plus haut degré les puissances de l'esprit', 'des facultés inconues'[3]]. Chastity and love relationships are in no way mutually exclusive in Balzac, where 'the thinker and the *viveur*' merge, as Gautier notes in connection with a portrait of the author that combines 'the monk' and the 'knave'.[4]

Let us now look at the paternal side. There is nothing traditional in the father as seen by Balzac. Balzac feminises the father at the same time as he energises him, through a form of maternal androgyny that is self-sacrificing and Christ-like in Goriot and perverse and satanic in Herrera. Whether mutating into a good or a bad father, the symbolic father is transgressed by being permeated by the mother. The abbé de Maronis, tutor to the young de Marsay, seeks to offer 'a virile substitute for the [latter's] mother' ['remplacer virilement la mère' (CH V 1056)]. Herrera, wishing to induce his adoptive son, Lucien de Rubempré, puts 'his arm under that of Lucien with maternal eagerness' ['son bras sous celui de Lucien avec un empressement maternel.' (CH V 691)] Order is undermined. Balzac, the subversive moraliser, creates amoral characters: is Goriot, overflowing with fusional sensuality, a father or a lover when he inhales, animal-like, the odours of his daughter? 'How good to touch against her dress, to imitate her step, to share her warmth?' ['Est-ce bon de se frotter à sa robe, de se mettre à son pas, de partager sa chaleur!' (CH III 197)] Possessive and abusive, his paternal passion is tyrannically carnal: 'I want my daughters! I made them! they are mine!' ['Je veux mes filles! je les ai faites! elles sont à moi!' (CH III 276)]; 'never marry your daughters if you love them ... No more marriages! That is what takes our daughters from us' ['ne mariez pas vos filles si vous les aimez ... Plus de mariages! C'est ce qui nous enlève nos filles' (CH III 278)]. Contravening patriarchal law, the father embodies no dynastic message; evil is victorious in a kind of patricide in *Le Père Goriot* and in a kind of suicide in *Illusions perdues*. In effect, the model for this new father, who is perverted rather than effeminised by being admixed with maternity, is money. 'Money is life', declares Goriot ['L'argent, c'est la vie.' (CH III 242)] Balzac modernises ancestral paternity by humanising it, and thus by weakening it. He illumines the spiritual decline of a society at the height of industrial and financial expansion. The symbolic skewing of the father in this brand new material civilisation of the nineteenth century is conveyed in the cynical advice offered by Herrera to Lucien: 'See men, and especially women, as mere instruments' ['Ne voyez dans les hommes, et surtout dans les femmes, que des instruments' (CH V 696)].

The will to power drives the whole of *La Comédie humaine*, but Balzac's unfailing lucidity unmasks the ineffectuality of this vicious social comedy: 'Man exhausts himself through two instinctively linked activities that drain the wellsprings of his existence. Two words express all the forms that can be taken by these two causes of death: 'DESIRE and POWER'/ 'I WANT and I CAN' ['VOULOIR et POUVOIR' (*La Peau de chagrin*, CH X 85)]. Breaking away from idealism, Balzac's novels are our realistic conscience, which does not prevent us from occasionally regretting a certain residual misogyny, racism and anti-Semitism that can be found in his pages. At the same time as he writes in a tone of condemnation, Balzac remains complicitous with that very society he so magisterially denounces but which he who inserted the aristocratic 'de' before his name, envies, fascinated as he was by the privileges attached to birth and fortune. But it is precisely thanks to his capacity for self-transformation that the novelist of the Universal overrides the complexes and the frustrations of his life as an individual.

Where does Balzac belong today? In the period 1960–70 the influence of structuralism and linguistics on literary criticism meant a certain dislocation of the fictional text. Writing and history went their separate ways. The function of myth was thereby impoverished. Too often, contemporary, commercially orientated novels simply tell stories and more literary novels simply talk about their own prose ... In an opinion poll in 2013 on book choice, 40 per cent of respondents felt that all that mattered was the topic, never the style. Their favourite author was Marc Lévy.[5] Industry replaces art. A recent French weekly magazine informed us that Bret Easton Ellis was abandoning the fictional form in favour of video formats, Twitter, TV series and cinema. According to Ellis, moreover, the literary world in the United States is on the verge of collapse, since people's interest in the novel has seriously diminished and now writers seem to be disappearing.[6] Our brains have been recalibrated by the internet. Might the young internet generation be alienated from literature? If that is the case, let them read Balzac before any more time is lost. And let us remain writers. The programme for the present and the future of literature can be found in a sentence in *La Femme de trente ans*: 'He was moved by one of those sensations that cannot be expressed in language.' ['Il était ému par une de ces sensations pour lesquelles il manque un langage.' (CH II 1132)] Language engenders further language. To stop writing would condemn it to the emptiness of unarticulated expression. The resistance of the novel works on our freedom to live where mere life is not enough. By reading Balzac, we become more and more alive.[7]

Epilogues

Living Balzac

ÉRIC JOURDAN

Does the Balzac who offers his panorama of a society with its multifarious facets have any descendants? There is, at the present time, one such descendant and it is the most tedious imaginable, since it simply means charting changes in fashion, thereby giving the false impression of bearing witness to a particular era. Amongst the prolific writers of the twentieth century – the Jules Romains, the Duhamels and the Martin du Gards of this world and those treading the murky waters of the twenty-first – Balzac's example has become sterile and pathetically imitative.[8] In the case of Proust, another victim to mimicry, *his* human comedy has suffered a similar fate. Mercifully, in Balzac as in Proust, what is behind the scenes is fascinating and conceals many a trap for the unwary. So let's forget their role of fathers giving birth to a miserable line of novelists with a greater or lesser interest in society, and let us talk about reality, about the real Balzac, the obscure brother of the suitor of Madame Hanska.

Farewell, paean to the people! The great man from the provinces buries himself in the murky depths of Paris, even including the salons of the Faubourg Saint-Germain. Vautrin is taking control. Sensuality is weaving its nocturnal way so as to spy on the shuttered house in an Auteuil cul-de-sac, in the quartier Saint-Lazare, the abode of the girl with the golden eyes.

Not yet the rabid *arriviste*, Rastignac is still a handsome, equivocal young man, a lover seeking out his own excitement, intrigued by his own pleasure. And *excitement* means everything, whether heart or hedonism. Over the remainder of his life (he appears in over twenty-five novels), his successes will give him regular access, like Bluebeard's key, to the secret boudoir where his body has no secrets in the half-light of alcoves. This is one of the few examples where Balzac explores the erotic life of a young man. It will be very similar in the early stages for Lucien de Rubempré, whose strange meeting with the abbé Herrera on their journey into the future is never really explained. Vautrin conceals the feelings, seemingly unavowed, that link the two strangers in the labyrinth of their silences.

Every possible sex is concealed in the minds of these young men, doubtless in order to counter the desires of their flesh; hence, at least for the young twenty-year-old, there is less likelihood of error. It is from these duplicitous narratives that the twentieth century has emerged, while at the same time, perhaps, losing its source in the imagination and, more especially, losing a certain *frisson* in the soul which betrays its convulsions better than actions in the nocturnal world of Balzac.

In the world of the French novel, literary antecedents are often ascribed either to Stendhal or to Balzac, who were both close and yet unrelated, whether in style or in imagination. For them, the planets turned around a different sun. Creators of this mould are never really reproducible since it is their isolation that keeps them alive, despite the attempts of their imitators to perpetuate them via their own blatherings. Those who want to repeat the past are non-existent!

In order to define this teeming Balzacian world, frozen in time despite its diversity, let us say: here is 'a magnificent spectacle, a world long gone, an Atlantis that is forever under the sea'. This is also true of Proust. Their successors, those who claim to follow in their wake, are merely indulging in photography, in other words – in clichés! The real Balzac is elsewhere, in the secret imagination whose heir bears the name of Sigmund Freud, and occasionally even that of Havelock Ellis. Tell me who haunts you and I will tell you who you are. That is the truth of the writer. The more he writes (and Balzac covers page after page), the more he hides from himself, with sudden underground explosions, a kind of Captain Nemo of the unconscious. The scenes that we can imagine through the silences of the *Histoire des Treize* tell us more than his purely external relationships, his pursuit of the Polish countess, the son he may or may not have had with Madame Visconti, and the unbridled letters between him and Jules Sandeau ....

Starting out from Tours, it is, therefore, an unknown Balzac who goes up to Paris to become something when he was in fact more, that unusual commodity: 'someone'. In *Splendeurs et misères des courtisanes*, Rubempré also leaves his provincial roots to seek fame and fortune in the capital. He will find love, despair and death. The very titles encapsulate the ambitions of these young men, starting with Balzac himself: *Un grand homme de province à Paris*! Real life, moreover, sometimes combines with pure invention: isn't Lucien's brother-in-law a printer by trade? In the background, the novel always has its roots in the real. The novelist conceals the excesses of his own ambitions, projecting them onto other men.

Everything is part of the whole. In order to launch the world he will bring together under the title *La Comédie humaine* (and the title itself is its own programme), Balzac exploits his own contradictions. He mingles what he sees and what he thinks he can see. The aristocracy, for example, which acts as a kind of roof over Balzac's society, is restricted to the whirl of its social calendar. This is also the case in Proust. Let me explain. The limits of Parisian society have nothing to do with the actual country squires who are expiring with boredom on their estates; ensconced in their prejudices, these noble families live in their own exclusive world and raise their drawbridges at the approach of anyone they consider not one of their own. Paris, however, belongs to jumped up dukes, to those whose titles are bought on the open market or to an ill-assorted bunch of ill-connected aristocrats (as

Saint-Simon had already insisted), who have saved themselves from disaster by marrying a pile of money, enabling them to restore their mansions and replace their tableware in gold.

Gold, that is what Balzac discovers; gold, the touchstone of the social unconscious. Having it or not having it is a game-changer for all dealings, whether psychological or commercial. Those who belong to the bourgeoisie, at the pinnacle of its success yet a motley crew according to normal criteria for success, are in power, since they are indeed a mixed crowd as possessions expand and take over commercial banking. Nothing has changed there. Owning things becomes an obsession, a necessity. Gold – the name given to the accumulation of money, whether public or private – buys individual ambition. No distinction is made between individual consciences, social rules, real possessions and fictional ones. This is a world that will soon lose its head and replace it with that of a golden calf. 'The calf of gold is still standing' ['Le veau d'or est toujours debout'] becomes the universal refrain and will become a catch phrase in our own time.[9] This refrain shows no sign of going out of fashion. We now have the choruses and the orchestras to give full resonance to these diabolical couplets. One of our duties now is to make them understandable in every language and in every form of writing, beginning with the global keyboard, *from one end of the earth to the other*.

Balzac will have been sufficiently prescient to see this sly river rise to the edge of its retaining walls. He even foresaw the way it would eventually burst those walls, reducing the importance of natural disasters since they did not affect human freedom.

Once this is revealed, our Balzac moves on, since a world poised precariously on gold bars leaves little room for individual mystery. Balzac does, therefore, need something else. Moving in from these external factors, he probes the potentialities of the hidden *self*. He has already delved into the unconscious of his characters; apart from the two young men (and we know that young men are always double), Rastignac and Rubempré, it initially behove young women (or girls) to mark out the dark walls of the well of truth, *Eugénie Grandet* and other *Lys* in this vale of tears ... Now Balzac is going to project himself into the unknown, while still hiding from himself, and since irony is not proper for French novelists who always take themselves seriously, Balzac is no exception. You have to be Anglo-Saxon to appreciate to what extent life laughs at poor humanity, and all the more so as everyone thinks they are unique!

Here then is Balzac confronting himself: a case for the couch in the Berggasse![10] Facing his own demons, he slips into the skin of one slim and youthful Rastignac, who, as in Rimbaud, is the twenty-year-old who ought to go naked, a Rastignac with his inimitable casual elegance, not like that of our Honoré who wants to look like a dandy (one of his weaknesses) and lives an ideal life vicariously, in the same way as Vautrin does through Lucien de Rubempré. His sensuality evaporates in dreams. It is not possible for every era to cross the horizon delimited by habit, it stops before most desires are fulfilled. The merit of confessing to the Viennese doctor is their anonymity and the slyness of confessing everything piecemeal, in the same way as a morsel of their victim's flesh is given to the hounds after the hunt.

I can well imagine Balzac watching the reactions from the sofa, in other words, the person who is confessing as they lie on the couch of Dr Freud. He would have been a peerless practitioner, anxious to discover a truth like an executioner, but in his case *mentally*, with neither pincers nor instruments of torture, with only the inquisitor's silence as weapon. He would have made short work of some, but others would have had the upper hand: young women and their tears, young men like Rastignac who, with a little extra imagination, could thwart those trying to smoke them out. For in a writer like Balzac there is both a prying eye and a listening ear. Balzac is a doctor of the unconscious despite himself, and what he discloses to us escapes him. Hence his restlessness in the midst of his many endeavours, in the plethora of his activities. What is he seeking? Here again, I would say: Balzac ...

Was it self-doubt that made Balzac hide from himself in this way, adding avatar to avatar in different facets of different characters (that is, though, what writers do) or was he looking for the hidden key that would enable him to look himself in the mirror without a fictional intermediary? Not everyone who wants to can be Sade or Montaigne. In any case, the obverse of the 'confessions' of 'le divin Marquis' will become in time a new mystery and illumination is no less blinding than pitch dark when the dark is *inhabited*.

Killing oneself through work is a form of suicide: one is afraid of time, one puts the mirror aside, refusing to look into it and erasing accumulated images of the self. One would, however, still like to lose oneself in it in order to recapture, just for a moment, for a split second, the self-image to which we are attached. There is no hypocrisy between one self and another self. Balzac is also part of those mirror images which reflect him in disturbing ways.

As regards Balzac's influence on me – there is none, no more than from Stendhal or any other writer of the last centuries. I am more *marked* as it were by the Anglo-Saxon world. French literature is the literature of my childhood – in the case of novels – Fairy Tales and the Knights of the Round Table: they belong to one's youthful years and they are with you for life. And then, aged fifteen, I discovered Laclos and Lautréamont, making me jettison everything else. As a novelist, the unnerving clarity of *Les Liaisons dangereuses* and the vision of brilliant darkness in the last two *Chants de Maldoror* cut into my soul like a blade. This never changed. And I will never forget Rimbaud's *La Saison en enfer*, that story of desires pursued by death ...

I certainly haven't read all Balzac. I chose what came naturally, as with Stendhal whose *Lamiel* I found unutterably tedious. Since, as far as novels are concerned, I have already mentioned Proust, I will not invite a lynching from his admirers by saying that, apart from the first few pages, his world leaves me completely cold. My character and my tastes draw me to Anglo-Saxon literature, at least where novels are concerned. Any Balzac influence is, therefore, very different from the one I have been asked to describe. It was not the official Balzac that interested me but Balzac's hidden compartments, like the numbered strongboxes in instinct's offshore accounts. And also the disciple of Swedenborg.[11] Was Balzac, too, visited by the invisible world? Does his interest in this offer a new direction? Will these questions from a non-believer fall on deaf ears? For these incursions into the unknown we need to have an angel's breath. All this is to the credit of the real Balzac, putting to one side the visible world of princesses, dukes and aristocratic crooks. ...

There is no need to write in the 'I' of the first person. We are in everything we write. I do not believe in the Punch and Judy man unless he is manipulating his own puppets. That is our glory and our weakness. Thus it is that Balzac reveals himself piecemeal, in snatches unknown *to himself*. And, to speak about another, true Balzac, concerned for other writers, let me imagine his reaction to the trials brought against Baudelaire and Flaubert.[12] How he would have leapt to their defence. My own position is rather unusual – if I have a place at all. My first book, which I wrote when I was just nineteen, was banned shortly after publication for thirty years and I nearly suffered a worse fate than Baudelaire and Flaubert combined, which in a sense would have put me really in the limelight.[13] I preferred to remain 'just me'. Be that as it may, I was banned and remained so for twenty-nine years for as long as the court order was maintained. As a result, the book was sold 'under the counter' and, in translation, published in paperback in the United States. I won't expand further.

Since Balzac was, despite his changes in political affiliations, in favour of writers' independence, he would have defended me. He was one of the first – Beaumarchais having blazed the trail – and even, it can be said, *the* first, to conceive of and develop a society of authors. This is greatly to his credit, even if, like all human endeavours, the initial idea was later somewhat distorted. I would add that in my case I would have exposed the hidden side of Rastignac or *how a handsome body becomes the trump card of an ambitious soul*. And it is actually a matter of 'soul' here, a word that also seems to be banned nowadays. We thus owe a great deal to Honoré de Balzac and what finer tributes than those of Baudelaire and Hugo ...

According to Baudelaire: 'Balzac is ... a novelist and a scholar, an inventor and an observer; a naturalist who also knows the laws for the creation of ideas and visible beings. He is a great man in the full sense of the word; he created a method and is the only one whose method is worth studying.'[14] ... And let us close with Hugo, going to see Balzac, whom he had been told was dying, one evening in August. Balzac was in the hôtel Beaujon, a residence he had bought and rescued, for him a source of pride. He had surrounded himself with fine possessions, various collections including paintings – he had a Holbein, Dutch painters, Pourbus ... Along the passages and even on the stairs it was a museum, an Ali-Baba's cave, his personal absolute ... Victor Hugo went up to the bedroom where Balzac lay dying. Imagine the lighting, the wavering candle-flames of the period. Hugo took the perspiring hand of the dying man. He clasped it. There was no reaction.

'I went back down, accompanied by the thought of these livid features; crossing the drawing room I came upon his bust, motionless, impassive, haughty and yet also glowing and I compared death with immortality.[15] Back at home ... I met several people waiting for me. I said: "Sirs, Europe is about to lose a great spirit."'[16]

The rest is silence.[17]

NOTES

1. S. Zweig, *Balzac: le roman de sa vie* (Paris: Albin Michel, 1950 [1946]), p. 397.
2. T. Gautier, *Balzac*, préface de J.-L. Steinmetz, postface de C. Brunerie (Paris: Le Castor Astral, 2011), p. 35.
3. Ibid., p. 43.
4. J.-L. Steinmetz, Préface, p. 7.
5. Marc Lévy: best-selling writer born in 1961. A number of his novels, such as *Et si c'était vrai*, have been made into popular box office films (translator's note).
6. See T. Mahler, 'Bret Easton Ellis: Confessions hollywoodiennes', *Le Point*, 2116 (March 2014), 148–150.
7. Text translated by Owen Heathcote. My thanks go to Maggie Allison for her comments on the translation.
8. Jules Romains (1885–1972), Georges Duhamel (1884–1966) and Roger Martin du Gard (1881–1958) are cited as examples of uptight, complacent, bourgeois writers. Similar figures can be found amongst *avant-garde* novelists who want to look as if they are close to the people. I will avoid giving a reverse hierarchy here ...
9. 'The calf of gold is still standing' is Mephisto's refrain in Gounod's *Faust* (1859). A more sinister equivalent can be found in Berlioz's *La Damnation de Faust* (1846). Gounod's rendering has an Offenbach ring, in the style of 'let's dance on a volcano'.
10. 19, Berggasse: Freud's last address in Vienna before his definitive exile in London for the final years of his life.

11. For Swedenborg's visions, see for example his personal journal *Diarum Spirituale*. Swedenborg influenced Balzac and Novalis amongst others. After Swedenborg's death, his disciples founded the 'New Church' in London.
12. The trial of *Madame Bovary* took place in 1856 and that of *Les Fleurs du mal* in 1857.
13. The book in question is *Les Mauvais anges*, banned from 1956 to 1984 but reprinted continuously thereafter.
14. See C. Baudelaire, 'Les Contes de Champfleury' in C. Pichois (ed.), *Œuvres complètes*, 2 vols (Paris: Gallimard, 'Pléiade', 1976), II, pp. 21–23 (p. 22).
15. Bust created by David d'Angers in 1844.
16. From Hugo's *Choses vues*. See R. Pierrot, *Honoré de Balzac* (Paris: Fayard, 1994), p. 503.
17. Text translated by Owen Heathcote. My thanks go to Maggie Allison for her comments on the translation.

GUIDE TO FURTHER READING

Editions of Works by Balzac

La Comédie humaine, eds P.-G. Castex et al., 12 vols (Paris: Gallimard, 'Pléiade', 1976–81).
Correspondance, eds R. Pierrot and H. Yon, 2 vols (Paris: Gallimard, 'Pléiade', 2006–).
Lettres à Madame Hanska, ed. R. Pierrot, 2 vols (Paris: Laffont, 'Bouquins', 1990).
Œuvres complètes de Honoré de Balzac, eds M. Bouteron and H. Longnon, 40 vols (Paris: Conard, 1912–40).
Œuvres diverses, eds P.-G. Castex, R. Chollet and R. Guise, 2 vols (Paris: Gallimard, 'Pléiade', 1990–).
Premiers romans, ed. A. Lorant, 2 vols (Paris: Laffont, 'Bouquins', 1999).
Le Faiseur, ed. P. Berthier (Paris: Flammarion, 2012).

Translations

Several attempts have been made to translate the entirety of *La Comédie humaine* into English, though all of these translations date from the nineteenth century. The most authoritative is *The Human Comedy* edited by George Saintsbury and translated by Clara Bell, Ellen Marriage, James Waring and R. S. Scott, 40 vols (London: Dent, 1895–99). However, this edition does not include *Physiologie du mariage, Sarrasine, La Fille aux yeux d'or, Une passion dans le désert* or *Petites misères de la vie conjugale*.

The thirty tales that Balzac completed for *Les Cent Contes drolatiques* appear under the title *Droll Stories Collected from the Abbeys of Touraine* translated by George R. Sims (London: Chatto & Windus, 1874).

The following key works from *La Comédie humaine* are also available in Oxford World's Classics (OWC) and/or Penguin Classics (PC): *La Peau de chagrin* (OWC, PC), *Eugénie Grandet* (OWC, PC), *Histoire des Treize* (PC), *Le Père Goriot* (OWC, PC), *César Birotteau* (PC), *Une ténébreuse affaire* (PC), *Ursule Mirouët* (PC), *La Rabouilleuse* (PC), *Illusions perdues* (PC), *Le Cousin Pons* (PC), *La Cousine Bette* (OWC, PC) and *Splendeurs et misères des courtisanes* (PC).

Originally part of the trilogy *Histoire des Treize*, *La Fille aux yeux d'or* appears in Oxford World's Classics accompanied by *Sarrasine* and *Le Chef-d'œuvre inconnu*. A volume of Balzac's short stories is also available in Penguin Classics and includes *El Verdugo*, *La Paix du ménage*, *Étude de femme*, *Un épisode sous la Terreur*, *Le Réquisitionnaire*, *L'Auberge rouge*, *La Bourse*, *La Grande Bretèche*, *Un drame au bord de la mer*, *La Messe de l'athée*, *Facino Cane* and *Pierre Grassou*.

Bibliographies, Chronologies and 'États présents'

Cosson, A. L., *Vingt ans de bibliographie balzacienne (1948–1967)* (Unpublished PhD thesis, University of Missouri, 1970).

Heathcote, O., 'État présent: Honoré de Balzac', *French Studies* 64.4 (October 2010), 463–470.

Royce, W. H., *A Balzac Bibliography: Writings Relative to the Life and Works of Honoré de Balzac* (University of Chicago Press, reprint edition, 1969).

Vachon, S., *Les Travaux et les jours d'Honoré de Balzac: chronologie de la création balzacienne* (Paris: Presses du CNRS and Presses universitaires de Vincennes; Presses de l'Université de Montréal, 1992).

Waggoner, M. W., *Bibliography of Balzac Criticism, 1930–1990* (Encinitas: French Research Publications, 1990).

L'Année balzacienne publishes an annual 'Bibliographie balzacienne' listing new work in the field. A similar update on Balzac studies also appears in the annual special bibliography issue of the *Revue d'histoire littéraire de la France*.

Electronic Resources

Kazuo Kiriu's vocabulary database 'Le Vocabulaire de Balzac' can be accessed via www.v2asp.paris.fr/commun/v2asp/musees/balzac/kiriu/concordance.htm.

Twelve volumes of Balzac's works are now available in the series 'Les Romans de Balzac' edited by Andrew Oliver and published by Éditions de l'originale. Each volume is accompanied by a CD-ROM containing critical resources. The most recent additions to the series include *Les Cent Contes drolatiques* (2011), *Le Médecin de campagne* (2012), *Eugénie Grandet* (2013) and a collection of stories from the *Scènes de la vie de province* (2013). The series website can be found at www.debalzac.com/collection2.htm.

An electronic edition of *La Comédie humaine* ('Explorer *La Comédie humaine*') was published on CD-ROM by Acamédia in 1999.

Critical Studies

Adamson, D., '*Le Père Goriot* devant la critique anglaise', AB 1986, 261–279.

Armstrong, A. H., *Genesis and Development of the Hero Figure in Honoré de Balzac's Early Novels: A Study in Patterns of Creativity* (Unpublished PhD thesis, University of London, 1993).

Aubert, N., 'En attendant les barbares: *La Cousine Bette*, le moment populaire et féminin de *La Comédie humaine*', *Women in French Studies*, 8 (2000), 129–37.
Barbéris, P., *Aux sources de Balzac* (Paris: Les Bibliophiles de l'Originale, 1965).
Barbéris, P., *Balzac et le mal du siècle: contribution à une physiologie du monde moderne*, 2 vols (Paris: Gallimard, 1970).
Bardèche, M., *Balzac romancier* (Paris: Plon, 1940).
Barel-Moisan, C. and J.-L. Diaz (eds), *Balzac avant Balzac* (Saint-Cyr-sur-Loire: Christian Pirot, 2006).
Baron, A.-M., *Balzac ou les hiéroglyphes de l'imaginaire* (Paris: Champion, 2002).
Baron, A.-M., *Balzac et la Bible: une herméneutique du romanesque* (Paris: Champion, 2007).
Baron, A.-M., 'Balzac au cinéma: *La Duchesse de Langeais* de Balzac à Rivette', AB 2007, 523–27.
Baron, A.-M., 'Balzac à l'écran', AB 2009, 349–355.
Baron, A.-M., *Honoré de Balzac à vingt ans: l'esclave de sa volonté* (Paris: Au Diable Vauvert, 2012).
Bellos, D., *Balzac Criticism in France 1850–1900: The Making of a Reputation* (Oxford: Clarendon Press, 1976).
Bellos, D., *Balzac: 'La Cousine Bette'* (London: Grant and Cutler, 1980).
Bellos, D., *Honoré de Balzac: 'Old Goriot'* (Cambridge University Press, 1987).
Bérard, S. J., *La Genèse d'un roman de Balzac: 'Illusions perdues'*, 2 vols (Paris: Armand Colin, 1961).
Bertault, P., *Balzac et la religion* (Paris: Boivin, 1942).
Bertini, M. and P. Oppici (eds), *Autour de 'Wann-Chlore': le dernier roman de jeunesse de Balzac* (Bern: Peter Lang, 2008).
Bordas, É., *Balzac, discours et détours: pour une stylistique de l'énonciation romanesque* (Toulouse: Presses universitaires du Mirail, 1997).
Borel, J., *Personnages et destins balzaciens: la création littéraire et ses sources anecdotiques* (Paris: Corti, 1958).
Brooks, P., *The Melodramatic Imagination: Balzac, Henry James, Melodrama, and the Mode of Excess* (New Haven and London: Yale University Press, 1976).
Brooks, P., *Reading for the Plot: Design and Intention in Narrative* (New York: Vintage Books, 1985).
Charpateau, I., *Le Fantastique balzacien: réflexions sur l'art* (Bordeaux: [N.P.], 1997).
Cheyne, M., 'No Longer Simply Black and White: Adaptation and the Representation of Female Vulnerability in Balzac's *Le Nègre*', *Lingua Romana*, 11.1 (Fall 2012), 78–102.
Chollet, R. and S. Vachon, *À l'écoute du jeune Balzac* (Montreal and Paris: Presses universitaires de Vincennes, 2012).
Chollet, R., *Balzac journaliste: le tournant de 1830* (Paris: Klincksieck, 1983).
Citron, P., *Dans Balzac* (Paris: Seuil, 1986).
Darnton, R., *Mesmerism and the End of the Enlightenment in France* (Cambridge MA: Harvard University Press, 2009).
Diaz, J.-L., *Devenir Balzac: l'invention de l'écrivain par lui-même* (Saint-Cyr-sur-Loire: Christian Pirot, 2007).
Dickinson, L. E., *Theatre in Balzac's 'La Comédie humaine'* (Amsterdam: Rodopi, 'Faux-Titre', 2000).

Diethelm, M.-B., Balzac et le roman de la jeune fille: scènes de la vie privée avant 'La Comédie humaine' (thèse de doctorat, Université Paris-Sorbonne, 2002) [microfiche available from the Atelier National de la Reproduction des Thèses].
Dosi, F., Trajectoires balzaciennes dans le cinéma de Jacques Rivette: 'Out 1', 'La Belle Noiseuse', 'Ne touchez pas la hache' (La Madeleine: LettMotif, 2014).
Dufour, P., Le Réalisme (Paris: Presses universitaires de France), 1998.
Falconer, G. (ed.), Autour d'un cabinet de lecture (Toronto: Centre d'Études du XIXe siècle, 2001).
Farrant, T., Balzac's Shorter Fictions: Genesis and Genre (Oxford University Press, 2002).
Frappier-Mazur, L. (ed.), É. Bordas (intr.), Genèses du roman: Balzac et Sand (Amsterdam: Rodopi, 2004).
Gaillard, F., 'La Stratégie de l'araignée' in F. van Rossum-Guyon and M. Brederode (eds), Balzac et 'Les Parents pauvres' (Paris: SEDES/CDU, 1981), pp. 179–187.
Ginsburg, M. (ed.), Approaches to Teaching Balzac's 'Old Goriot' (New York: MLA, 2000).
Guise, R., 'Un grand homme du roman à la scène ou les illusions reparaissantes de Balzac', AB 1966, 171–216; AB 1967, 177–214; AB 1968, 337–368, and AB 1969, 247–280.
Guyon, B., La Création littéraire chez Balzac (Paris: Armand Colin, second edition, 1969).
Heathcote, O., Balzac and Violence: Representing History, Space, Sexuality and Death in 'La Comédie humaine' (Oxford: Peter Lang, 2009).
Heathcote, O., 'Balzac and Theory, Balzac as Theory', Paragraph, 32.2 (2009), 197–213.
Hemmings, F. W. J., The Theatre Industry in Nineteenth-Century France (Cambridge University Press, 1993).
Hulme, P., 'Balzac's Parisian Mystery: La Cousine Bette and the Writing of Historical Criticism', Literature and History, 11.1 (1985), 47–64.
Hutcheon, L., A Theory of Adaptation (Abingdon and New York: Routledge, 2006).
Jameson, F., 'La Cousine Bette and Allegorical Realism', PMLA, 86.2 (1971), 241–254.
Jameson, F., The Political Unconscious: Narrative as a Socially Symbolic Act (Ithaca: Cornell University Press, 1981).
Kanes, M., 'Père Goriot': Anatomy of a Troubled World (New York: Twayne, 1993).
Kelly, D., Fictional Genders: Role and Representation in Nineteenth-Century French Narrative (Lincoln NE: University of Nebraska Press, 1980).
Knight, D., Balzac and the Model of Painting. Artist Stories in 'La Comédie humaine' (London: Legenda, 2007).
Labouret, M., 'Méphistophélès et l'androgyne: les figures du pacte dans Illusions perdues', AB 1996, 211–230.
Le Yaouanc, M., Nosographie de l'humanité balzacienne (Paris: Maloine, 1959).
Lee, S., Traces de l'excès: essai sur la nouvelle philosophique de Balzac (Paris: Champion, 2002).
Lefebvre, A.-M., 'Fleurs du mal balzaciennes', AB 1997, 91–132.
Lucey, M., The Misfit of the Family: Balzac and the Social Forms of Sexuality (Durham NC: Duke University Press, 2003).

Lukács, G., *Studies in European Realism: A Sociological Survey of the Writings of Balzac, Stendhal, Zola, Tolstoy, Gorki, and Others* (New York: Grosset and Dunlap, 1964).
Lukács, G., *Balzac et le réalisme français*, trans. P. Laveau, pref. G. Gengembre (Paris: La Découverte, 1999 [1967]).
Macherey, P., *A Theory of Literary Production* (London: Routledge, 1978).
Mahieu, R., 'Une insertion problématique: *Le Lys dans la vallée* et les *Scènes de la vie de campagne*' in C. Duchet and I. Tournier (eds), *Balzac, Œuvres complètes. Le 'Moment' de 'La Comédie humaine'* (Saint-Denis: Presses universitaires de Vincennes, 1993), pp. 191-202.
Massonnaud, D., *Faire vrai: Balzac et l'œuvre-monde* (Geneva: Droz, 2014).
McCall Saint-Saëns, A., 'De la haine épistolaire ou "la fatale puissance de la lettre" dans les *Lettres à Madame Hanska*' in L. Frappier-Mazur and J.-M. Roulin (eds), *L'Érotique balzacienne* (Paris: SEDES, 2001), pp. 41-50.
McCormick, J., *Popular Theatres of Nineteenth-Century France* (London and New York: Routledge, 1993).
McCracken, S., '*Cousin Bette*: Balzac and the Historiography of Difference', *Essays and Studies*, 44 (1991), 88-104.
McGuire, J. R., 'The Feminine Conspiracy in Balzac's *La Cousine Bette*', *Nineteenth-Century French Studies*, 20.3-4 (1992), 295-304.
Mehta, B. J., 'La Prostitution ou cette triste réalité du corps dans *La Cousine Bette*', *Nineteenth-Century French Studies*, 20. 3-4 (1992), 305-316.
Méra, B., *Balzac et la figure mythique dans 'Les Études philosophiques'* (Paris: L'Harmattan, 2004).
Michel, A., *Le Mariage chez Honoré de Balzac: Amour et féminisme*, 4 vols (Paris: Les Belles Lettres, 1978).
Mikhalevitch, A., *Balzac et Bianchon* (Paris: Champion, 2014).
Miller, D. A., 'Balzac's Illusions Lost and Found', *Yale French Studies*, 67 (1984), 164-181.
Monteilhet, V., 'Les Adaptations balzaciennes sous l'Occupation: un cinéma de collaboration ou de résistance?', AB 2002, 327-347.
Mortimer, A. K., 'Balzac and Poe: Realizing Magnetism', *Dalhousie French Studies*, 63 (2003), 22-30.
Mortimer, A. K., *For Love or for Money: Balzac's Rhetorical Realism* (Columbus: Ohio State University Press, 2011).
Moscovici, C., *Gender and Citizenship: The Dialectics of Subject-Citizenship in Nineteenth-Century French Literature and Culture* (Lanham MD: Rowman and Littlefield, 2000).
Mounoud-Anglés, C., *Balzac et ses lectrices: L'affaire du courrier des lectrices de Balzac: Auteur/lecteur, l'invention réciproque* (Paris: Indigo and Côté-Femmes, 1994).
Mozet, N., *Balzac au pluriel* (Paris: Presses universitaires de France, 1990).
Mura-Brunel, A., *Silences du roman: Balzac et le romanesque contemporain* (Amsterdam: Rodopi, 2004).
Neefs, J., '*Illusions perdues*: Représentations de l'acte romanesque' in R. Le Huenen and P. Perron (eds), *Le Roman de Balzac: Recherches critiques, méthodes, lectures* (Montreal: Didier, 1980), pp. 119-130.

Nesci, C., *La Femme, mode d'emploi: Balzac, de la 'Physiologie du mariage' à 'La Comédie humaine'* (Lexington, KY: French Forum, 1992).
Paraschas, S., *The Realist Author and Sympathetic Imagination* (London: Legenda, 2013).
Parent-Lardeur, F., *Lire à Paris au temps de Balzac: Les cabinets de lecture à Paris, 1815–1830*, second revised edition (Paris: Éditions de l'École des Hautes Études en Sciences Sociales, 1999).
Pasco, A., *Balzacian Montage: Configuring 'La Comédie humaine'* (University of Toronto Press, 1991).
Péraud, A., *Le Crédit dans la poétique balzacienne* (Paris: Garnier, 2012).
Petrey, S., *Realism and Revolution: Balzac, Stendhal, Zola, and the Performance of History* (Ithaca: Cornell University Press, 1988).
Peylet, G., 'De la manie à la mélancolie: les souffrances du créateur balzacien dans la correspondance et dans les romans de 1830', *Eidôlon*, 52 (1999), 147–160.
Pierrot, R., *Ève de Balzac* (Paris: Stock, 1999).
Prendergast, C., *The Order of Mimesis: Balzac, Stendhal, Nerval, Flaubert* (Cambridge University Press, 1986).
Reid, R., *Families in Jeopardy: Regulating the Social Body in France, 1750–1910* (Palo Alto: Stanford University Press, 1993).
Robb, G., *Balzac* (London: Picador, 1994).
Rothfield, L., *Vital Signs: Medical Realism in Nineteenth-Century Fiction* (Princeton University Press, 1995).
Rovere, M. (ed.), 'Balzac: le génie moderne du roman classique', special issue of *Le Magazine littéraire*, 509 (June 2011), 54–91.
Sanders, J., *Adaptation and Appropriation* (London and New York: Routledge, 2006).
Schehr, L. R., 'Fool's Gold: The Beginning of Balzac's *Illusions perdues*', *Symposium*, 36.2 (1982), 149–165.
Schehr, L. R., 'A Queer Theory Approach: Gender and Genre in *Old Goriot*' in M. P. Ginsburg (ed.), *Approaches to Teaching Balzac's 'Old Goriot'* (New York: MLA, 2000), pp. 118–125.
Schuerewegen, F., *Balzac contre Balzac: les cartes du lecteur* (Toronto: Paratextes; Paris: SEDES, 1990).
Spang, R. L., *Stuff and Money in the Time of the French Revolution* (Cambridge MA: Harvard University Press, 2015), pp. 173–183, 190–194.
Sprenger, S., 'Balzac, Archaeologist of Consciousness' in V.-A. Deshoulières et P. Vacher (eds), *Archéomanie: la mémoire en ruines* (Clermont-Ferrand: Université Blaise Pascal, 2000), pp. 97–114.
Sterne, L., *The Life and Opinions of Tristram Shandy, Gentleman*, ed. I. C. Ross (Oxford University Press, 2009).
Swahn, S., *Balzac et le merveilleux: étude du roman balzacien 1822–1832* (Lund University Press, 1991).
Szypula, E., 'An Aesthetics of Indirection in Novels and Letters: Balzac's Communication with Évelina Hanska' in R. Sell, A. Borch and I. Lindgren (eds), *The Ethics of Literary Communication: Genuineness, Directness, Indirectness* (Amsterdam: John Benjamins, 2013), pp. 229–246.

Tilby, M., 'Honoré de Balzac (1799–1850): "Realism" and authority' in M. Bell (ed.), *The Cambridge Companion to European Novelists* (Cambridge University Press, 2012), pp. 192–208.

UNESCO, *Hommage à Balzac* (Paris: Mercure de France, 1950).

Vachon, S. (ed.), *Balzac: une poétique du roman* (Montreal and Saint-Denis: XYZ éditeur et Presses universitaires de Vincennes, 1996).

Vachon, S. *1850. Tombeau d'Honoré de Balzac* (Montreal and Saint-Denis: XYZ éditeur et Presses universitaires de Vincennes, 2007).

Van Rossum-Guyon, F. (ed.), *Balzac, 'Illusions perdues': 'l'œuvre capitale dans l'œuvre'* (Groningen: Rodopi, 1988).

Van Rossum-Guyon, F. *Balzac: la littérature réfléchie. Discours et autoreprésentations* (Montreal: Département d'Études françaises, 'Paragraphes', 2002).

Vanbremeersch, M.-C., *Sociologie d'une représentation romanesque: les paysans dans cinq romans balzaciens* (Paris: L'Harmattan, 1997).

Vanoncini, A., 'Balzac, Tocqueville, Michelet: du roman à l'histoire' in R. Mahieu and F. Schuerewegen (eds), *Balzac ou la tentation de l'impossible* (Paris: SEDES, 1998), pp. 37–46.

Vogel, U., *Balzac als Briefschreiber: ein Romancier Zwischen Realität und Fiktion* (Frankfurt am Main: Haag & Herchen, 1986).

Von Mises, L., *The Theory of Money and Credit*, trans. H. E. Batson (Indianapolis: Liberty Fund, 1981).

Watts, A., *Preserving the Provinces: Small Town and Countryside in the Work of Honoré de Balzac* (Bern: Peter Lang, 2007).

Watts, A., 'Diamond Thieves and Gold Diggers: Balzac, Silent Cinema and the Spoils of Adaptation' in K. Griffiths and A. Watts, *Adapting Nineteenth-Century France: Literature in Film, Theatre, Television, Radio and Print* (Cardiff: University of Wales Press, 2013), pp. 47–79.

White, N., *The Family in Crisis in Late Nineteenth-Century French Fiction* (Cambridge University Press, 1998).

Wurmser, A., *La Comédie inhumaine: la signification de l'œuvre et de la vie d'Honoré de Balzac* (Paris: Gallimard, 1964).

INDEX OF CHARACTERS

Adeline *see* Hulot, Adeline
Adrien *see* Genestas, Adrien
Aiglemont, Julie d' 77, 78
Ajuda-Pinto 91
Annette 33
Argow 32, 33, 34, 35, 36
Arthez, Daniel d' 98, 101, 102, 104, 105, 107

Bargeton, Madame de 97, 98, 99, 101, 105, 108
Beauséant, Madame de 83, 84, 86, 90, 92, 94, 148
   on film 162
   model of struggle 91
Benassis, Dr 23, 47, 132, 136, 136–8, 139
   protecting marginals 136
Bette 4, 117, 124, 125, 166
   independence 113–14
   jealousy 112
   mistreatment of 112, 113, 119
   non-normative gender identity 111
   relationship with Steinbock 115–16, 116
   relationship with Valérie 116–17, 118–19, 120–1
   on television 166, 167
   ugliness 111, 112, 113, 114
Bianchon, Horace 23, 124
Birotteau, César 75, 76–7
Birotteau, François 168
   on television 168
Bixiou 67, 141, 149
Blondet, Émile 22, 61, 63, 67, 102, 107, 129, 132, 137, 149
Bonnet 134, 135, 138
Brossette 129, 133, 138
Butifer 136

Camusot 103, 105, 149
Camusot, Madame 176

Cane, Facino 146, 148
Cardot 63
Chabert, Colonel 16, 146
Chaulieu, Louise de 49
Chrestien, Michel 99, 103
Claës, Balthazar van 12, 19, 20, 97, 145
Claparon 75
Cochet, Mlle 130
Coralie 99, 102, 103, 105
Corentin 171
Cornoiller 172
Couture 67, 149
Crevel 72, 79, 120, 121, 122, 123, 124
   on television 166
Crevel, Célestine 121, 124

Dauriat 103
David *see* Séchard, David
Delphine *see* Nucingen, Delphine de
Derville 17
des Grassins 74
Dey, Comtesse de 17, 145, 154
Doni, Massimilla 148
du Tillet 75
Dudley, Lady 131, 132
Dutheil 135

Émile *see* Blondet, Émile
Ernest de la Brière 49
Esgrignon, Victurnien d' 76, 87, 88
Esther 109
Eugène *see* Rastignac, Eugène de
Eugénie *see* Grandet, Eugénie
Ève *see* Séchard, Ève

Félix *see* Grandet, Félix; Vandenesse, Félix de
Finot 67, 149
Fischer, Lisbeth ('Bette') *see* Bette

207

INDEX OF CHARACTERS

Florine 103
Foedora, Countess 62–4, 65
Frenhofer 13, 70, 97, 144

Gamard, Mlle 168
Gambara 97
Gaubertin 129
Gaudin, Pauline 62, 64
Gaudissart 72, 77
Genestas, Adrien 136, 138
Genestas, Pierre-Joseph 136, 137, 138
Gérard 134, 137
Gobseck 17, 67, 76, 77, 79, 143, 148
Godeau 77, 78, 79
Goguelat 136
Goriot 82, 86, 90–1, 92, 93, 109, 115, 147, 191
  on film 162
Goulard 76
Grandet, Charles 36, 67, 71, 74
  adaptations
    film 159
    radio 170
Grandet, Eugénie 18, 36, 70–2, 147, 173
  and Charles 36, 159
Grandet, Félix 72, 75, 147, 159, 180
  love of gold 71, 73–5, 77
  radio adaptation 172
Grandet, Guillaume 75
Graslin, Pierre 134
Graslin, Véronique 134, 135, 139
Grassou, Pierre 148
Gravier 137
Guénic, Calyste du 87, 88
Guillaume, Augustine 169, 169–70
Guillaume, Monsieur 169
Guillaume, Virginie 169

Henriette *see* Mortsauf, Henriette de
Herrera, Carlos 105, 191
Hortense *see* Hulot, Hortense
Hulot, Adeline 79, 117, 119, 121, 122–3, 166
  beauty 114, 120
  marriage to Hulot 113
  privileged by family 112
  selling herself 124
  submissiveness 121–2, 122–3
Hulot, baron 73, 113, 114, 115, 118, 121, 124, 180
  on television 166
Hulot, Hortense 113, 118, 121, 123, 124

Hulot, maréchal 113, 115, 120
Hulot, Victorin 121, 123, 124

Janvier, Abbé 137, 138
Joseph 32, 36
Josépha 122, 124
Julie *see* Aiglemont, Julie d'

Keller 74

La Fosseuse 136
Laguerre, Mlle 130
Lambert, Louis 19, 23, 97
Langeais, Antoinette de 18, 91
  on film 163
L'Estorade, Renée de 49
Listomère, Madame de 168
Louise *see* Chaulieu, Louise de
Lousteau, Étienne 71, 98, 100, 101, 102, 103, 107
Lucien *see* Rubempré, Lucien de

Magnan, Prosper 161, 171
Manerville, Natalie de 40, 131, 132, 148
Marneffe, Valérie 111, 116, 118, 120, 123, 124, 166
  and Hulot 118
  lesbian(?) relationship with Bette 116–17, 118–19, 120–1
  power over men with Bette 120
  queen of speculation 72–3
  and Steinbock 123
Marsay, Henri de 18, 87
Matifat 103
Maucombe, Renée de 49
Mélanie 32
Mercadet 67, 76, 77–8
Mercadet, Madame 78–9
Michaud 129
Michonneau, Mlle 162
Michu 171
Mignon, Modeste 49
Minard 77, 79
Minoret, Dr 24
Mirouët, Ursule 24
Montcornet, Comte de 129, 130, 131, 138
Montcornet, Comtesse de 129, 130, 138
Montéjanos 36
Montriveau 163
  on film 163
Morillon, Victor 103
Mortsauf 131, 132, 139

INDEX OF CHARACTERS

Mortsauf, Henriette de 88, 131, 132, 135,
    141, 154
  death 131
  and Félix 131, 132

Nanon 74, 173
Nathan 102, 103, 150
Nucingen 67, 75–6, 78, 87, 92, 148
Nucingen, Augusta de 88
Nucingen, Delphine de 67, 87, 88, 90, 148
  on film 162

Pauline *see* Gaudin, Pauline
Peyrade 171
Poiret 162
Pons 114
Popinot, Anselme 77
Portenduère, Madame de 72
Portenduère, Savinien de 87

Raphaël *see* Valentin, Raphaël de
Rastignac, Eugène de 4, 62, 109, 176, 177,
    193, 196
  as *arriviste* 82, 84, 85, 87, 88, 89–90, 93–4
  and Balzac's use of reappearing characters
    81–3
  development of character 88
  on film 162
  immorality 183–5
  moral/social education 81, 86, 90–1
  natural qualities 91
  in Paris 84–5, 87
  reader's judgement of 93
  struggle 85, 92, 93
Rastignac, Gabriel de 135
Renée *see* L'Estorade, Renée de; Maucombe,
    Renée de
Restaud, Anastasie de 76, 84, 86, 162
  on film 162
Rigou 129
Roguin 75
Rosann, Marquise de 31–2
Rubempré, Lucien de 4, 17, 176, 191, 193,
    195, 196
  arriviste and poet 97–9
  and the *Cénacle* 97–8
  as commodity 105
  death 109, 182
  femininity 104
  life in Paris 87, 88
  lost illusions 106
  prostitution and book trade 103–4
  taking mother's name 101, 108
  theatre and book trade 100–2, 109
  writing and acting 102–3

San-Réal, Mariquita de 111
Sarrasine 12, 111
Sauviat 134
Séchard, David 98, 107, 109
Séchard, Ève 98, 105, 106
Séraphîta 18
Sommervieux, Théodore de 169
Steinbock, Wenceslas 111, 115–16, 116, 118,
    119, 123
  on television 166

Taillefer 60, 63, 161
Tascheron, Francis 134
Tascheron, Jean-François 134
Tonsard, Catherine 129, 130
Trailles, Maxime de 67, 76, 92
Troisville, Virginie de 129
Troubert, Abbé 168

Valentin, Raphaël de 87, 88, 147, 172, 177
  contemplating suicide 54–5
  and Countess Foedora 62–4
  in the curiosity shop 57–8
  death 65
  dinner and orgy 60–1
  gambling 56
  magical illness 23
  pact motif 54, 58
  and Pauline 64
  philosophical reflections 61
  and the wild ass's skin 58–9, 59–60,
    64, 65
  wish fulfilment 58, 59, 63
Valérie *see* Marneffe, Valérie
Vandenesse, Félix de 40, 49, 88, 131, 132,
    133, 137, 138
Vandenesse, Marie-Angélique de 150
Vautrin 4, 17, 24, 29, 74, 107, 108, 111, 147,
    176, 177, 186, 193, 196
  arrest (on film) 162
  and Goriot 109
  and Rastignac 83, 85, 86, 90, 92, 108–9
  similarity with Bette 119
  on television 165
Vautrin cycle 36
Véronique *see* Graslin, Véronique

Walhenfer 144, 171

209

GENERAL INDEX

Footnotes are indicated by the page number followed by the letter 'n' and the note number.

Abrantès, Duchesse d' 29, 190
adaptations 157–74
  cinema 158–64
  radio 157, 170–3
  television 164–70
  theatre 157
Alain 31, 131, 132
Andréoli, Max 153, 156n13
Angelo, Yves 163
Année balzacienne, L' (journal) 9
Appelboom, Thierry 22
Arago, Étienne 27, 29, 35
arrivisme 82, 85–90
Artiste, L' 143
assignat 68, 73
Axel, Gabriel 168

Balzac, Bernard-François (Honoré's father) 1
Balzac, Honoré de
  admiration of Scott 14
  ambition to document society 3
  childhood 2
  chronology of life xiv–xvii
  core values 4, 128, 138
    see also monarchy; religion
  correspondence 40–51
    with Berny, Laure de 43, 44
    business letters 41
    'citing' Chénier 44
    epistolary fiction 40–1
    with Hanska, Eveline 41, 42, 45–7, 50–1, 189–90
      gifts 46–7
      money 51
      novelistic 45–6

  novels as tributes 47–8
  taking many forms 46
  with Latouche 42
  with Laure (sister) 43–4
  misunderstandings 49–50
    in novels 49–50
  publications 7, 51
  with Sand, Georges 41, 42
  as self-creation 43–4
  self-interest 42
  showing creative imagination 40
  significance 40
  studies 40
  to borrow money 42
  to family 41
  to female friends 43
  to female readers 41
  to friends 42, 43
  debts 2, 17, 51, 176, 178
  early failure 2
  education 2
  first literary works 2–3, 43
  first writing success 2
  influence of Cuvier 21
  marriage with Eveline Hanska 45
Balzac, Honoré de, œuvre
  Adieu 18–19, 143, 146, 167, 175
  Agathise 30, 34, 37
  Albert Savarus 49, 82, 150
  Auberge rouge, L' 79, 142, 144, 146, 159–60
    adaptations 159–60, 171, 173
  Autre étude de femme 151, 154
  'Avertissement du "Gars"' 103
  Béatrix 87, 185
  Bourse, La 170

210

GENERAL INDEX

Cabinet des antiques, Le 82, 87, 176, 180
Chef-d'œuvre inconnu, Le 70, 97, 144, 154, 181
Chouans ou la Bretagne en 1799, Les 42
Colonel Chabert, Le 16, 17, 143, 144, 145, 146, 147, 153, 175
   adaptations 161, 163, 170
Comédie humaine, La 1
   adaptations 157–74
   admiration of Oscar Wilde 182
   ambiavalence 178
   'Avant-Propos' 12, 18, 20, 21, 128, 175
   Balzac, Honoré de, *œuvre* style 178, 181, 182
   characters
     identification with 4
     marginalised 111, 116
     reappearance 4, 8, 81, 87, 176, 178
   criticism
     Barthes 184
     New Novelists 183–4
   detailed description 176–7
   as history 14–15
   influence on Flaubert 178, 178–9
   influence on Henry James 180–2
   influence on modern writers 7, 184–5
   influence on Proust 183–4
   influence on Zola 179–80
   influenced by other writers 175
   multiple voices 7
   neo-gothic influences 13
   observation of society 3, 4, 12, 12–13, 175–6
   publication 108
   realism 182
   references to Cuvier 21
   references to Saint-Hilaire 22
   setting within living memory 14
   'short' or 'shorter' fiction 140
   structure 107, 175
   translation 5
Comédiens sans le savoir, Les 151
Comment aiment les filles 108
Contes drolatiques, Les Cent 146
Contrat de mariage, Le 87, 142, 148
Cousin Pons, Le 112, 140, 142, 181, 186
Cousine Bette, La 7, 36, 72, 76, 111–26, 142, 173, 176, 177, 179, 180, 190
   abnormality and labelling 113
   adaptations
     film 163

     radio 171
     television 165–6
   Bette's belated fashion 117–18
   envy 120
   film adaptations 159
   gender identity 115
   hysteria 122
   inheritance 121
   jealousy 113
   lesbian relationship 116–17, 118–19
   marriage 113, 121, 122
   masculinity of Bette 114
   money 124
   power of Bette and Valérie 120–1
   ugliness and beauty 112
Cromwell (play) 2, 29, 43
Curé de Tours, Le 140, 142, 144, 180, 181
   television adaptation 168
Curé de village, Le 127, 128, 132, 134–5, 135, 138, 177
   clergy 135
   religion 135
   town text 134
David Séchard ou Les Souffrances de l'inventeur 108
Début dans la vie, Un 82
Dernier Chouan ou la Bretagne en 1800, Le (*Les Chouans*) 3, 14, 27, 28, 42, 142, 143, 170
Deux Poètes, Les 107
Deux Rêves, Les 143
Dom Gigadas 27, 28
Duchesse de Langeais, La 16, 158, 161, 163, 169, 185
Élixir de longue vie, L' 53, 144, 145
Employés, Les 82
Envers de l'histoire contemporaine, L' 14
Épisode sous la Terreur, Un 143
Études analytiques 107, 141
Études de mœurs 15, 81, 107, 128, 141, 153, 178
Études philosophiques 12, 98, 107, 141, 153
Eugénie Grandet 3, 17, 74, 79, 141, 143, 145, 147, 175, 177, 195
   adaptations 157, 159
   radio 170, 172
   television 164, 168, 169
   money and speculation 70–1, 73–5
Excommunié, L' 27, 28
Facino Cane 12
Faiseur, Le (play) 8, 76, 77–8, 78

211

Balzac, Honoré de, œuvre (cont.)
  Falthurne 30, 37
  Fausse maîtresse, La 150, 161
  Femme abandonnée, La 91, 143, 144, 148
  Femme de trente ans, La 175, 192
  Ferragus 16, 185
  Fille aux yeux d'or, La 16, 17, 111, 116, 170, 176, 185
  Fille d'Ève, Une 81, 88, 133, 147, 149, 150, 152
  Gambara 97, 99
  Gobseck 17, 67–8, 76, 79, 148, 177
  Grande Bretèche, La 144, 154, 161, 170
  Grenadière, La 144
  Heure de ma vie, Une 32
  Histoire de France pittoresque 14, 28, 152
  Histoire de la grandeur et de la décadence de César Birotteau 75, 76, 76–7, 147, 177
  Histoire des Treize 16, 24, 36, 145, 184, 194
  Histoire impartiale des Jésuites 29
  Histoire intellectuelle de Louis Lambert 29
  Homme d'affaires, Un 151
  Honorine 150
  Illusions perdues 1, 17, 42, 60, 87, 97–110, 141, 146, 175, 177, 191
    author as performer 100–1
    business of literature 99
    Cénacle 98
    commodification of genius 100
    fictional illusion 106
    first reception 97
    fragmentation and unity 108
    journalism 98, 99
    as model of *La Comédie humaine* 106
    performance 101–2
    prostitution 102–3
    reflexivity 106, 109
    structure and publication 107–8, 109
    television adaptations 164
    theatre 100
      and authorship 100
  Illustre Gaudissart, L' 72
  Interdiction, L' 148, 168, 169
  Louis Lambert 97, 177, 181
  Lys dans la vallée, Le 23, 40, 49, 127, 128, 131–4, 137, 138, 140, 154, 179, 185, 195
    countryside 132
    religion and politics 132–3
    television adaptation 167

  Madame Firmiani 143, 144, 146, 147, 181
  Maison du chat-qui-pelote, La 143, 152, 153, 169, 170
  Maison Nucingen, La 22, 67, 75, 87, 141, 147, 148, 149, 150, 151
  Maître Cornélius 14
  Marie Stuart (attrib. to Raisson) 28
  Médecin de campagne, Le 23, 47, 49, 127, 128, 132, 134, 136–8, 138
    centralised power 137–8
    influence of town 137
    plural voices 136–7
    religion 137
    rural revival 137
  Melmoth réconcilié 177
  Mémoires de deux jeunes mariées 40, 49
  Message, Le 13
  Messe de l'athée, La 141, 148
  Modeste Mignon 49, 190
  Muse du département, La 71, 148
  Nègre, Le (play) 29
  Parents pauvres, Les 142
  Paysans, Les 15, 127, 129–31, 132, 133, 137, 138, 139
    conditions of peasants 177
    impotence of the law 130
    religion and monarchy 131
  Peau de chagrin, La 12, 21, 36, 45, 52–66, 81, 87, 88, 142, 144, 177, 192
    allegorical reading 65
    ass's skin 36, 52, 54, 58–65, 141, 144
    conception 52
    difficulties 52, 53
    fantasy 53, 53–4, 55
    fantasy and drab reality 55
    Gothic 63, 64
    influence of Hoffmann 53
    influence of Mesmer 23, 61–2
    liminal moments 54–5, 59
    and limitations of science 23
    money and gambling 56
    pact motif 54, 58
    radio adaptation 171–2
    serialisation 52–3
    wish fulfilment 58, 59, 64
    wonder 64–5
  Père Goriot, Le 4, 74, 81–96, 97, 108, 118, 147–8, 149, 176, 177, 181, 186, 191
    adaptations
      film 162, 164
      radio 170

GENERAL INDEX

television 164, 169
theatre 157
arrivisme 82, 85–90
boue 84–5
composition 81
corrupt values 91–2, 93–4
dedication 22
fatherhood 191
morality 88, 92–3
'nerve centre' of *La Comédie humaine* 81
novel of instruction, *Erziehungsroman* 86
Parisian setting 83–5
realism 176, 181
reappearing characters 81, 176
struggle 85, 91, 94
symbol of Western culture 186
wealth and class 82, 177
Petites misères de la vie conjugale 152, 170
Physiologie du mariage 29, 46, 90, 122, 142, 143
Pierre Grassou 148
Pierrette 41, 112, 142, 167, 180
Balzac, Honoré de, œuvre
premiers romans
Annette et le criminel (Saint-Aubin) 30, 31, 34, 35
Centenaire, ou les Deux Béringheld, Le (Saint-Aubin) 31, 34
Clotilde de Lusignan, ou Le Beau Juif (Lord R'Hoone) 31, 34, 37
Dernière Fée, ou la nouvelle lampe merveilleuse, La (Saint-Aubin) 27, 30, 31, 33, 34
Héritière de Birague, L' (Lord R'Hoone (et al?)) 27, 31, 32, 34, 35
Jean Louis, ou la fille trouvée (Lord R'Hoone (et al?)) 27, 31, 33, 35
Vicaire des Ardennes, Le (Saint-Aubin) 31, 33, 34, 35
Wann-Chlore (Saint-Aubin) 28, 31
Balzac, Honoré de, œuvre
Rabouilleuse, La 42, 161, 185
Recherche de l'absolu, La 20, 53, 97, 145
Réquisitionnaire, Le 17, 146, 154
Sarrasine 12, 111, 141, 142, 144, 145, 146, 153
Barthes' criticism 184
Scènes de la vie de campagne 15, 127–39
calmness of characters 127
presence of town and bourgeoisie 137
Religion and Monarchy 128–9, 138
transition to 'core values' 128

villages appraised by outsiders 137
Scènes de la vie de province 15, 107, 128, 141
importance of money 71
Scènes de la vie parisienne 16
Scènes de la vie privée 3, 141, 142, 143, 146, 152
Séraphîta 46, 47, 48, 111, 135, 177
Souffrances de l'inventeur, Les 141
Splendeurs et misères des courtisanes 87, 108, 116, 140, 148, 149, 151, 165, 194
Sténie ou Les Erreurs philosophiques 30, 40
Sur Catherine de Médicis 14, 16
Ténébreuse affaire, Une 167, 171
Théorie de la démarche 19
Théorie de la volonté 24
Traité de la vie élégante 21
Ursule Mirouët 24, 87, 167, 186
Vieille fille, La 142, 150
Z. Marcas 82
Balzac, Laure (Honoré's mother) 2
Balzac, Laure (Honoré's sister) 43, 43–4
bankruptcy and debt 17, 72, 74–9, 77–8
Barbéris, Pierre 5, 13, 25n4, 49n4, 53, 124, 126n27, 129, 138, 139n12
Bardèche, Maurice 53, 80n1, 80n3
Baron, Anne-Marie 40, 158, 174n2
Baroncelli, Jacques de 161, 163
Barrès, Maurice 83, 89
Barthes, Roland
Degré zéro de l'écriture 17
S/Z 6, 10n7, 12, 111, 153, 156n12, 184
Baudelaire, Charles 12, 53, 66n2, 154, 177, 185, 197
Art romantique, L' 12, 14, 25
Beaumarchais, Pierre-Augustin Caron de 29, 197
Berkeley, George 69
Berny, Laure de 43, 44, 139n6
Berthier, Patrick 110n11, 138, 139n10
Bichat, Marie François Xavier 68
Billard, Pierre 171
biology 20, 20–1
Blanchar, Pierre 161
Blix, Gören 61, 66n6
Bolshoi Ballet 1
Bordas, Éric 7, 10
Borel, Jacques 22–3, 26n16
Borget, Auguste 41

213

Bory, Jean-Louis 165
Boudet, Alain 167
Bourdieu, Pierre 6, 112, 125n4
bourgeoisie, rise of 14, 18, 130
  and capitalism 56, 176-7
  in the country 137, 138
  and July Monarchy 74, 139n3, 144
Bourget, Paul 89, 153, 156n16
Brachet, Jean-Louis 123
Brontë, Charlotte 4
Brooks, Peter 89, 95n17, 110n4, 153, 154, 155
Brunetière, F. 178, 187n8
Buffon 3, 19, 20, 21
Butler, Ronnie 94, 95n26

Cabanis, Pierre Jean Georges 22, 68
Calvino, Italo 1
  'City as Novel in Balzac, The' 184-5, 188n38
capitalism 13, 70, 176-7, 177, 186-7
  and bourgeoisie 56, 176
  and individualism 144
Carpenter, Scott 153
Carraud, Zulma 41, 43, 137
Carrière, Jean-Claude 165
Castex, Pierre-Georges 16, 38, 49n6, 73, 80n9
Castle, Terry 116, 125n14
Catholicism 24
celibacy 112, 141-2
characters
  as ideas 69
  identification with 4
  marginalised 111, 116
  personae of Balzac 107
  reappearance 2, 8, 81, 87, 149, 176, 178
  wide range of 15
Chasles, Philarète 178
Chatterton, Thomas 99, 99-100
Citron, Pierre 82, 95n6, 155n6, 156n12
Clark, Pricilla P. 86, 95n12, 95n14
class 5, 17-18
Collier, Peter 153, 156n10
Comte, Auguste 68
Condorcet, Nicolas de 68
Conquering Power, The (film) 159
Cooper, James Fenimore 2
Coster, Claudine 166
countryside 127, 131, 136
Cousin, Victor 29, 35
Cravenne, Marcel 167
creationism 22

criticism
  Marxist interpretations 5
  nineteenth century 4, 5
  structuralists and post-structuralists 6
Custine, Marquis de 41
Cuvier, Georges 20, 21, 21-2

d'Alembert 62
Darnton, Robert 62
  Mesmerism and the End of the Enlightenment in France 61
David, Jacques-Louis 36
Depardieu, Gérard 163
Descartes, René 30
Diaz, José-Luis 40, 53
Dictionnaire Balzac 10
Diderot: *Jacques le fataliste* 106
doctors 22-3
Dombasle, Arielle 169
Dostoevsky, Fyodor 1, 177
  Brothers Karamazov, The 177
  Crime and Punishment 177
Ducray-Duminil: *Lolotte et Fanfan* 31
Dumas, Alexandre (*père*) 3

Ellis, Bret Easton 192
Ellis, John 168, 174n11
Ellison D.R. 94, 95n27
energy and movement 21
Engels, Friedrich 3, 5, 13
Enlightenment 19, 58, 65
Epstein, Jean 159-61, 171, 173
evolutionary theory 21-2

families
  breakdown 121-2
  dependence on 113
  dissolution of 69
  and money and individualism 186-7
  as pillar of society 69
  privileging one member 112, 119-20
  and unfaithfulness 124
fantasy 12, 53, 53-4, 55
  as aesthetic necessity 55
  and drab reality 55
  and reality 64
  wild ass's skin 36, 52, 54, 58-65, 144
Fénelon: *Les Aventures de Télémaque* 86
film adaptations 158-64
  during German occupation of France 161
  escapism 162
  reasons for 158-9
  silent films 158-61, 173

GENERAL INDEX

flashback technique 4
Flaubert, Gustave 1, 12, 42, 43, 89, 93, 150,
    178–9, 185, 187n11,12, 197
  Bouvard et Pécuchet 179
  Cœur simple, Un 179
  Éducation sentimentale, L' 86, 97, 179
  Madame Bovary 122, 178–9
Fortassier, Rose 86, 138, 139n9
Foucault, Michel 6, 113, 125n9
Four Horsemen of the Apocalypse, The
    (film) 159
French economy 77–8, 78, 177
French Revolution 4
Frolich, Juliette 82, 94n5

Galdós, Benito Pérez 1
gambling 54, 55, 56, 72
Gaskell, Elizabeth 4, 10n3
Gasset, José Ortega y 52, 65n1
Gautier, Théophile 3, 41, 66n2, 143, 178,
    190, 191, 198n2
gender
  affiliation 18
  ambiguity 115
  at the heart of conflict 111
  Balzac's treatment of 17, 18
  fathers feminised 191
  identities 111, 115, 144
  and inheritance 121
  roles 130–1, 145
  and sex 18
  stereotypes 6–7
gender theory 6–7
'*generative idea*' 142
Gide: *Faux-Monnayeurs, Les* 89
Giraudoux, Jean 161
Goethe 31, 32, 60
  Werther 30
gold 16, 67, 68, 71, 74, 78, 195
  'spirituality of current societies' 79
Griffiths, Kate 165, 174n8
Groupe d'études balzaciennes (GEB) 9
Groupe international de recherches
    balzaciennes (GIRB) 9
Guérin 33

Hanska, Eveline 5, 21, 40, 41, 43, 45–7,
    106, 189
Harkness, Margaret 5
Heathcote, Owen 40, 51n1, 153, 156n13
Hirsch, Marianne 92, 95n24
history 11–12, 12, 14
  'distortion' 16

and nation-building 16
onward march of 16
present as 70
and society 14–15
history of manners 81
Hoffmann, E.T.A. 13, 53, 65, 142, 175, 177
Holbach, Baron d' 30
homme social 187
homosexuality 116
  see also gender; sexuality
Hubert, Yves-André 165, 173
Hugo, Victor 3, 4, 13, 14, 41, 179, 197, 198,
    199n9
  Hernani (play) 3
Humanity and Animality 20
Hutcheon, Linda 158

'idea' (philosophy) 69
identity
  fluidity of 187
  and gender 111, 115, 144, 184
  inherently flawed 122
  marginalised 116
  sense of 48
images 69–70
immorality 90, 178, 181
individualism 135, 144, 186
inheritance
  and gender 121
  and money 71, 72, 79
interconnectedness of world 21

James, Henry 1, 153, 156n14, 180–2, 182,
    187n17
  Ambassadors, The 181
  'Lesson of the Master, The' 181
  Spoils of Poynton, The 181
Joyce, James 184
  Dubliners 184
July Revolution (1830) 4, 16, 53, 54, 68, 74,
    76, 79, 123, 176, 179

Kelly, Dorothy 6, 18, 155n6
Kerouac, Jack 185
Kiriu, Kazuo 10
Knight, Diana 120, 125n20, 153, 156n13
Kock, Paul de 30, 33, 179
  Georgette ou la nièce du tabellion 30

La Fontaine: 'Les Loups et les Brebis' 169
Laforgue, Jules 153, 156n13
Lagrange 19
Lamarck, Jean-Baptiste 20, 21

215

Lamartine, Alphonse-Marie-Louis de Prat de 41
land and wealth 67, 68, 70, 77
landscape in literature 127
Latouche, Henri de: *Fragoletta* 42
Leitch, Thomas 158, 173, 174n14
Lepoitevin de l'Égreville, Auguste (Viellerglé) 27, 29, 30, 36
  Charles Pointel 30, 32, 33, 35
  Corrupteur, Le 28
  Deux Hector, Les 35
  Stanislas, ou La Suite de Michel et Christine 29
  see also Balzac, Honoré de, œuvre, *premiers romans*
Leroux, André 165
lesbianism 116–17, 118–19, 154
  see also Balzac, Honoré de, œuvre; *Cousine Bette, La*; sexuality
Lewes, George Henry 4, 10n2
Locke, John 70
Louis-Philippe 16
love 71, 77
Lucey, Michael 6, 18, 110n8, 111, 112, 113, 114, 119, 125n1
Lucien de Rubempré (radio serial) 170
Lukács, Georg 5, 13, 53, 70, 80n4, 109, 110n12, 129

Macherey, Pierre 129
magnetism 23, 24
Maison de Balzac, Passy 9
Malebranche, Nicolas 30
marginal characters 111, 116, 136
marginalised by family 121, 125
marginalised society 116, 120
Marx, Karl 5, 6, 10n1, 13
  Das Kapital 5, 177
Massonaud, Dominique 10
Matlock, Jann 113, 123, 125n7
Maturin, Charles Robert
  Melmoth the Wanderer 31, 53
  Women 31
Maupassant, Guy de 93
  Bel-Ami 89
medicine 22–3
mental illness 23
Merville, Jean-Baptiste Guillonnet de 2
Mesmer, Franz Anton 19, 23, 24, 61, 61–2
mesmerism 61–2, 64, 65
Michon, Pierre 185
  Trois auteurs 185
Millet, Richard 185

Écrivain Sirieix, L' 185
Lauve le pur 185
'Octavian' 185
Milton, John 61
monarchy 16, 138
  as core value 4
  and religion 128, 131, 133
money 17, 67–8, 181, 191, 195
  behind plots 40
  borrowing 76, 78
  and currency 68, 78
  Great Recoinage (1696) 68
  'hyperconcentration of capital' 177
  inflation 68
  and inheritance 71, 72, 79
  National Bank of France 78
  as new religion 71, 73
  and power 68, 79
  religion of Mammon 67, 73
  and society 70, 177
  speculation 72–5
  value of banknotes 68
  as yardstick 124
  see also bankruptcy and debt
Moore, Thomas 32
Mozet, Nicole 7, 120, 121, 122, 125n19, 126n21

Nacquart, Jean-Baptiste 23, 29, 42, 43
Napoleon 2, 13, 16, 24, 36, 116, 136, 137, 138
  Balzac's view of 13
  repatriation of body 16
naturalism 5, 179
Ne touchez pas la hache (film) 163, 164
Nesci, Catherine 18
New Novelists 6, 183–4, 185
Nodier, Charles 3, 32, 41, 42

occult 23, 24
Ormesson, Jean d' 94, 95n25

Paglia, Camille 184, 188n36
Panckoucke: *Encyclopédie méthodique* 23
Paris 16, 17, 22, 83–5, 116, 117
  boue 84–5
Pasco, Allan H. 85, 95n10, 187n4
Passion in the Desert (film) 163
Pigault-Lebrun, Charles-Antoine-Guillaume 31
Piketty, Thomas 71, 79, 80n7
  Capital in the Twenty-First Century 177
Poe, Edgar Allan 1

poverty 17, 116, 117
power 192
  and money 68, 79
premiers romans 27–39
  editions 38–9
  see also under Balzac, Honoré de, œuvre
Prendergast, Christopher 112, 115, 125n3
Proulx, François 87, 89, 89–90, 95n7, 95n22
Proust, Marcel 1, 183–4, 193, 194, 197
  À la recherche du temps perdu 183
  Contre Sainte-Beuve 182
psychic energy 24

Rabelais, François 3, 32, 37, 155, 175
Radcliffe, Ann 13, 30
radio adaptations 158, 170–3
  Balzac's evocation of sound 170–1
  BBC 170, 171–2
  sounds evoking thoughts and feelings 171
  USA 170
Raisson, Horace-Napoléon 28, 29, 39
  Blonde, Une 28
  Code des gens honnêtes 29
  Marie Stuart 28
Raitt, Alan 153, 156n10
Rambaud, Patrick: *La Bataille* 186
realism 3, 6, 12, 18–19, 53, 175
  and fantasy 111
  and rewriting the real 182
reality, substance of 69
Reign of Terror 18
religion 137
  as core value 4, 138
  faith and ritual 137
  'great facilitator' 135
  and law 130
  and monarchy 128, 131, 133, 138
  money as 67, 71, 73
  and politics 127–8, 131, 132–3, 134, 135
Revue de Paris 142
Revue des deux Mondes 142
Revue parisienne, La 69
R'Hoone, Lord (Balzac's pseudonym) 2, 27–8, 31, 33, 34, 35, 37, 38–9
  see also Balzac, Honoré de, œuvre, *premiers romans*
Rivette, Jacques 163–4
Robb, Graham 176
Robbe-Grillet, Alain 6, 10n5, 12, 183, 188n35
Romanticism 3
Rossum-Guyon, Françoise van 90, 95n23

Rousseau, Jean-Jacques 19
  Discours sur l'origine et les fondmens de l'inégalité parmi les hommes 34
  Nouvelle Héloïse, La 30

Saché, Château de 10
Saint Simon, Henri de 68, 69, 80n2, 137, 195
Saint-Aubin, Horace (Balzac's pseudonym) 2, 27, 31, 34, 35, 38–9
  see also Balzac, Honoré de, œuvre, *premiers romans*
Saint-Hilaire, Étienne Geoffroy 3, 20, 21, 21–2, 24
Saint-Pierre, Bernardin de: *Paul et Virgnie* 31
Saintsbury, George 5, 25n1
Sand, George 13, 16, 41, 42, 185
Sandeau, Jules 194
  Vie et Malheurs de Horace de Saint-Aubin 27
Sanson 29
  see also Vidocq
Scher, Lawrence R. 6
Schiller, Friedrich von 31, 32
Schuerewegen, Franc 188n29
  Balzac contre Balzac 7
sciences 11, 20–4, 65
  and mesmerism 61–2
  and unity 20
Scott, Walter 2, 14, 16, 28, 29, 31, 32, 92, 175
  Ivanhoe 28
Seul amour, Un (film) 161
sex and marriage 124
sexed identity 190
  see also gender; homosexuality; lesbianism
sexuality 111
  commodification of 124, 125
Shakespeare, William 3
Sijie, Dai: *Balzac and the Little Chinese Seamstress* 186
slave trade 67
social philosophy 68–9
social species 21
Société des Amis de Balzac 9
society
  Balzac as historian of 7, 14–15
  Balzac's wish to observe and document 3, 12
  disintegration of 4
  forces shaping 17, 24, 69
  as market 70
  pillars of 69
  taxonomy of 15

217

society (cont.)
  total vision of 3
  in transition/motion 25, 70
sociology 68
Souverain, Hippolyte 38, 41
speculation 72–5, 77
Spinoza, Baruch 30
spiritualism 23–4
Stendhal 13, 185, 193, 196
  Lamiel 197
  Rouge et le noir, Le 97
Sterne, Laurence 31, 56, 175
  Tristram Shandy 32, 33, 55–6, 58
structuralism 192
  and post-structuralists 6
Sue, Eugène: *Mystères de Paris, Les* 38
supernatural forces 23, 53
  in Balzac's works 177

Taine, Hippolyte 179
television adaptations 164–70
  domestic life 164
  realism 164–5
  reorganisation of French television 166–7
  scholarly approach: *Cousine Bette* 164–5
  technical developments 1970s and 80s 167–8
  Vautrin 165
  visual observation 164–5
triage grouping 22
Tulard, Jean 161, 174n5

unity 21
unity of composition 20, 22

urban life 151, 176–7, 184
  see also Paris

Valentino, Rudolph 159, 160
Verhaeghe, Jean-Daniel 169, 169–70
Vidocq 29
  see also Sanson
Viellerglé *see* Lepoitevin de l'Égreville, Auguste (Viellerglé)
Vigny, Alfred de: *Chatterton* 99, 99–100
virtue and vice 77, 90
Voltaire 35

Wild Ass's Skin Reloaded, The (radio) 171–2
Wilde, Oscar 1, 182, 188n27
Wittig, Monique 116
wives as capital 67
women 18
  see also gender; lesbianism; sex and marriage; sexuality
wonder 64–5
working class 18
  see also marginalised society; poverty
Wurmser, André 5, 42, 51n3, 70, 76, 80n6, 129

Zola, Émile 1, 5, 17, 177, 179–80, 187n14,16
  Conquête de Plassans, La 180
  'Differences between Balzac and myself' 180
  Fortune des Rougon, La 180
  Nana 180
  Pot-Bouille 97
  Rougon-Macquart, Les series 89, 179–80
Zweig, Stéfan 190

Cambridge Companions to . . .

AUTHORS

Edward Albee edited by Stephen J. Bottoms
Margaret Atwood edited by Coral Ann Howells
W. H. Auden edited by Stan Smith
Jane Austen edited by Edward Copeland and Juliet McMaster (second edition)
Balzac edited by Owen Heathcote and Andrew Watts
Beckett edited by John Pilling
Bede edited by Scott DeGregorio
Aphra Behn edited by Derek Hughes and Janet Todd
Saul Bellow edited by Victoria Aarons
Walter Benjamin edited by David S. Ferris
William Blake edited by Morris Eaves
Boccaccio edited by Guyda Armstrong, Rhiannon Daniels and Stephen J. Milner
Jorge Luis Borges edited by Edwin Williamson
Brecht edited by Peter Thomson and Glendyr Sacks (second edition)
The Brontës edited by Heather Glen
Bunyan edited by Anne Dunan-Page
Frances Burney edited by Peter Sabor
Byron edited by Drummond Bone
Albert Camus edited by Edward J. Hughes
Willa Cather edited by Marilee Lindemann
Cervantes edited by Anthony J. Cascardi
Chaucer edited by Piero Boitani and Jill Mann (second edition)
Chekhov edited by Vera Gottlieb and Paul Allain
Kate Chopin edited by Janet Beer
Caryl Churchill edited by Elaine Aston and Elin Diamond
Cicero edited by Catherine Steel
Coleridge edited by Lucy Newlyn
Wilkie Collins edited by Jenny Bourne Taylor
Joseph Conrad edited by J. H. Stape
H. D. edited by Nephie J. Christodoulides and Polina Mackay

Dante edited by Rachel Jacoff (second edition)
Daniel Defoe edited by John Richetti
Don DeLillo edited by John N. Duvall
Charles Dickens edited by John O. Jordan
Emily Dickinson edited by Wendy Martin
John Donne edited by Achsah Guibbory
Dostoevskii edited by W. J. Leatherbarrow
Theodore Dreiser edited by Leonard Cassuto and Claire Virginia Eby
John Dryden edited by Steven N. Zwicker
W. E. B. Du Bois edited by Shamoon Zamir
George Eliot edited by George Levine
T. S. Eliot edited by A. David Moody
Ralph Ellison edited by Ross Posnock
Ralph Waldo Emerson edited by Joel Porte and Saundra Morris
William Faulkner edited by Philip M. Weinstein
Henry Fielding edited by Claude Rawson
F. Scott Fitzgerald edited by Ruth Prigozy
Flaubert edited by Timothy Unwin
E. M. Forster edited by David Bradshaw
Benjamin Franklin edited by Carla Mulford
Brian Friel edited by Anthony Roche
Robert Frost edited by Robert Faggen
Gabriel García Márquez edited by Philip Swanson
Elizabeth Gaskell edited by Jill L. Matus
Goethe edited by Lesley Sharpe
Günter Grass edited by Stuart Taberner
Thomas Hardy edited by Dale Kramer
David Hare edited by Richard Boon
Nathaniel Hawthorne edited by Richard Millington
Seamus Heaney edited by Bernard O'Donoghue
Ernest Hemingway edited by Scott Donaldson
Homer edited by Robert Fowler
Horace edited by Stephen Harrison
Ted Hughes edited by Terry Gifford
Ibsen edited by James McFarlane

Henry James edited by Jonathan Freedman
Samuel Johnson edited by Greg Clingham
Ben Jonson edited by Richard Harp and Stanley Stewart
James Joyce edited by Derek Attridge (second edition)
Kafka edited by Julian Preece
Keats edited by Susan J. Wolfson
Rudyard Kipling edited by Howard J. Booth
Lacan edited by Jean-Michel Rabaté
D. H. Lawrence edited by Anne Fernihough
Primo Levi edited by Robert Gordon
Lucretius edited by Stuart Gillespie and Philip Hardie
Machiavelli edited by John M. Najemy
David Mamet edited by Christopher Bigsby
Thomas Mann edited by Ritchie Robertson
Christopher Marlowe edited by Patrick Cheney
Andrew Marvell edited by Derek Hirst and Steven N. Zwicker
Herman Melville edited by Robert S. Levine
Arthur Miller edited by Christopher Bigsby (second edition)
Milton edited by Dennis Danielson (second edition)
Molière edited by David Bradby and Andrew Calder
Toni Morrison edited by Justine Tally
Alice Munro edited by David Staines
Nabokov edited by Julian W. Connolly
Eugene O'Neill edited by Michael Manheim
George Orwell edited by John Rodden
Ovid edited by Philip Hardie
Petrarch edited by Albert Russell Ascoli and Unn Falkeid
Harold Pinter edited by Peter Raby (second edition)
Sylvia Plath edited by Jo Gill
Edgar Allan Poe edited by Kevin J. Hayes
Alexander Pope edited by Pat Rogers
Ezra Pound edited by Ira B. Nadel
Proust edited by Richard Bales
Pushkin edited by Andrew Kahn
Rabelais edited by John O'Brien
Rilke edited by Karen Leeder and Robert Vilain
Philip Roth edited by Timothy Parrish
Salman Rushdie edited by Abdulrazak Gurnah
John Ruskin edited by Francis O'Gorman
Shakespeare edited by Margareta de Grazia and Stanley Wells (second edition)
Shakespearean Comedy edited by Alexander Leggatt
Shakespeare and Contemporary Dramatists edited by Ton Hoenselaars
Shakespeare and Popular Culture edited by Robert Shaughnessy
Shakespearean Tragedy edited by Claire McEachern (second edition)
Shakespeare on Film edited by Russell Jackson (second edition)
Shakespeare on Stage edited by Stanley Wells and Sarah Stanton
Shakespeare's History Plays edited by Michael Hattaway
Shakespeare's Last Plays edited by Catherine M. S. Alexander
Shakespeare's Poetry edited by Patrick Cheney
George Bernard Shaw edited by Christopher Innes
Shelley edited by Timothy Morton
Mary Shelley edited by Esther Schor
Sam Shepard edited by Matthew C. Roudané
Spenser edited by Andrew Hadfield
Laurence Sterne edited by Thomas Keymer
Wallace Stevens edited by John N. Serio
Tom Stoppard edited by Katherine E. Kelly
Harriet Beecher Stowe edited by Cindy Weinstein
August Strindberg edited by Michael Robinson
Jonathan Swift edited by Christopher Fox
J. M. Synge edited by P. J. Mathews
Tacitus edited by A. J. Woodman
Henry David Thoreau edited by Joel Myerson
Tolstoy edited by Donna Tussing Orwin
Anthony Trollope edited by Carolyn Dever and Lisa Niles
Mark Twain edited by Forrest G. Robinson
John Updike edited by Stacey Olster

Mario Vargas Llosa edited by Efrain Kristal and John King
Virgil edited by Charles Martindale
Voltaire edited by Nicholas Cronk
Edith Wharton edited by Millicent Bell
Walt Whitman edited by Ezra Greenspan
Oscar Wilde edited by Peter Raby
Tennessee Williams edited by Matthew C. Roudané
August Wilson edited by Christopher Bigsby
Mary Wollstonecraft edited by Claudia L. Johnson
Virginia Woolf edited by Susan Sellers (second edition)
Wordsworth edited by Stephen Gill
W. B. Yeats edited by Marjorie Howes and John Kelly
Zola edited by Brian Nelson

TOPICS

The Actress edited by Maggie B. Gale and John Stokes
The African American Novel edited by Maryemma Graham
The African American Slave Narrative edited by Audrey A. Fisch
African American Theatre by Harvey Young
Allegory edited by Rita Copeland and Peter Struck
American Crime Fiction edited by Catherine Ross Nickerson
American Modernism edited by Walter Kalaidjian
American Poetry Since 1945 edited by Jennifer Ashton
American Realism and Naturalism edited by Donald Pizer
American Travel Writing edited by Alfred Bendixen and Judith Hamera
American Women Playwrights edited by Brenda Murphy
Ancient Rhetoric edited by Erik Gunderson
Arthurian Legend edited by Elizabeth Archibald and Ad Putter
Australian Literature edited by Elizabeth Webby
British Literature of the French Revolution edited by Pamela Clemit
British Romanticism edited by Stuart Curran (second edition)
British Romantic Poetry edited by James Chandler and Maureen N. McLane
British Theatre, 1730–1830, edited by Jane Moody and Daniel O'Quinn
Canadian Literature edited by Eva-Marie Kröller
Children's Literature edited by M. O. Grenby and Andrea Immel
The Classic Russian Novel edited by Malcolm V. Jones and Robin Feuer Miller
Contemporary Irish Poetry edited by Matthew Campbell
Creative Writing edited by David Morley and Philip Neilsen
Crime Fiction edited by Martin Priestman
Early Modern Women's Writing edited by Laura Lunger Knoppers
The Eighteenth-Century Novel edited by John Richetti
Eighteenth-Century Poetry edited by John Sitter
Emma edited by Peter Sabor
English Literature, 1500–1600 edited by Arthur F. Kinney
English Literature, 1650–1740 edited by Steven N. Zwicker
English Literature, 1740–1830 edited by Thomas Keymer and Jon Mee
English Literature, 1830–1914 edited by Joanne Shattock
English Novelists edited by Adrian Poole

English Poetry, Donne to Marvell edited by Thomas N. Corns
English Poets edited by Claude Rawson
English Renaissance Drama edited by A. R. Braunmuller and Michael Hattaway (second edition)
English Renaissance Tragedy edited by Emma Smith and Garrett A. Sullivan Jr.
English Restoration Theatre edited by Deborah C. Payne Fisk
The Epic edited by Catherine Bates
European Modernism edited by Pericles Lewis
European Novelists edited by Michael Bell
Fairy Tales edited by Maria Tatar
Fantasy Literature edited by Edward James and Farah Mendlesohn
Feminist Literary Theory edited by Ellen Rooney
Fiction in the Romantic Period edited by Richard Maxwell and Katie Trumpener
The Fin de Siècle edited by Gail Marshall
The French Enlightenment edited by Daniel Brewer
French Literature edited by John D. Lyons
The French Novel: from 1800 to the Present edited by Timothy Unwin
Gay and Lesbian Writing edited by Hugh Stevens
German Romanticism edited by Nicholas Saul
Gothic Fiction edited by Jerrold E. Hogle
The Greek and Roman Novel edited by Tim Whitmarsh
Greek and Roman Theatre edited by Marianne McDonald and J. Michael Walton
Greek Comedy edited by Martin Revermann
Greek Lyric edited by Felix Budelmann
Greek Mythology edited by Roger D. Woodard
Greek Tragedy edited by P. E. Easterling
The Harlem Renaissance edited by George Hutchinson
The History of the Book edited by Leslie Howsam
The Irish Novel edited by John Wilson Foster
The Italian Novel edited by Peter Bondanella and Andrea Ciccarelli
The Italian Renaissance edited by Michael Wyatt
Jewish American Literature edited by Hana Wirth-Nesher and Michael P. Kramer
The Latin American Novel edited by Efraín Kristal
Latin Love Elegy edited by Thea S. Thorsen
Literature and the Posthuman edited by Bruce Clarke and Manuela Rossini
The Literature of London edited by Lawrence Manley
The Literature of Los Angeles edited by Kevin R. McNamara
The Literature of New York edited by Cyrus Patell and Bryan Waterman
The Literature of Paris edited by Anna-Louise Milne
The Literature of the First World War edited by Vincent Sherry
The Literature of World War II edited by Marina MacKay
Literature on Screen edited by Deborah Cartmell and Imelda Whelehan
Medieval English Culture edited by Andrew Galloway
Medieval English Literature edited by Larry Scanlon
Medieval English Mysticism edited by Samuel Fanous and Vincent Gillespie
Medieval English Theatre edited by Richard Beadle and Alan J. Fletcher (second edition)
Medieval French Literature edited by Simon Gaunt and Sarah Kay
Medieval Romance edited by Roberta L. Krueger
Medieval Women's Writing edited by Carolyn Dinshaw and David Wallace
Modern American Culture edited by Christopher Bigsby
Modern British Women Playwrights edited by Elaine Aston and Janelle Reinelt
Modern French Culture edited by Nicholas Hewitt

Modern German Culture edited by Eva Kolinsky and Wilfried van der Will
The Modern German Novel edited by Graham Bartram
The Modern Gothic edited by Jerrold E. Hogle
Modern Irish Culture edited by Joe Cleary and Claire Connolly
Modern Italian Culture edited by Zygmunt G. Baranski and Rebecca J. West
Modern Latin American Culture edited by John King
Modern Russian Culture edited by Nicholas Rzhevsky
Modern Spanish Culture edited by David T. Gies
Modernism edited by Michael Levenson (second edition)
The Modernist Novel edited by Morag Shiach
Modernist Poetry edited by Alex Davis and Lee M. Jenkins
Modernist Women Writers edited by Maren Tova Linett
Narrative edited by David Herman
Native American Literature edited by Joy Porter and Kenneth M. Roemer
Nineteenth-Century American Women's Writing edited by Dale M. Bauer and Philip Gould
Old English Literature edited by Malcolm Godden and Michael Lapidge (second edition)
Performance Studies edited by Tracy C. Davis
Piers Plowman by Andrew Cole and Andrew Galloway
Popular Fiction edited by David Glover and Scott McCracken
Postcolonial Literary Studies edited by Neil Lazarus
Postmodernism edited by Steven Connor
The Pre-Raphaelites edited by Elizabeth Prettejohn
Pride and Prejudice edited by Janet Todd
Renaissance Humanism edited by Jill Kraye
The Roman Historians edited by Andrew Feldherr
Roman Satire edited by Kirk Freudenburg
Science Fiction edited by Edward James and Farah Mendlesohn
Scottish Literature edited by Gerald Carruthers and Liam McIlvanney
Sensation Fiction edited by Andrew Mangham
The Sonnet edited by A. D. Cousins and Peter Howarth
The Spanish Novel: from 1600 to the Present edited by Harriet Turner and Adelaida López de Martínez
Textual Scholarship edited by Neil Fraistat and Julia Flanders
Theatre History by David Wiles and Christine Dymkowski
Travel Writing edited by Peter Hulme and Tim Youngs
Twentieth-Century British and Irish Women's Poetry edited by Jane Dowson
The Twentieth-Century English Novel edited by Robert L. Caserio
Twentieth-Century English Poetry edited by Neil Corcoran
Twentieth-Century Irish Drama edited by Shaun Richards
Twentieth-Century Russian Literature edited by Marina Balina and Evgeny Dobrenko
Utopian Literature edited by Gregory Claeys
Victorian and Edwardian Theatre edited by Kerry Powell
The Victorian Novel edited by Deirdre David (second edition)
Victorian Poetry edited by Joseph Bristow
Victorian Women's Writing edited by Linda H. Peterson
War Writing edited by Kate McLoughlin
Women's Writing in Britain, 1660–1789 edited by Catherine Ingrassia
Women's Writing in the Romantic Period edited by Devoney Looser
Writing of the English Revolution edited by N. H. Keeble

Printed in Great Britain
by Amazon